Europe's Classical Balance of Power

Europe's Classical Balance of Power

A Case History of the Theory and Practice of One

of the Great Concepts of European Statecraft

By Edward Vose Gulick

Department of History, Wellesley College

PUBLISHED FOR

The American Historical Association

Cornell University Press, Ithaca, New York

CORNELL UNIVERSITY PRESS
LONDON: GEOFFREY CUMBERLEGE
OXFORD UNIVERSITY PRESS

First published 1955

THIS VOLUME IS PUBLISHED FROM A FUND CONTRIBUTED TO THE AMERICAN
HISTORICAL ASSOCIATION BY THE CARNEGIE CORPORATION OF NEW YORK.

PRINTED IN THE UNITED STATES OF AMERICA BY THE
VAIL-BALLOU PRESS, INC., BINGHAMTON, NEW YORK

Preface

THE balance of power, as a subject for historical research, is something like the weather: everybody talks about it, but few do anything about it. It is likely that no other single phrase of statecraft, except perhaps "divide and rule," has been used and misused on such a vast scale in the western world. Professor Pollard, a distinguished English historian, has written:

Like "liberty," "independence," the "freedom of the seas" or of the straits, the balance of power may mean almost anything; and it is used not only in different senses by different people, or in different senses by the same people at different times, but in different senses by the same person at the same time.[1]

Seeking to clarify his thinking on this elusive expression, he consulted one of the best modern dictionaries. He reports

[1] A. F. Pollard, "Balance of Power," *Jour. of the British Institute of International Affairs,* II (March, 1923), 58.

whimsically that he looked up each word separately and found that twenty different uses were listed for the word "balance," sixty-three for "of," and eighteen for "power." According to the law of permutations and combinations, it follows that the possible meanings of the entire phrase are somewhere in the thousands.

Although the expression has attracted widespread attention and use, the professional historian may well be astonished to discover that members of his own guild have never spelled out the origins of the idea of the balance of power, have overlooked studying it from the point of view of case histories of its application as an important principle of European diplomacy, have ignored the extent to which it has figured in intellectual history, and have misused the term in their own writings. For one of the great principles of European statecraft, such a situation is surprising and unfortunate. The present study is directed, therefore, toward furthering our knowledge of the balance of power by seeking insights into two of its aspects. The study contains first an essay on the theory of balancing power and then a case history illustrating the doctrine in operation.

For the theory the best starting point is the European and English writers of the eighteenth century, when balancing power achieved a kind of crescendo of development; the era of these writers was in all likelihood the century of greatest enthusiasm for, and most widespread practice of, the balance of power in European affairs and probably in world history.

With regard to the handling of this theoretical material, an approach may be made in two useful ways. One may describe the theories of individual writers; or, after examination of many writers, one may work out the propositions of a general balance-of-power theory for their period. The former is the type of work which Carleton Hayes, in *The Historical Evolution of Modern Nationalism,* has done for nationalist writers, or Friedrich Meinecke and G. P. Gooch for German thinkers. The latter approach is what the Swedish economic historian,

Eli Heckscher, did for an important branch of economics in early modern Europe by showing in his *Mercantilism* the outlines of a systematic approach to economics after examining the scattered materials of the subject.

In the present study the second approach has been selected—that is, the attempt to present a system rather than a group of essays on individual writers. There were strong reasons for such a choice.

In general, there have not been outstanding writers on the balance of power of the stature of a Machiavelli, a Hobbes, a Montesquieu, or a Bentham. These writers themselves nibbled at the edges of the subject but never dug into it, so far as we know. Secondly, the real balance-of-power writers have not, as a rule, written very much on their subject. Many admitted the importance of the principle; most stated it rather simply and with considerable accuracy; but few summoned up remarks that filled more than a very few pages of text. For example, Vattel, an influential writer on the balance of power, an able man with a wide audience, assigned a position of great importance to the principle of the balance of power in international law, yet he covered his discussion of it in a handful of scattered pages. There are, to be sure, longer studies, but they, too, are often long merely by comparison—Hume's rather well-known essay "Of the Balance of Power" is a scant nine pages in length.

We have, then, the curious situation that scarcely a writer denies the significance of the balance of power as a principle of international law or as a great historic practice in international relations, yet none has written in adequate detail about it. Consequently, a handling of the subject which concentrated on the individual writers and on the origins, development, and refinement of their special points of view would find inadequate material and might well emerge, after the last second-rate writer had been lovingly put to bed by the author, as chloroform in print.

Thus, the "systematic" approach, as opposed to the "individual" approach, was dictated by necessity and interest. Certain positive advantages also recommend it: it shows the consensus of opinion of the ablest writers on the balance of power; it contains an inner logic of its own, once the theory has been put together; and it benefits both from a bird's-eye view of the subject and from historical perspective.

One should recognize that the generalizations of the present study are not a reproduction of the thinking of any single earlier writer, but that they attempt to fill out and rationalize a system which earlier writers themselves never filled out or rationalized to any appreciable degree.

Once one has assembled the elements of the balance-of-power theory during the era of its greatest popularity and most general application, the next logical step is to observe the balance of power in operation in a great crisis of European affairs to see if the theory was put to work, and if so, with what results. That story comprises the related essay on the case history and begins with the fatal Napoleonic invasion of Russia in 1812, follows through the Emperor's defeat and abdication in 1813–1814, picks up the tale of peacemaking in 1814–1815, continues with the re-creation of a reinforced balance-of-power system in the fall of 1815, and ends with a brief epilogue on the experiment during the subsequent decade with an improved system for maintaining a continental equilibrium. Emphasis is placed upon the years from 1812 to 1815 because they offer special advantages for a case history of the practice, just as the eighteenth century does for the theory: they stand in intimate relation to the eighteenth-century theory of balancing power; they embrace a fascinating and terrible period when European states were being consumed by the glittering and misdirected genius of Napoleon; they include examples of the common implements of equilibrist practice—alliances, intervention, coalitions, and warfare; they witness a great development in balancing technique; and they end with a great peace settlement, in the drafting of which statesmen consciously attempted to re-create a Europe of balanced power.

Although a number of scholars have worked on the diplomatic history of these years, none of them has yet devoted sufficient attention to either the theory or the practice of the balance-of-power system to demonstrate its real importance or exact nature in the period. Furthermore, none has brought together more than a fraction of the important facets of the problem. For example, Albert Sorel, the greatest of all diplomatic historians, believed as Rousseau did before him that a restoration of the balance of power was virtually predictable, that a threat to the balance would stimulate opposition which, sooner or later, would be irresistible. Nevertheless, his work is deficient both in its exposition of the role which Castlereagh played in that restoration and in the recognition of the significance of the Treaty of Chaumont to the development of the balance-of-power system. While C. K. Webster filled gaps in our understanding of Castlereagh's role and showed the importance of Castlereagh's contribution to the new development of diplomacy by conference, he did not demonstrate the connection between either of those phenomena and the antecedent conception of balance of power. A similar lack of attention to the various aspects of balance of power has been shown by the other students of the period. By such statements the present writer does not mean to disparage the superb work of these two great scholars but merely to point out the need for a detailed examination of the balance of power in the 1812–1815 period which will supplement the splendid work which has already been done.

It should be understood that the present study does not pretend to be the political, military, or intellectual history of the years under scrutiny. It attempts to examine, analyze, and trace the history of a particular conception and show how it related to, and affected, the larger context of historical events of the time. On the basis of the material which has been assembled, it is argued that the balance of power has a recognizable body of theory which has been largely ignored by historians and which is to be distinguished from simple rules of thumb which any statesmen might use in any state system. It is shown that theory and practice were closely related in the period of 1812–1815 and consequently that the theory was more than just a group of airy, unobserved maxims. Material has been presented to illustrate the neglected, idealistic side of the balance of power, a side long forgotten in our day. Moreover, the present work argues that the balance of power has evolved from primitive to more sophisticated forms and that the years from 1812 to 1815 were crucial years in that evolution, when statesmen attempted to make of the coalition a regular peacetime instrument for enforcing the balance-of-power system. It is argued that the concert is simply a "refined" form of balance of power; and that collective security, contrary to the assertions of nineteenth-century liberals and the Wilsonian liberals of the twentieth century, is indeed the ideal, long enunciated by balance-of-power theorists, toward which the balance-of-power system has been moving for more than two centuries.

My great debt to writers on the balance of power and on the Napoleonic period is shown in the bibliographical essay at the end of this volume. Here I have the pleasure of recording my debt and my thanks to others. It is through the generosity of the Carnegie Revolving Fund Committee of the American Historical Association that this manuscript has been brought to publication. Professor Raymond P. Stearns of that committee has been most helpful and discreet in passing on suggestions for changes. Professor Harry Rudin of Yale University was inspiring as a teacher and generous with time and ideas when this study was being prepared as a dissertation. In 1949–1950 financial support in the form of a grant from the Louise S. McDowell Research Fund freed me from certain academic commitments and made possible further work in research and rewriting.

The following publishers graciously granted permission to quote from their works: G. Bell & Sons, Ltd., for passages from Sir Charles Webster's *British Diplomacy;* the Carnegie Endowment for International Peace for quotations from the English translation of Emmerich de Vattel's *Le droit des gens;* J. M. Dent & Sons, Ltd., and E. P. Dutton & Co., Inc., for excerpts from W. K. Marriott's translation of Machiavelli's *The Prince* (Everyman's Library); and J. M. Dent & Sons, Ltd., for quotations from *De Monarchia,* in *A Translation of the Latin Works of Dante Alighieri* (Temple Classics).

Betty Gulick put up with the usual, and always harrowing, difficulties which attend a book and contributed generously as a typist. Finally, I remember with particular pleasure a wartime visit to Professors Felix Gilbert and Theodore Von Laue, when I was just embarking on a study of the balance of power, and their very moving courtesy and generosity in showering me with ideas and assistance.

Edward Vose Gulick

Wellesley, Massachusetts
March, 1955

Contents

PART 2.   APPLICATION

Maps

Europe's Classical Balance of Power

PART 1 ∽ THEORY

Catechist: Hold, my pretty Child—one Word more.—You have been ask'd concerning the Ballance of Power.—Tell me what it is?

Europa: It is a such an equal Distribution of Power among the Princes of Europe, as makes it impracticable for the one to disturb the Repose of the other.

Catechist: Pray who was it that formed that excellent Plan?

Europa: The immortal King *William,* the *Dutch,* and other wise Men.

Catechist: Tell me wherein consists the Safety of Europe?

Europa: In this same Ballance of Power.

Catechist: What is it that generally causes War in her Bowels?

Europa: It is occasion'd by the Ballance of Power being destroy'd.

Catechist: And how may that Ballance be destroy'd?

Europa: That Ballance may be destroyed by Force or Fraud; by the Pusillanimity of some, and the Corruption of all.

Catechist: When any Potentate hath arriv'd to an exorbitant Share of Power, ought not the Rest to league together in order to reduce him to his due Proportion of it?

Europa: Yes, certainly.—Otherwise there is but one Potentate, and the others are only a kind of Vassals to him.

—*Europe's Catechism* (London, 1741), 11–12.

Chapter I

___

Assumptions

IF WE contemplate two roped climbers on a mountain top, we make certain assumptions—usually by a lightning process of mind that does not draw our attention. We assume that there is a mountain which solidly fills the space between their advanced position and the security of the valleys below. We assume further that the mountain, although composed of such various things as snow slopes, glaciers, and rock masses, will not separate out suddenly into its component parts like a pyramid of gymnasts and walk away but that it is committed to its role of stationary and composed support of our climbers. Similarly, when writers have viewed the balance of power, they have unconsciously and habitually made (and often ignored) numerous assumptions. They have assumed, for example, the initial existence of the state, a unit of power based upon land and people, which was capable of exerting influence beyond its own borders;

3

they have assumed also that power existed; that it could be measured by men; that men, having measured it, could balance it; that their balancing policies could affect the lives of states and the movement of history; and that the state system could be, and would be, perpetuated through human analysis, direction, and action.

For present purposes, it is enough to single out four important assumptions which demand special comment.

STATE SYSTEM

Balance of power theorists assumed, first of all, the existence of a *state system,* that is, a group of independent "neighboring states more or less connected with one another" [1] and of relatively equal power. In the present examination, emphasis is placed not so much upon the individual state as upon the group of states in contact with one another, or "the general union . . . of all European powers in one connecting system." [2] Grouping is the cardinal condition; we view the family and not the individual.

The European state system of 1815 extended from the Atlantic to the Urals and included some fifty members. There were five major powers (Great Britain, France, Russia, Prussia, and Austria), four secondary powers (Portugal, Spain, Holland, and Sweden), more than forty lesser powers of very unequal size—chiefly in Germany and the Italian peninsula, and four free cities.[3] These states were jealously independent; they were neighboring, if not neighborly; they had interlacing connections with one another; and the larger states, the chief components of the system, were not widely unequal in power. Together

[1] Friedrich von Gentz, *Fragments on the Balance of Power* (London, 1806), 55. Hereafter cited as Gentz, *Fragments.*

[2] Henry, Lord Brougham and Vaux, "Balance of Power," *Works* (London and Glasgow, 1855–61), VIII, 12–13.

[3] For the sake of simplicity the figures have been taken from the year 1815, because of the fluctuations attendant upon the breakup of the Napoleonic Empire.

the states, large and small, comprised a system of states for all of the above reasons. There was a certain cohesiveness—derived largely from common cultural experiences in the past—which bound them together and which meant that they had more in common with each other than they had with others which lay outside the group—a point which will be dealt with later.[4]

This assumption of a state system is basic to any theory of political and military equilibrium among states. Just as one person does not make a crowd, one state cannot make a state system; and without a state system, one can have no balance of power among states. One should not be misled by the simplicity of this observation. The state system has obtained for so long in Europe that westerners have been prone to regard it as an inescapable, necessary, and even desirable condition of life—as common as drawing one's breath and as inevitable as taxes. It has often been forgotten that the whole apparatus of the European state system, with its carefully contrived concepts of sovereignty, independence, nationalism, and legal equality, all meshed more intricately than the elements of a Swiss watch, is by no means a common historical circumstance. The European system has had an unusual history in its singularly high development, making it unique in this respect so far as the historical record yet shows. There have been other state systems, to be sure—writers usually name the Carthage and Rome of the third century B.C., the China of Confucius' time, and Athens, Sparta, and Corinth of the fourth century B.C.[5]—but the historian can readily point to

[4] See below, p. 10 ff.

[5] See for illustration, David Hume, *Essays: Moral, Political, and Literary* (London, 1875), I, 348–356, where the author in an essay, "Of the Balance of Power," discusses ancient Greece, Carthage, and Rome. See also Quincy Wright, *A Study of War* (Chicago, 1942), II, 762–763, for observations both on ancient China and ancient Europe; and Frederick Schlegel, *A Course of Lectures on Modern History* (London, 1849), 8–10, where the author comments on the ancient Greek and post-Alexandrine balance-of-power system. Schlegel's lectures were originally delivered in Vienna in 1810. Another essay on the balance-of-power system in the ancient world appears in one of the exceptional, book-length treatments of the balance: F. J. von Hendrich,

other times and places, equally famous, where a state system has
not existed, the most obvious example in western experience
being the Roman Empire. Quite obviously, and quite importantly, the Roman world of 100 A.D. sported no system of
jealous, independent states, each responsible for its own security; Rome controlled the Mediterranean lands. Nor did medieval Europe in 1200 A.D. really enjoy a fully developed state
system. The vogue was for imperial unification of one form or
another, and a state system was generally considered anarchic
and undesirable—as indeed it is in many respects. The arguments against it and in favor of empire were expressed for all
time by Dante in a well-known passage:

It is evident that in the quiet or tranquillity of peace the human
race is most freely and favourably disposed towards the work proper
to it (which is almost divine, even as it is said "Thou hast made him
a little lower than the angels"). Whence it is manifest that universal peace is the best of all those things which are ordained for
our blessedness. . . . If we consider the family, the goal of which
is to prepare its members to live well, there must needs be one to
guide and rule. . . . If we consider a district, the end of which is
helpful co-operation both in persons and in appliances, one must
needs be the guide of the rest, whether he be imposed upon them by
another or rise to eminence out of themselves, with the consent of
the rest. Else not only do they fail to attain the mutual support they
aim at, but sometimes when several strive for pre-eminence, the
whole district is brought to ruin. And if we consider a city, the end
of which is to live well and suitably, there must be a single rule,
and this not only in a rightly ordained polity, but even in a wrong
one. For if it be otherwise not only is the end of civil life missed,
but the very city itself ceases to be what it was. If finally we consider
a special kingdom, the end of which is the same as that of the city,
only with better assurance of tranquillity, there must be one king to
rule and govern, else not only do they in the kingdom fail to reach
the goal, but the kingdom itself lapses into ruin, according to that

*Historischer Versuch über das Gleichgewicht der Macht bei den alten und
neuen Staaten* (Leipzig, 1796), 74–143.

saying of the infallible truth, "every kingdom divided against itself shall be laid waste." . . . Therefore there must be one guiding or ruling power. And this is what we mean by monarch or emperor. Thus it appears that for the well-being of the world there must be a monarchy or empire.[6]

One need not grope among parchment and broken monuments for evidence of a time when state systems did not exist. For an even more telling example of this general pattern, one looks to the Far East in 1815, at a time exactly contemporaneous to the high development of the European state system itself. Where Europe in that year had five important centers of power and several lesser ones, each sovereign and independent and responsible for its own survival, the Far East had one such center—Manchu China, ruled from Peking by an imperial court and a scholar bureaucracy and supported by garrisons of Manchu bannermen at key points throughout China. Surrounding states—Japan, Korea, Laos, Burma—were of distinct inferiority, like small chicks clustered around a big hen. Where powerful European states had perforce to face formidable neighbor states of equal or greater power, Manchu China held overwhelming power relative to her Japanese, Korean, Burmese, and other neighbors. Where European states recognized fellow states as equal before international law and capable of receiving and exchanging missions and embassies on the basis of that equality, Manchu China accepted no such relationship with outside powers. Equality among states had no factual basis in the Far East and consequently made no sense in that context. A state which sought permanent relations with Manchu China could do so only on a basis of what was known as "tribute relations," i.e., the acceptance of a status of inferiority and the rendering of tribute at regular intervals to the Emperor of China by way of special emissaries who publicly kowtowed to him and his officials. When one considers that the kowtow was not a simple

---

[6] *De Monarchia*, bk. I, chs. iv and v, *A Translation of the Latin Works of Dante Alighieri* (J. M. Dent and Sons, London, 1904).

bow before an acknowledged superior but consisted of kneeling and knocking one's forehead on the ground three times before the Emperor, of standing briefly before kneeling again for three knocks, and of a third round of three, all performed before the entire court and to the shouted commands of a court function-ary, one understands why Europeans protested. Merely this one eastern ceremony suggests, and with accuracy, that international relations in the Far East at the time of Napoleon and the Congress of Vienna were almost antithetical to those in Europe. We now read with amusement of the repeated snubs visited by the Manchus upon eager European diplomatists who sought 150 years ago to open regular intercourse, European style, with the Orient. The kowtow was a particular stumbling block for stiff-backed westerners, and much thought was given to the problem of whether or not to perform it. The Dutch bent; the British did not.[7]

Placed in the wider vistas of world history, the Europe of that period, with its cluster of armed states, its specialized concepts of international relations, its brochures on the balance of power, and its eagerness to preserve all the trappings of such a system, looks surprisingly parochial. Moreover, it is evident that such a system is by no means too commonplace to describe systemat-ically. One even wishes that more description had been done, just as one sometimes wishes that William Gilbert and Arthur Sullivan might have turned their attention to the eighteenth-century European state system. They would not have lacked material.

FRAMEWORK

The second major premise is implied in the first, where we have already assumed the existence of a state system. By the second, we assume a *framework*—that is, a generally recognized

---

[7] For a brief description in English of the system of tribute relations under the Manchus, see H. B. Morse's impressive work, *The International Relations of the Chinese Empire* (London, 1910–18), I, 48–62.

size of the system and therefore a limited number of entities to be balanced. In other words, the state system must possess a rather clearly defined territory; it cannot consist of a wholly indeterminate area and therefore of a wildly fluctuating number of states. A statesman could not deal with an infinite or ever-varying number of imponderables, any more than an expert juggler, accustomed to keeping five eggs in the air, could be asked to keep five dozen going. At the same time, there are, indeed, only rough limits to the size of a balance-of-power system. Logically, one may say there is a precise minimum—that is, two states with relatively equal power could theoretically comprise a balance-of-power system. The fact that neither possessed an overwhelming preponderance of power would act as a check on their actions. But while it might seem possible for the state system to consist of no more than two powers in order to permit the existence of a balance of power, this number should properly be regarded as improbable, unusual, and even dangerous for the continuance of the equilibrium. With only two, a statesman would have to pray for several special conditions in order to avoid the growth of disparity; assuming an equality of power to begin with, unlikely in itself, he would hope for either a static maintenance of this condition or a parallel development in power for the two states, also unlikely. A happy minimum would therefore include more than two states, but it need not embrace a large number. The answer is rather like an answer to the query of how many eggs make an omelet.

There is also no exact numerical limit to the maximum membership of a state system, as long as there is some kind of workability. For example, Europe in the seventeenth and eighteenth centuries embraced some three hundred sovereign entities [8] and yet was rendered a workable equilibrium through the domination of the system by the small group of large powers and a tacit

---

[8] The Chinese state system of 700 B.C. was similarly large, including perhaps 200 sovereign units, a number later reduced to seven (Wright, *A Study of War*, II, 763, n. 48).

understanding of the areal extent of the system. History has been kind in the sense that the historical experience of states has been such as to limit the number of eggs which statesmen have had to juggle. The obvious facts of geography and communications have usually dictated the determinate number of members in a system and therefore the outlines of the framework. For example, Europe in the early nineteenth century had such irregular relations with the Far East and was so far removed from it by the difficulties of travel that there was no question as to whether Great Britain and France were members of the same state system as China and Japan. Although no Great Wall surrounded the European states in 1800, we may say that a kind of diplomatic fence divided the European state system from the rest of the world. The fence may have been broken here and there; it may have permitted rather easy ingress and egress; it may sometimes have moved around; but it existed, and it was a fact of demonstrable importance in the balance-of-power system.

The existence of such a framework may be shown by reference to several types of evidence, some of them rather unusual: the writings of balance-of-power theorists emphasizing the common culture of Europe, the relations of the Ottoman Porte to Europe, the speeches of statesmen, the distribution of diplomatic representatives, and the alliance structure of European states.

Writers on the balance of power have repeatedly stressed the common ground of culture in European states. They have pointed out that in addition to proximity, which undergirds a balancing system, there is a conception of a common destiny, a conception of a certain unity in spite of wars and differences. Martens suggested it when he wrote that

the resemblance in manners and religion, the intercourse of commerce, the frequency of treaties of all sorts, and the ties of blood between sovereigns, have so multiplied the relations between each particular state and the rest, that one may consider Europe (particularly the Christian states of it) as a society of nations and states, each of which has its laws, its customs, and its maxims, but which it cannot put in execution without observing a great deal of delicacy towards the rest of the society.[9]

The Abbé de Pradt found that Europe formed "a single social body which one might rightly call the European Republic" [10] and which was on a large scale what the family of German states was on a smaller scale. He held that all the sovereigns of Europe formed a kind of commonwealth, reciprocally guaranteeing each other's continuance. Vattel declared that the practice of balance-of-power policies "make of modern Europe a sort of Republic." [11] To Gentz, it was the "European commonwealth." [12] A careful reading of these and numerous other writers leaves a strong impression of a recognized framework for the balance of power which existed either consciously or unconsciously in the minds of statesmen and political theorists.

The social historian would find himself comfortably at home with the emphasis of the balance-of-power writers on European unity—or "diversity in ideal unity," to use von Ranke's phrase for the Italian state system of the fifteenth century.[13] The social historian might point to Europe's common experience of the medieval Christian church, to the use of Latin as a European

[9] G. F. von Martens, *Summary of the Law of Nations* (Philadelphia, 1795), 27–28.

[10] Dominique de Fourt de Pradt, *La Prusse et sa neutralité* (London, 1800), 86–87 (translations from this work are mine); Niklas Vogt (1756–1836), historian at the University of Mainz, teacher of Metternich, and prolific writer on the balance of power, used this phrase as a title for one of his works, *Über die europäische Republik* (5 v., Frankfurt am Main, 1787–92). For an analysis of his work and its bearing on the balance of power, see Magdalene Herrmann, *Niklas Vogt, ein Historiker der Mainzer Universität aus der 2. Hälfte des 18. Jahrhunderts* (Giessen, 1917), *passim*.

[11] Emmerich de Vattel, *The Law of Nations* (Washington, 1916), III, 251, #47.

[12] *Fragments*, 69.

[13] Leopold von Ranke, *History of the Latin and Teutonic Nations, 1494–1514* (London, 1887, trans. by P. A. Ashworth from *Geschichten der lateinischen und germanischen Völker*, Leipzig, 1885), 38.

language, to the universal ideals of the medieval period, to the general European opposition to Islam and the Ottoman Empire, to the general effects of the Renaissance, to the diffusion of the great architectural fashions, to the similarity of many traditions in music, painting or sculpture, to the spread of Roman law and to the general similarity of wedding, funeral, and family mores. A complete list of shared experiences would inundate the reader. It is worth noting that in the case of each of these items, western scholarship has been impressive and detailed, with the result that we have more often noted the differences between Paris and Rome and less often the vast and impressive similarities which stand out so conspicuously when comparison is made with other and different parts of the world. When the social historian has finished with his exegesis of "diversity in ideal unity," the balance-of-power writer of the eighteenth or early nineteenth century might add that the member states of his "Republic" shared a generally similar institution of autocracy (Great Britain was the notable exception) and that their diplomatic customs, their military and naval organizations, their strategy and tactics, their economic practices, and their ruling classes all had a great deal in common. Again, the similarities within Europe are impressive when comparison is made between European and non-European areas: "no citizen of Europe could be altogether an exile in any part of it." [14] The "unity" within the framework is important to our argument because it shows how this group of states was crisscrossed with a network of interrelationships and ties which were not duplicated in the relations of those states with the non-European

[14] Edmund Burke in *Letters on a Regicide Peace;* see Ross J. S. Hoffman and Paul Levack (eds.), *Burke's Politics, Selected Writings and Speeches of Edmund Burke on Reform, Revolution, and War* (New York, 1949), 459. See *ibid.,* 458–459, for Burke's well-expressed discussion of "the similitude throughout Europe of religion, laws and manners." See also Rousseau on the same subject in C. E. Vaughan (ed.), *The Political Writings of Jean Jacques Rousseau* (Cambridge, 1915), I, 366–368.

world. In other words, unity drew a line around the state system and indicated where the framework began and ended.

The framework was a flexible conception, as mentioned. It had to grow like anything else, and it had changed in size a good deal since its birth in Italy in the fifteenth century. For example, the Italian Renaissance state system in the 1400's rounded out its century of "diversity in ideal unity" by witnessing its own collapse through a fatal flexibility—the invited intrusion of Charles VIII of France in 1494 which led to the destruction of the fragile network of the Italian system. French power, thrust among the small states of Italy, was like a crowbar dropping through cobwebs.

Furthermore, a certain flexibility of the framework was necessarily introduced by the overseas expansion of European powers [15] and by the tendency in Europe to develop a larger and larger framework. The pan-European framework, which by 1815 included everything from Portugal to the Urals, emerged slowly in modern history, its place being held from time to time by smaller, local frameworks, or "inferiour balances," as an anonymous eighteenth-century writer expressed it.[16] For example, the Baltic powers were often engaged in a framework distinct from that of the western European powers, as indicated by the relatively separate existence of two wars in Europe, the War of the Spanish Succession and the Great Northern War, at the same time at the beginning of the eighteenth century. This separation of orbits was recognized in both the British and Prussian cabinets by the presence there of two secretaries of state, one

[15] For a discussion of the effect of overseas expansion upon the European framework, see pp. 76 ff. of Adolf Rein's article "Über die Bedeutung der überseeischen Ausdehnung für das europäische Staaten-system," *Hist. Zeit.*, 137, pt. I (1927), 28–90. This is one of the few outstanding articles on the balance of power. The author utilizes material largely neglected by previous writers.

[16] *Appendix to the Memoirs of the Duke de Ripperda* (London, 1740), 357.

for each framework. By the end of the same century, the two structures had been permanently amalgamated, and there was a general European framework, which embraced Britain and the Christian countries of the Continent.

Flexibility is further illustrated by a curious point. It was debatable whether or not the Ottoman Empire was inside or outside the framework of the European balance of power in our period. One may, indeed, find this very point at issue in debates on the floor of the House of Commons in the early 1790's, when Pitt and the government were interested in sending British aid to Turkey to check the Russian advance on the shores of the Black Sea. Burke and Grey, pillars of the opposition and advocates of balance-of-power policies, sought to block Pitt's plans by speeches which emphasized the limited and exclusive membership in the European framework and which insisted that Turkey should not be considered a party to the European balance of power. Grey felt that the "maintenance of the balance of power was certainly a laudable object, when not pursued to too great an extent. . . . That Great Britain had pursued this object too far would not be denied, when it was considered that in her progress after it she had traveled as far as the banks of the Black Sea." [17] Burke's objections to the same attempt on the part of the government, uttered almost a year before Grey's, were more vigorously pointed:

The considering the Turkish empire as any part of the balance of power in Europe was new. . . . He had never before heard it held forth, that the Turkish empire was ever considered as any part of the balance of power in Europe. They had nothing to do with European power; they considered themselves as wholly Asiatic. Where was the Turkish resident at our court, the court of Prussia, or of Holland? They despised and contemned all christian princes,

---

[17] Speech in House of Commons, Feb. 29, 1792, in T. C. Hansard, *The Parliamentary History of England from the Earliest Period to the Year 1803* (London, 1806-20), XXIX, 929; quoted in Cobden, *Political Writings*, I, 271–272.

as infidels, and only wished to subdue and exterminate them and their people.[18]

On the other hand, in spite of what Burke said, the malignant and turban'd Turk obviously had one leg over the European fence, since he controlled the Balkans, an important sector of Europe, and since as recently as 1683 his armies had been encamped around Vienna. On the other hand, Islam, polygamy, the governmental slave hierarchy of the Ottoman Empire, and a plenitude of other differences stuck in the European craw, and the diplomatic position of the Ottoman with relation to the European framework remained a peculiar one.[19] While both Great Britain [20] and France maintained ambassadors in Constantinople throughout the eighteenth century, the Turks did not reciprocate until 1793, when their westernizing Sultan, Selim III, took the radical step of establishing permanent diplomatic missions at Paris, Vienna, London, and Berlin. This policy did not work out as smoothly as the Sultan must have hoped. Ruling an ancient empire steeped in tradition, he was beset with difficulties in his attempts to westernize. Here he had personnel problems, and he soon dropped the use of ambassadors.[21] In this case, however, the reciprocal maintenance of missions was not enough to render the Porte a bona fide member of the European framework. When Castlereagh, at the Congress of Vienna in February, 1815, offered the Porte an opportunity to join a general European guarantee, the Sultan refused.[22] It

[18] Speech in House of Commons, March 29, 1791, in Hansard, XXIX, 75–77.

[19] See F. L. Baumer, "England, the Turk, and the Common Corps of Christendom," *AHR*, L (Oct., 1944), 26–48, for a careful scrutiny of diplomatic relations between Turkey and Christian states in the sixteenth and seventeenth centuries.

[20] D. B. Horn (ed.), *British Diplomatic Representatives, 1689–1789* (London, 1932), Camden 3d ser., XLVI, 150–155.

[21] A. J. Toynbee, *A Study of History* (London, 1934–39), III, 72, n. 1.

[22] C. K. Webster, "Some Aspects of Castlereagh's Foreign Policy," *Trans. Royal Hist. Soc.* (London, 1912), 3d ser., VI, 69.

was, indeed, not until the Congress of Paris in 1856 that the Porte was officially accepted as a member of the European framework.[23] Cobden, as late as 1836, was asking, "Upon what principle is Turkey made a member of this European system? The Turks, at least, will be admitted by everybody to form no party to this 'union.' "[24]

From the relationship of the Ottoman Empire to the European state system, one gathers that the balance-of-power system, so given to precise data, to weights and measures, to tidy calculations of power, to measuring out its life with coffee spoons, was at least moderately imprecise. The fence of the framework was occasionally obscured or in disrepair. At the same time, Burke's aroused concern over the inclusion of the Turks reminds us of the evident reality of some kind of framework of the European balance, and the heat of his argument in this case illuminates the conceptual framework of the balance of power.

A much more revealing type of evidence on the framework is the distribution of diplomatic representatives. A balance-of-power system depends for operability on the watchfulness of foreign offices over the various important member states. This fact has been recognized from the very beginning of equilibrist strategy in the Renaissance. The importance which has attached to the ambassador as a diplomatic watchdog is evidence of it.[25]

The historian, assuming this much—namely, that the presence of diplomatic watchdogs is important to the balance of power—may at this juncture suggest that the pattern of distribution of the representatives is an equally significant fact: if the assigning of an individual ambassador or minister is important, is not the pattern of assignment of the whole group a good piece of evidence on the confines of a state system? Take, for example, Great Britain. A list of the personnel of the British

[23] Edouard Gourdon, *Histoire du congrès de Paris* (Paris, 1857), 10; see Article 7 of the General Treaty of March 30, 1856.

[24] Cobden, *Russia* (1836), in *Political Writings* (London, 1867), I, 269.

[25] See below, p. 55.

diplomatic service between 1792 and 1815 reveals that there were some thirty of His Majesty's missions abroad, twenty-five of which were in Europe.[26] The remaining five were scattered among countries of the western hemisphere and the Near East, and these missions were intermittent in character—the Persian mission, for example, being listed for only 1811–1815. This distribution, overwhelmingly European in character, may be taken as good evidence for the presence of a European framework, because England, as a seafaring and trading nation, tended to have wider and more permanent non-European contacts than the continental countries, and the fact that her diplomatic contacts were still dominantly European argues for her primary concern with European countries.[27]

Evidence of a similar character for France shows that French foreign missions were all European with two exceptions—the United States and the Ottoman Empire, which received French representatives from time to time in these years, depending on the shifting course of events.[28] For the period prior to the French

[26] See Great Britain, House of Commons, *Parliamentary Papers*, 1822, XVIII, 285, 4–5; also, S. T. Bindoff, E. F. Malcolm-Smith, C. K. Webster (eds.), *British Diplomatic Representatives, 1789–1852* (London, 1934), Camden 3d ser., vol. L, *passim*.

[27] There are other indications of the presence of a framework for the balance of power at the end of the eighteenth and beginning of the nineteenth centuries in some helpful, although inconclusive, evidence on the economic side. See the treaties and conventions which determined the commerical relations of England with her overseas markets. Hertslet, outstanding authority on British commercial relations, lists for the period under discussion seventeen overseas countries which were embraced by Britain's commercial treaty structure. Of these only two—Persia and the United States—were non-European in character, while a third, Turkey, was only partially European and occupied an ambiguous position in the European framework, as already noted (Lewis Hertslet, *A Complete Collection of the Treaties and Conventions and Reciprocal Regulations at present Subsisting between Great Britain and Foreign Powers* [London, 1840–1925], I, II, *passim*).

[28] A list of French ambassadorial posts is to be found in *Liste des noms et demeures de messieurs; les pairs de France; les membres de la Chambre des Députés* (Paris, 1815?). For evidence of the French eighteenth-century

Revolution, France maintained only one non-European mission, and that in Turkey, which had been an irregular and peripheral member of the European framework since the time of Francis I. The regular posts for French ministers and ambassadors, however, lay in Spain, England, Austria, Prussia, Russia, Poland, the German Diet, and so forth. All the foreign missions maintained by other countries in France were European, with two exceptions, a United States legation and a Turkish chargé d'affaires.

The final, clinching argument for a European framework is based on the treaty structure from 1792 to 1815, and we find conclusive documentation for the presence of a framework for the balance of power. The easiest rule of thumb for discovering the local framework of the balance of power is, indeed, to examine the treaty structure. Typically, a treaty of alliance is made between two states and directed against a third. A perusal of several treaties will soon disclose the number of states which are potential (or actual) enemies and allies. If we can uncover this number, we have virtually defined the framework within which their equilibrist diplomacy must operate. Our concern, then, lies primarily with the membership of the coalitions between 1792 and 1815, for this is the information which will determine the groupings of enemies and allies and therefore the extent of the framework. The pattern of the coalition wars may be stated briefly as follows: expansionist France opposed by a stubborn and war-weary England throughout the period; England, the nucleus of opposition, being joined in its struggle from time to time by Spain, Russia, Prussia, Austria, the Netherlands, Sardinia, and a host of lesser German states.[29] The con-

---

European framework for the balance of power, see Commission des Archives Diplomatiques, *Recueil des instructions données aux ambassadeurs et ministres de France depuis les traités de Westphalie jusqu'à la révolution française* (26 v., Paris, 1884–1929), which is packed with European material but contains very little concerning non-European areas.

[29] There were usually many members of these coalitions; for example, the First Coalition included Austria, Prussia, Great Britain, Spain, Sardinia, Sicily, Hesse-Darmstadt, Baden, United Provinces, Brunswick, Tuscany,

flict, while it had its overseas side shows, was neither a local war over one part of Europe nor a struggle that ranged over the entire world. It was European, a fact underlined by the almost exclusively European character of the treaty structure for the period. In four volumes covering the period 1800–1815, Martens listed about 2,900 pages of treaty texts, nearly 2,800 of which dealt with treaties between European countries (Great Britain included). About fifty of the remaining pages contain the agreements between Great Britain and East Indian potentates, and some seventy-five pages list the few agreements between European and non-European states which were made in those years.[30]

There can be no substantial doubt that a kind of diplomatic framework existed at that time. It was definitely European, comprised most of the continent, treated the Ottoman Empire as peripheral and the rest of the world as nonmembers.

RELATIVE HOMOGENEITY

In studying the international relations of the eighteenth century, the student finds that Europe was an in-group of states which excluded non-European countries and which displayed a high degree of homogeneity within itself, as shown. Relative

---

Parma, Venice, Portugal, etc. For purposes of simplicity, only the principal members are usually mentioned in studies of the period.

The essential details of the coalitions against France may be followed in Adalbert Wahl, *Geschichte des europäischen Staatensystems im Zeitalter der französischen Revolution und der Freiheitskriege* (Munich and Berlin, 1912), 34 ff., 93 ff., 145 ff., and 220 ff.

Different students of the period find varying numbers of coalitions. They usually agree on the number (3) as far as 1807, and then strike off in different directions, often counting the Franco-Austrian War of 1809 as a coalition war.

[30] G. F. von Martens, *Recueil des principaux traités d'alliance, de paix, . . . conclus par les puissances de l'Europe . . . depuis 1761 jusqu'à présent* (Göttingen, 1817–35), VII (1831), 1800–03; VIII (1835), 1803–08, *passim;* and G. F. von Martens, *Nouveau recueil de traités d'alliance . . . depuis 1808 jusqu'à présent* (Göttingen, 1817–42), I (1817), 1808–14; II (1818), 1814–15, *passim.* These works will hereafter be cited as Martens, *Recueil,* and Martens, *Nouveau recueil.*

homogeneity was a demonstrable fact; it existed and it bestowed certain benefits upon the European balance of power. The question remains as to whether or not such homogeneity was a necessary precondition for a workable equilibrium. An unequivocal affirmative is found among many theorists in that period.

One cannot read the above selections concerning the "European commonwealth" [31] without realizing that these writers assumed such homogeneity to be a necessary condition of a balance-of-power system. The impression gained from their writing is strengthened by reference to the work of another commentator on the European state system—Immanuel Kant. Kant is not commonly thought of as a writer on the balance of power, and he was certainly not a conventional writer on the subject. Histories rarely refer to his work on the balance of power as such; and just one writer, and that in an unpublished manuscript, has suggested that Kant was the "greatest of all those . . . [who wrote on] the theory of the balance of power." [32]

Kant (1724–1804) lived in Königsberg, East Prussia, in the classical period of the balance of power. During the latter years of his life he was a distant witness of the convulsions of the French Revolution and a much closer observer of the second and third partitions of Poland of 1793 and 1795, ominous events at the end of a rather settled century. During his sixty-ninth year, the wars of the French Revolution began. In the second year of warfare he drafted a long essay entitled *Zum ewigen Frieden*,[33] in which he touched on some of the basic problems

[31] See above p. 11.

[32] A. F. Kovacs, "The Development of the Principle of the Balance of Power from the Treaty of Westphalia to the Congress of Vienna" (unpubl. MS, University of Chicago Library), 79.

[33] Immanuel Kant, *Zum ewigen Frieden* (1795) in *Sämmtliche Werke* (Leipzig, 1867–1869), VI (1868), 405 ff.; available in English translations by Hastie, Campbell Smith, Friedrich, and others. Page references below are to the translation by M. Campbell Smith, *Perpetual Peace; A Philosophical Essay* (London, 1903).

of the state system of Europe. Although perceptive, this work is a curious offering to include under the theory of the balance of power. It does not define the balance of power, save by implication; it does not attempt to assess the partitions of Poland in relation to the tenets of balancing theory; it does not discuss the use of specific alliances, coalitions, barriers, or wars as devices or evidences of the balance of power; and it does not even use the words balance of power extensively. In short, Kant did not oblige us with a treatise written, as it were, just to illuminate our particular interests and problems at this particular moment. Nevertheless, he did include ideas and analyses which a student of balance of power cannot afford to ignore. While unorthodox, the essay does take up matters germane to balance-of-power analysis—for example, the author was writing about the European state system. He rejected universal monarchy, favored retention of freedom by individual states, and opposed the preponderant power of any one state; [34] and he recognized the selfish and disruptive impulses of rulers and states. Kant faced the usual problems of balance-of-power writers and statesmen; and he had in mind a standard aim of these men, namely the continued freedom and security of the individual state. It was here, however, that he departed from their more conventional approach: where they dealt with specific policies and devices of particular states, he dealt more loftily with the historic tendencies of the state system as a whole; where they continued as political analysts and commentators on technique, he ascended the heights of long-range historical judgment and prophecy.

His assertions concerning the tendencies within the European state system make very interesting reading. He argued, for example, that the state system, far from being a hopelessly brutish and anarchic form of institutionalized disorganization, tended toward stability and peace in spite of the aggressive capacities of men and states; their universal selfishness bred so many checks and counterchecks that individual states found their

[34] *Ibid.*, 128 ff.

hands tied.[35] Human nature, he felt, did not have to be per-
fected before improvement was possible in international relations, because there existed an evolutionary movement within
the state system tending automatically toward improvement. It
all added up to a kind of "predetermined design to make harmony spring from human discord." [36] We must grant that considerable success attended this prophecy of improvement, because a rough approximation of his guess appeared within a
generation in the concert system of 1814–1822 and to a lesser
degree in the remainder of the nineteenth century, when the
concert existed in an abortive form. Any attentive reader will
find that Kant's essay casts penetrating shafts of insight into the
darkness of the subject. The essay also reveals its share of oddi-
ties and mistakes—for example, Kant's overlooking the tendencies which were destined to destroy the European framework of
the balance of power and create in its place a world framework.
Although one need not approach the essay with the air of entering a cathedral, Kant has given us a stimulating interpretive
essay by which we are measurably enriched.

In the course of the development of his arguments, Kant
made it perfectly apparent that one of his basic assumptions
was the relative homogeneity of the states within the European
system. He found it clearly necessary that European governments possess a rough homogeneity, and he thought that such
necessary similarity would arise through a prevalence of republican forms of government (by which he meant the separation of
executive and legislative functions). A minimal homogeneity
was necessary, and basic dissimilarity was dangerous.[37] By assuming such a degree of uniformity among states in the framework, he relied on a regional framework for the balance of
power and risked the breakup of his system whenever that
framework should give way. He was, therefore, strictly European in point of view; and his treatise was palpably a product
of his environment, by being European and not universal in its

[35] *Ibid.*, 134–135.   [36] *Ibid.*, 143.   [37] *Ibid.*, 120 ff.

assumptions. In this sense, it was dated and would demand re-thinking for relevance to later periods.

The case in favor of assuming a necessary homogeneity among the members of a state system was a persuasive one.[38] With similar outlooks on international law,[39] it was easier to effect the exchange of ambassadors, ministers, and attachés, all of whom were important to the preservation of the balance of power; given similar concepts of military organization, of strategy and tactics, it was easier for statesmen to measure the power of foreign members of the system in the ceaseless game of counter-weighting and balancing; and, given similar cultural traditions, it was easier to respect the institutions of other states and be moderate toward those states in peace settlements.

In addition, homogeneity meant a kind of advantageous group-consciousness for the members of the state system; it meant a uniformity of assumptions which in turn facilitated the perpetuation of a balance of power. A statesman could count on the existence among other states of a virtually instinctive will to resist attempts at domination; he could assume that states within the system possessed the will to compete and the desire to survive as free states; he could assume that they had a varying, but considerable, capacity to survive. If Europe was an un-weeded garden with things rank and gross possessing it merely, there was at least the predictable process of growth and competi-

---

[38] The points which follow are presented here without embellishment and in summary form, since they require space for development below. They may appear obscure when treated in such brief and anticipatory fashion but ought to be clear after a reading of the appropriate sections below.

[39] Burke indicated that he regarded relative homogeneity as indispensable to the European balance of power; see for example, his reference to "the scheme of public law, or mass of laws, upon which that independence and equilibrium are founded" (Hoffman and Levack, *Burke's Politics,* 407). He again, and very clearly, implied this indispensability in his argument in favor of intervention in French affairs (*ibid.,* 443, par. 4), where he speaks of certain rights of European states as a body, referring to Europe as a "federative society—or, in other words, . . . [a] diplomatic republic of Europe."

tion. One plant did not yield its place without a struggle, and relative homogeneity in the governing institutions of European states tended to supply something approaching a constant in the flux of international politics.

The arguments in favor of a relative homogeneity within a state system do not prove that such similarity was, or is, an essential precondition to the existence of a balance-of-power system. The absence of homogeneity would not be destructive of the balance of power in the same way that the absence of the first assumption, that of the state system itself, would be. If you took away the state system, you would simply have no possibility of a balance of power among states; it would be like depriving the omelet of eggs. The absence of homogeneity, on the other hand, could be described more accurately as crippling to the balance of power, not destructive of it. An equilibrium perhaps could be preserved among states which were essentially different, but such an equilibrium would be seriously handicapped and its future in all probability rendered deeply obscure and highly unstable. The balance-of-power system was, as will shortly be shown, an old and oft-repaired machine, which creaked badly enough as it was; without a lubricating homogeneity it might well have broken down.

RATIONAL SYSTEM OF ESTIMATING POWER

There are a number of aspects of balance of power which make its eighteenth-century and early nineteenth-century popularity seem no accident. One of these is the fourth major assumption. An age of mechanistic philosophy in which Newton was king, Locke, Voltaire, and Montesquieu the royal advisers, and in which the religious vogue of Deism, plausible and arid, had relegated God to the role of retired watchmaker of the universe —this age was anything but hostile to the logic of balancing power. The power of individual states was conceived to be susceptible of measurement by certain well-defined factors: "Their populations, their territories, their finances—i.e. 'the balance of trade'—and by the state of their armies and navies." [40]

A good example of this approach is seen in the project which Talleyrand submitted to Napoleon on the eve of the battle of Austerlitz in October, 1805. In that year Napoleon was approaching his peak. His southeastern policies had brought control of the Italian peninsula to France. The boundaries of western and southern Germany had recently been arbitrarily redrawn to satisfy his aims, and incidently to line the ample pocketbook of Talleyrand, who is said to have received bribes from the petitioning German delegations. The year 1805 was for Napoleon a kind of hinge date; he was not yet committed to a grandiose imperial plan for France in Europe; Europe itself still contained a state system not yet utterly out of balance; and Napoleon might still have swung in either of two directions in his over-all strategy—toward balance of power or toward empire. He could keep France a powerful, but restrained, member of the European state system—a strong state in the company of other strong states; or he could attempt to push French control over as much of Europe as his resources would permit. We remember what he did but have largely forgotten that there was a time when his ultimate aims were still undeveloped. The year 1805 was such a time. In October of that year Napoleon was about to wind up a whirlwind military campaign against Austria. There would soon be a peace settlement between a victorious Napoleon and a defeated Austria. Talleyrand, his principal adviser on foreign affairs, was aware of the importance of the coming settlement and was concerned lest its stipulations weaken and humiliate Austria, one of the chief supports of the European equilibrium, and thereby compromise the future of the state system. In other words, Talleyrand was eager to swing Napoleon in the direction of a balance-of-power strategy.

He argued in his letter to Napoleon that French power must not be immoderately increased; that Austria must be compen-

[40] Theodore H. Von Laue, "History of Balance of Power, 1494–1914" (unpubl. MS), 2; see also Wright, *Study of War*, II, 743.

sated for losses; and that new boundaries should be made, by careful adjustment, to strengthen the future balance of the system rather than distort it. He wanted to remove the basis for future Franco-Austrian antagonism. The areas in which their interest overlapped and conflicted might be taken by France with one hand, but liberal Eastern compensation must be offered to Austria with the other. Such a program would tend to fasten Austrian eyes on the new areas, divert her from conflict with France, and also maintain her as an undiminished power in the general equilibrium. This proposed exchange of lands was worked out by the French minister in terms of population, territorial extent, and income, and an attempt was made to indicate the comparable power value of each.[41]

Again, during the Congress of Vienna, statesmen resorted to a similar system of measurement to determine the exchange and distribution of German and Polish territories to Prussia, Russia, and Austria.[42] Castlereagh had recommended this technique as a means of helping to break the deadlock in the Saxon-Polish question in late December, 1814.

Throughout Talleyrand's letters and the charts and figures of 1814–1815 there breathes the easy conviction that the power of states could be estimated with sufficient accuracy for the additions and subtractions of balance-of-power diplomacy. In actual fact, a singularly complex problem is presented by the measurement of power, and such measurement is not at all a trustworthy process, as it is assumed to be by equilibrists. Indeed, Cobden pointed out, and not without some justice, that the theory of the

[41] Talleyrand to Napoleon, Oct. 17, 1805, in Pierre Bertrand, ed., *Lettres inédites de Talleyrand à Napoléon, 1800–09* (Paris, 1889), 171.

[42] For evidence of the importance which statesmen attached to population as one of the major ingredients of the balance of power, see the elaborate statistical tables employed by Austria, France, and Prussia at the Congress of Vienna in the negotiations concerning compensation for Prussia and Austria. See Comte d'Angeberg (J. L. B. Chodzko), *Le congrès de Vienne et les traités de 1815* (Paris, 1864), I, 509–510, 582–585, 602–604, 681–683; II, 1884–1885, 1936–1939, 1947–1952, 1957–1960. This work will hereafter be cited as d'Angeberg, *Congrès de Vienne*.

balance of power "could . . . be discarded as *fallacious,* since it gives no definition—whether by breadth or territory, number of inhabitants, or extent of wealth—according to which, in balancing the respective powers, each state shall be estimated." [43]

If he had lived in the twentieth century, Cobden might have gone on to say that the complexity of power is attested by ample books which have discussed it and disagreed over it, after the unending pastime of scholars. The strength of a state now depends upon its population, birth rate, and death rate; its geographical location, configuration, and supply of raw materials; its entire economic system, including production, transportation, and markets; its government, leadership, traditions, and outlook; and the whole matter of its military, naval, and air instruments, which in turn include a vast array of important factors, such as rate of production, methods of recruitment and training of personnel, morale, fire power, electronic instruments for detection, rockets, guided missiles, and atomic weapons. And how, indeed, is a statesman to measure these elements of power? Cobden put his finger on a sensitive point but then pressed too hard and injured his case. He was perhaps justified in his hostility to balance-of-power policies, and he was unquestionably right in indicating a certain vagueness in their conception, but power (according to the equilibrist), whether it can be accurately measured or not, does exist, and can be observed to exist, in variable amounts. In short, a greater or lesser aggregate of power may be possessed by a given state, and such possession is a fact of great importance to neighboring states which may be deficient in power. Their statesmen, whether accurate in their estimates or not, must measure power, regardless of the primitive character of the scales at their disposal.

In defense of the assurance of statesmen in the palmy days of balance of power, we can say that the problem of power in the eighteenth and early nineteenth centuries was less intricate than it is today, simply because the instruments of power were them-

[43] Cobden, *Political Writings,* I, 269.

selves less complex. War was two-dimensional rather than three-dimensional, as with the airplane and guided missiles. Power was more directly a matter of territory and of the number of men with muskets which governments could put on the field and less a matter of which state could produce the largest amounts of specialized material and highly trained personnel. By and large, a statesman in 1750 or 1815, if he possessed information on the size of armies, on the men who led them, and on the relative wealth of the rulers, probably had a better chance of estimating the power of a foreign state than he would have today. Much of the necessary information was actually common knowledge in the chancelleries of Europe. These circumstances do not mean that Metternich or Castlereagh had accurate means of assessing the absolute power of France in 1805 or 1815, but they do mean that statesmen used a rough guess, which confined itself largely to armies and military potential and which was capable of giving them some idea of French power in relation to that of other states. That they could have made accurate power estimates was impossible, just as it is today. That they were compelled to rely on half-truths was one of the weaknesses of their system.

One may, then, dismiss the question of "power" with the admission, on the one hand, that it is impossibly complex and the assertion, on the other hand, that the statesmen themselves were reduced to making guesses. These guesses have themselves become historical facts and are valuable evidence in assisting us to arrive at an understanding of what their authors understood by "power." For our purposes, it is enough to understand their meaning, to be aware of the difficulties of achieving an understanding of absolute power, and to realize that the estimation of power was, and is, one of the common mental processes of a balance-of-power statesman.

The precise point at which the scales of power turn, like that of the solstice in either tropic, is imperceptible to common observation: and, in one case as in the other, some progress must be made in the new direction, before the change is perceived. They who are in the sinking scale, for in the political balance of power, unlike to all others, the scale that is empty sinks, and that which is full rises; they who are in the sinking scale do not easily come off from the habitual prejudices of superior wealth, or power, or skill, or courage, nor from the confidence that these prejudices inspire. They who are in the rising scale do not immediately feel their strength, nor assume that confidence in it which successful experience gives them afterwards. They who are the most concerned to watch the variations of this balance, misjudge often in the same manner, and from the same prejudices. They continue to dread a power no longer able to hurt them, or they continue to have no apprehensions of a power that grows daily more formidable.[44]

[44] Lord Bolingbroke, *Works* (Philadelphia, 1841), II, 258.

Chapter II

Aims

NO ONE who has watched a boat being built would regard a barnacle as essential to its structure. In similar fashion, once the edifice of aims of the balance of power is exposed, the observer, seeing what its main elements are, can easily distinguish what is germane from what is incidental.

PRESERVE INDEPENDENCE AND SECURE SURVIVAL

The basic aim of the balance of power was to insure the survival of independent states. This may be taken as fundamental to the classical balance-of-power system and should be distinguished from those goals, such as "peace" and (to a lesser degree) the "status quo," which were incidental to it.[1]

Writers on the balance of power expressed their recognition of this basic aim in various ways. Brougham, for example, held

[1] See below, pp. 35–42, for comment on these points.

that "the whole object of the [balance of power] system is to maintain unimpaired the independence of nations." [2] Heeren spoke of the balance of power as the "mutual preservation of freedom and independence, by guarding against the preponderance and usurpation of an individual." [3] Vattel, in elucidating the "general Principles of the Duties of a Nation to Itself," summarized them with the dictum: "To preserve and perfect one's existence is the sum of all duties to self." [4] We find in all three a repeated emphasis on the primacy of the survival of independent states. Similarly, where the old British Mutiny Act provided for the levy of troops, it was associating an instrument of war (the levy) with the two ideas of "the Safety of the United Kingdom . . . and the Preservation of the Balance of Power in Europe," and was by implication asserting that survival took precedence over peace as an aim of the balance of power.[5]

PRESERVE THE STATE SYSTEM

Taking the survival of the independent state as his base, the equilibrist erected his aims by piling two more blocks on top of the first. The second block consisted of the argument that the best way to preserve the individual state was to preserve the system of which it was a part. Self-interest, according to this line of reasoning, could best be pursued by attention to group interest. By preserving the state system you would preserve the parts thereof. For a superb illustration of this second block, carefully aligned and cemented by the master mason himself, we look at a famous passage in the *Mémoires* of Prince Metternich, creator and preserver of intricately balanced structures:

[2] Brougham, *Works,* VIII, 80.

[3] A. H. L. Heeren, *History of the Political System of Europe and Its Colonies* (Northampton, Mass., 1829), I, 12–13.

[4] Vattel, *Law of Nations,* III, 13, no. 14.

[5] Cited by T. J. Lawrence, *Principles of International Law* (Boston, 1910), 130. Text may be found in George K. Rickards (ed.), *The Statutes of the United Kingdom of Great Britain and Ireland* (London, 1804–69), XXVIII, pt. I, 34.

Politics is the science of the vital interests of States in its widest meaning. Since, however, an isolated state no longer exists, and is found only in the annals of the heathen world . . . we must always view the *society* of states as the essential condition of the modern world. . . . The great axioms of political science proceed from the knowledge of the true political interests of *all states;* it is upon these general interests that rests the guarantee of their existence. . . . What characterizes the modern world and distinguishes it from the ancient is the tendency of states to draw near each other and to form a kind of social body based on the same principle as human society. . . . In the ancient world isolation and the practice of the most absolute selfishness without other restraint than that of prudence was the sum of politics. . . . Modern society on the other hand exhibits the application of the principle of solidarity and of the balance of power between states. . . . The establishing of international relations, on the basis of reciprocity under the guarantee of respect for acquired rights, . . . constitutes in our time the essence of politics.[6]

The same concern for the state system was mirrored in the first secret article of the treaty of April 11, 1805, between Russia and Great Britain, which spoke of "the establishment in Europe of a federative system to ensure the independence of the weaker states by erecting a formidable barrier against the ambition of the more powerful." [7] Gentz also had it in mind when he wrote:

The fate of Europe depends upon the fortunes and political relations of the powers which preponderate in the general system. If the balance be preserved among these; if their political existence and *international organization* be safely established; if, by their mutual action and reaction, they protect and secure the independence of the smaller states . . . ; if there is no dangerous prepon-

[6] Prince Metternich, *Mémoires, documents et écrits divers* (Paris, 1880–84), I, 30; cited by H. du Coudray, *Metternich* (New Haven: Yale University Press, 1936), 167–168.

[7] French text in J. Holland Rose (ed.), *Select Despatches . . . relating to the Third Coalition against France, 1804–05* (London, 1904), App., 273; quoted by W. Alison Phillips, *The Confederation of Europe* (2d ed., New York, 1920), 40–41.

derance to be perceived, which threatens to oppress the rest, or to involve them in endless war; [then] we may rest satisfied with the *federal constitution* which fulfills these most essential points, notwithstanding many errors and defects. And such was the federal constitution of Europe before the French revolution.[8]

This quotation fairly radiates concern for the *group* of states comprised in the state system.

These selections indicate the structure built by the supporters of balance-of-power policy. It will be observed, however, that their reasoning was not derived by a strict logic but had a certain admixture of faith, the cement between the first two blocks being two parts logic and one part faith, in spite of what the masons might protest to the contrary. Where a writer found balance of power to be an obvious maxim of self-interest, a careful scrutiny of his statement will reveal it to be merely a plausible half-truth. There are, to be sure, circumstances in which equilibrist policies would be obvious self-interest, especially those times when the balance of power was in danger of being upset to the disadvantage of the state. There are, however, numerous occasions when a violation of the principles of the balance of power would undeniably be self-interest: for example, when an opportunity for safe conquest and annexation appeared. Under such circumstances, balance-of-power theory demanded restraint, abnegation, and the denial of immediate self-interest.

NO ONE STATE SHALL PREPONDERATE

Once the second block was in place, there was no choice about the third. If one granted that the survival of independent states was the primary aim and added that the best chance of achieving it resided in preserving the state system, a relentless logic led

[8] Friedrich von Gentz, *The State of Europe before and after the French Revolution* (pamphlet, London, 1801; trans. from *Von dem politischen Zustand von Europa vor und nach der französischen Revolution,* Berlin, 1801), 93; quoted by Von Laue, "History of the Balance of Power," 93.

to the obvious axiom of preventing the preponderance of any one member of the state system. "Nations [should] unite, or . . . prepare for their defense, as soon as they perceive anyone becoming dangerously powerful." [9] Failure to do so was "an inexcusable breach of duty." [10] Similar formulations have often been made by writers, typical of whom again was Friedrich Gentz in his assertion "That if the states system of Europe is to exist and be maintained by common exertions, no one of its members must ever become so powerful as to be able to coerce all the rest put together." [11]

There has never been any divergence of opinion among equilibrist writers on this third general proposition. Their statements vary a bit in phraseology and tone, but they convey the same substance. The position is well stated by Gaspard de Réal de Curban, writer on government in the middle of the eighteenth century:

For several centuries Europe has been worrying about the smallest manifestation of ambition which it perceived in a Power. Each nation, while it tries to rise above the others, is occupied with maintaining a certain balance, which bestows upon the smallest states the force of a large section of Europe, and preserves them in spite of the weakness of their armies and the defects of their governments. This equilibrium of power is based on the incontestable principle that the greatness of one Prince is, properly speaking, only the ruin or the diminution of the greatness of his neighbor, and that his might is but another's weakness.[12]

[9] Brougham, *Works,* VIII, 73.   [10] *Ibid.,* 72.

[11] Gentz, *Fragments,* 61–62.

[12] *La science du gouvernement* (Paris, 1765), VI, 442; hereafter cited as Réal, *Science du gouvernement.* Quoted in Von Laue, "History of the Balance of Power," 37–38. See also *Appendix to the Memoirs of the Duke de Ripperda,* 357–358. Another eighteenth-century writer defined the balance of power as "the expressed or tacit union of several states of lesser power in order to secure their existence, their freedom and their possessions, and to prevent . . . the . . . too far-reaching designs of any other power which . . . has already become too overwhelming" (Ewald Friedrich, Graf von Hertzberg, *Über den wahren Reichtum des Staaten, das Gleichgewicht des Handels und der Macht* [Berlin, 1786], 9). Hertzberg (1725–1795) was a

COMMENTS

Peace

We may say that survival, a degree of co-operation, and the prevention of a hostile predominance were all germane to the balance-of-power theory, as indicated. We may also say that peace was not germane. However desirable it may have been, however passionately the theorist may have longed for it, however devotedly he may have consecrated his life to its realization, peace was no more essential to equilibrist theory than the barnacle to the boat.

An appreciable amount of confusion has arisen on this point as the result of mistaken analysis of balance-of-power theory. Indeed, peace has occasionally been urged as the pre-eminent aim of balance-of-power policies: "A balance of power aims primarily to preserve peace and the *status quo*." [13] The same idea is often found in treaties when the balance of power is mentioned; witness one of the treaties of Utrecht, that between Great Britain and Spain (July 2/13, 1713), which contains the following phrase: "in order to secure and stabilize the peace and tranquility of the Christian world by a just equilibrium of power (which is the best and most solid basis of mutual friendship and durable harmony)." [14] Although many who have written on the balance of power have adopted this point of view, there are reasons why their position is untenable.

Consider, for example, the striking content of the diplomatic history of the last five hundred years in Europe, from the Italian Renaissance to the present, which has literally brimmed with parallel evidence of both balance of power and war, during the very period when the balance of power was at its height. Ac-

prominent Prussian statesman, chief minister to the king from 1763 to 1791, and author of many works on history and political science.

[13] Sidney B. Fay, "Balance of Power," *Encyclopaedia of the Social Sciences* (New York, 1937), I, 397.

[14] J. Dumont, *Corps universel diplomatique du droit des gens* (Amsterdam, 1731), VIII, 391, col. 7.

cepting such a finding, it is possible to deal with this coincidence in two ways: one may say that the balance of power aimed at peace but perennially failed, or that balance-of-power theory aimed at the survival of the state system and regarded war as a means of preventing the breakdown of that system. With regard to the first of these propositions, we cannot help asking if the balance-of-power system was, in the period of its most consistent practice, as ineffectual as the proposition suggests. It is tempting to say yes and drive another nail into the balance-of-power coffin, but the answer surely lies in the direction of the second proposition, and for several reasons.

It is noticeable that wars were fought in the name of balance of power against Charles V, Louis XIV, and Napoleon, to mention only the most outstanding and to ignore myriad examples of lesser importance. One also notices that the clearest-headed theorists of equilibrium have not only *not* claimed peace as the principal aim, but have actually envisaged war as an instrument for balancing power: Vattel, Gentz, Brougham, Christian Wolff, in company with such practical statesmen as Talleyrand, Metternich, and Castlereagh, all thought of war as an instrument to preserve or restore a balance of power. One observes also the almost placid acceptance by Rousseau and Kant of the hideous nature of competition within the state system and their obvious belief in a successful balancing system in spite of it. The argument of these advocates conforms to theory and fact by showing that the incidence of war was not evidence of the ineffectiveness or absence of balance-of-power policies but that such incidence indicated widespread practice (often malpractice, to be sure) of the balance of power, of which war was an instrument. Their contention explains where the first proposition obscures, and, by explaining, effectively cuts the ground from under the "peace" point of view.

We would be correct in listing peace as one of the incidental by-products of equilibrist policy, or as one of its secondary aims. There is no doubt that peace has often been temporarily preserved as a result of balance strategy; but we may also be sure that a system of independent, armed, and often mutually hostile states is inherently incapable of remaining at peace over a considerable period of time merely by the manipulation of balance techniques.

Status Quo

Returning to the assertion that a balance of power system "aims primarily to preserve peace and the *status quo*," we must still examine the *status quo* as an admissible, primary aim of balancing theory. In this case we may not say that one finds merely a casual connection between the two, as in the case of "peace" and the balance of power. We are not dealing with a barnacle on the hull of the theory; rather, the design of the ship itself is at stake, for here we find separate groups of writers arguing separate interpretations of the relationship between balance of power and *status quo*. Some assert and some deny the need to preserve the *status quo*, their disagreement being most vividly illustrated in their different attitudes toward the partitions of Poland in the eighteenth century, when Poland was, by 1795, extinguished as an independent state. There were writers who found this act a hideous breach of balance-of-power precepts, which were designed to preserve, rather than dissolve, the independence of states.[15] Others argued that Poland was weak, a prey to outside interference, and an area doomed to ultimate absorption; consequently, a series of partitions which distributed Polish areas among three neighboring powers was a desirable and even outstanding achievement of balance-of-power policy; war was avoided and a political vacuum was eliminated from eastern Europe.[16] Thus some writers abhorred the political

[15] Metternich found the partition "contrary to all principles of sound policy." (The phrasing is that of the English translation of the memoirs: *Memoirs of Prince Metternich, 1773–1815* [New York, 1880], II, 9). Vergennes regarded the First Partition as the work of a clique of powers against the system of general equilbrium (Siour Favier, *Politique de tous les cabinets de l'Europe* [Paris, 1802], III, 162).

[16] The Abbé de Pradt is an example of those writers who favored and

extinction of an independent state, others even applauded it. The latter writers obviously regarded the *status quo* as untenable or unrealistic.

The matter may be clarified by a return to first principles. The first aim of balancing theory called for the survival of independent states. Without such states, there could be no state system; and without the system, there could be no balance of power. Although so much may be said without cavil, the aim is quite general and invites interpretation. What, for example, was meant by the "survival of independent states"? Did this phrase mean all states in the system? Or did it mean merely some? Could a theorist legitimately, according to balance-of-power theory, insist on the survival of key states only, or did he have to preserve each and every member of the state system? It was at this crossroads that writers marched off in different directions. If a theorist argued for the preservation of all states, he was arguing for the *status quo;* if he argued for the survival of some only, he was disregarding the *status quo.* The arguments in favor of each position demand scrutiny before judgment may be passed on their relative value.

In support of the *status quo* as the proper interpretation of the primary aim of balance-of-power theory, one may argue both from the theoretical position and from the historical record. In theory, if the *status quo* of the Europe of 1648 or 1713, when Europe was dissected into many states, could have been pre-

---

even extolled the partitions as a balance achievement: "The dismemberment of Poland . . . never disturbed the equilibrium of Europe. . . . The extinction of the Polish anarchy, instead of being a loss for Europe, was on the contrary a real gain for it, and a confirmation of its equilibrium" (*La Prusse et sa neutralité,* 87–88. See also Gould Francis Leckie, *An Historical Research into the Nature of the Balance of Power in Europe* (London, 1817), 324–340, where the author argues that the partitioning was "one of the most useful lessons of its kind to be drawn from history" (324); "[Poland's] dissolution was long foreseen, and we think ought not to be regretted" (325); "Poland seemed to cherish a government incompatable with the very intention of human society" (328).

served indefinitely, it would have assured forever that there could be no preponderant power. Neither France nor Austria, both of them prominent at those dates, was sufficiently powerful to dominate the continent. Moreover, England, Prussia, Spain, Sweden, and others were not negligible in the equilibrium. A freezing of such a divided Europe for all time would have meant the perpetuation of a state system and the avoidance of preponderance. Under those circumstances, "the survival of independent states" (meaning all states) would have involved the fighting of wars to maintain or restore the territorial framework which existed before the war. The logic of this interpretation is satisfactory, if somewhat superficial; furthermore, the historical record has some encouraging words to add. For example, in the period from 1648 to 1792, there were, generally speaking, no great territorial changes in continental Europe, except for the first partition of Poland. We note some minor changes: the "corrections" of European territory by Louis XIV, the Spanish Netherlands becoming the Austrian Netherlands, Gibraltar and Minorca being taken by Britain, Silesia seized and secured by Prussia, and certain Ottoman areas going to Russia. But it would be no mistake to disregard these as outstanding changes in general European territories. The major impression which the observor receives from the state system of 1648–1792 is one of relative stability, although Poland offers contrary evidence, because the first partition of that unhappy land witnessed the loss of about one-third of her territory, together with the loss of considerable prestige, the important grain areas of Galicia, and her access to the Baltic. Nevertheless, one may treat that partition as an unfortunate exception to general practice in the period before 1792. The record is, indeed, a remarkable one for preservation of the *status quo*. Wars, an all-too-familiar disfigurement of the seventeenth and eighteenth centuries, repeatedly ended in restoration of either the *status quo* or a close approximation of it. More dramatic changes were a characteristic of the overseas phases of the wars to a much greater degree than of the continental theater itself. Indeed, the trifling changes in Europe, where Frederick the Great fought two wars within twenty-three years to secure for Prussia at great risk no more than the province of Silesia, were in dramatic juxtaposition to the Gargantuan slabs of territory which changed hands overseas. In the peace treaty at the end of the Seven Years' War, Great Britain swept France from the great subcontinent of India and gutted the French empire in North America, only to lose the American colonies herself within another twenty years. The apogee of the theory of balance of power, or at least an important part of it, was indeed contemporary to a notable retention of the general outlines of the *status quo* in Europe over a period of many years. So much may be accepted. There remain, however, powerful arguments against acceptance of the *status quo* interpretation as the only legitimate one.

The second interpretation, that is, the one which rejects slavish attention to the *status quo,* focuses attention on the unavoidable movement of history (as opposed to the possible freezing of a state system into a given *status quo*) and tends to emphasize the preservation of key members of the system at the expense, if necessary, of smaller or weaker powers. According to this point of view, one must take into account the dynamism of history, the flow of power and wealth from one area to another, the decadence of once-great powers in the general equilibrium, and the emergence of new, dynamic powers. The Greeks had a word for it—flux. Indeed, one of the great justifications of studying history is the insights which one gets into the process covered by this word. One of the few things that we can be sure of in all history is that everything changes. In the long run, flux will upset the best-laid plans of an earlier epoch. What once balanced nicely will for another generation hang as awkwardly as a wet toga. There is, then, a theoretical justification, and a strong one, for the reading of the phrase "survival of independent states" as some states, or key states, and not all states. With regard to the historical record, this school of thought can point an accusing finger at the opposition for its selection of 1792 as a terminal date for evidence. The use of evidence chosen only from the period before 1792 is arbitrary in the extreme, because such selectivity avoids the necessity of dealing with the awkward facts of 1793–1814, when Europe went through the most violent phase of the French Revolution, as well as two partitions of Poland, the excesses of Napoleonic imperialism, the violence of coalition warfare, a great modern broadening of warfare itself, the consolidation of German states, and the creation (coupled with the later destruction) of a great continental empire under Napoleon.

When the time came for peacemakers to discuss the restoration of the European state system, the unresolved controversy over the *status quo* bubbled at once to the surface. Some voices were raised for the restoration of the frontiers of 1789, 1790, or 1792, but there was vigorous rejection of such reasoning by many others. Times had changed, it was asserted by the latter, and the reconstruction of outworn boundaries would not serve the purposes of a new Europe which had been deeply modified and invigorated by the French dynamism of the 1790's and the Napoleonic period. We see here the typical cleavage in interpreting the phrase "survival of independent states"—the supporters of the *status quo* against those of flux. The latter could show with cogency how a restoration of the old state system of the period before 1792 was impossible under the circumstances. For one thing, it was impossible to prevent further Russian gains in what had been Poland—Russia was one of the victorious powers; Russian policy was adamant in seeking to place a new small Poland under the Russian tsar; and, most persuasive of all, Russian troops effectively occupied Polish soil.

One may show that, although both had their weaknesses, the flux doctrine was better adapted to the harsh realities of history than the *status quo* position, particularly in the era of pronounced and fundamental changes from 1792 on. The supporters of the *status quo* represented a kind of idealistic conservatism, at once more artificial, more legalistic, and more anachronistic than its tougher cousin. The theorists who rejected the *status quo* in favor of a more fluid equilibrium represented a point of view which was more tenable as a long-term adjustment to the flow of history, tougher and more workable in the harsh world of statecraft by diplomacy. The former was more a short-term policy and a typical small-power attitude; the latter, a safer long-term one and more an expression of a big-power point of view.

Balance of Power and Machiavellianism

Balance-of-power policies have often eventuated in singularly sordid diplomatic acts and practices. No one denies this, but such an unsavory history has given rise to further confusion, this time with regard to the "Machiavellian" aims of the balance of power. In the twentieth century one lives, as far as equilibrist theory is concerned, in the shadow of an able and violent denunciation of balance-of-power policies by nineteenth- and twentieth-century liberals. Richard Cobden, for example, reeled off one of the most pungent bits of invective when he shouted in print: "The balance of power is a chimera! It is not a fallacy, a mistake, an imposture—it is an undescribed, indescribable, incomprehensible nothing; mere words, conveying to the mind not ideas, but sound." [17] Woodrow Wilson, an intellectual descendent of Cobden in his attitude toward the balance of power, helped greatly to consolidate its bad reputation in utterances like the following characterization of the balance as "a thing in which the balance was determined by the sword which was thrown in on one side or the other; a balance which was determined by the unstable equilibrium of competitive interests; a balance which was maintained by jealous watchfulness and an antagonism of interests." [18] The criticism of these and other men

[17] *Political Writings*, I, 258.

[18] Wilson in his response to an address at the Guildhall, London, Dec. 28, 1918, in Ray Stannard Baker and William E. Dodd (eds.), *The Public Pa-*

was so thundering that it succeeded in identifying balance of power with "Machiavellianism," both of which terms have now long been used and abused as derogatory. There is an appreciable gulf between the two as theoretical systems, and the matter is best settled at once. Attention is called to their respective aims, which are signally different.

Balance-of-power aims begin with the survival of the independent state and go on to group concern and the thwarting of preponderance of any one state. Where balance-of-power theory asserts that self-interest is best served by group interest, we have shown the argument to be partly a matter of faith. No such faith is apparent in Machiavelli, who accepts proposition number one (the survival of the independent state) and rejects propositions number two (group concern) and number three (preventing the preponderance of any single state). He may be said to argue, not that self-interest is best served by group interest, but that self-interest is best served by more and better attention to self-interest. His distillation of political advice in *The Prince* is a good illustration of this point.

There is, first of all, no direct concern with the state system in *The Prince*. The author, having lived in a time of troubles, when thrones were quickly won and lost, was primarily concerned with two things—how a prince could get and keep his crown and how he could get on in the world. *The Prince* thereby becomes a document for the individual state or the individual ruler, and not for the state system. The balance of power is neither discussed nor referred to in any important passage, although Machiavelli does urge something closely akin to it under certain circumstances:

Again, the prince who holds a country differing in the above respects [language, customs, or laws] ought to make himself the head and defender of his less powerful neighbours, and to weaken the

---

pers of Woodrow Wilson: War and Peace (New York and London, 1927), I, 342.

more powerful amongst them, taking care that no foreigner as powerful as himself shall, by any accident, get a footing there; for it will always happen that such a one will be introduced by those who are discontented.[19]

Here again, however, the concern of the author is not with the preservation of a system, but merely with the prince, who must maintain himself in adversity that he may be ready when opportunity should knock. An opportunity to conquer the world, a wholesale heresy to the equilibrist, would have been acceptable to Machiavelli, whose advice was directed toward possible aggrandizement, with no element of self-discipline which the balance theory would impose. The fact that *The Prince* was avidly read and greatly admired by Bonaparte is an accurate index to its essential incompatibility with the principles of balance of power, just as the disdain of Vattel—the careful and rational equilibrist—for Machiavelli is a similar indication of the same antithesis between the latter's ideas and equilibrist principles.

Moreover, *The Prince* is overwhelmingly concerned with domestic policy, typical examples of the author's advice being:

It is necessary for a prince wishing to hold his own to know how to do wrong, and to make use of it or not according to necessity.[20]

Injuries ought to be done all at one time, so that, being tasted less, they offend less; benefits ought to be given little by little, so that the flavour of them may last longer.[21]

The chief foundations of all states, new as well as old or composite, are good laws and good arms; and as there cannot be good laws where the state is not well armed, it follows that where they are well armed they have good laws.[22]

Those who solely by good fortune become princes from being private citizens have little trouble in rising, but much in keeping atop.[23]

[19] *The Prince* (trans. by W. K. Marriott, London and New York, 1908), 20; for a passage which virtually trespasses upon the balance of power see *ibid.,* 178–179.

    [20] *Ibid.,* 122.   [21] *Ibid.,* 73.   [22] *Ibid.,* 97.   [23] *Ibid.,* 53.

The Prince, then, is not a balance-of-power document. It assumes the desirability of greatness for the individual state, whatever the cost to the system, and urges the unmitigated self-interest of the state.[24] The balance-of-power theory, on the other hand, can be shown to be, at best, a theory of the general good, a theory of self-discipline, a theory of survival for the group and a theory of moderation; witness, for example, the following illuminating quotation from Koch, early nineteenth-century writer on the balance of power:

This system [balance of power] has for its object the preservation of the public tranquillity, the protection of the weak against the oppression of the strong, the blocking of the ambitious projects of conquerors, and the prevention of discord, which in turn leads to the calamities of war. Uniting [the powers] . . . by one interest, it compels them to sacrifice their personal views to the general welfare, and it makes them . . . a single family.[25]

None of these benevolent characteristics may properly be claimed for the policies urged by Machiavelli. Compared to the nakedly "realistic" Machiavelli, the theorists of the balance of power appear as pure as an angel's intention—in theory, let us remember. It is perhaps possible that *The Prince* might have been substantially different, possibly even a balance-of-power handbook, if it had been written thirty years earlier, when the Italian peninsula still enjoyed a balance-of-power framework sufficient unto itself. Its author might even have made notable

---

[24] Friedrich Meinecke, *Die Idee der Staatsräson in der neueren Geschichte* (Munich and Berlin, 1925), 31–60, offers a lucid and illuminating discussion of Machiavelli's relationship to the development of the idea of national interest. Meinecke develops the thesis that we tend to identify Machiavelli with just a part of his outlook (p. 56), rather than with the whole, and that what we regard as the ruthless severity of his outlook was mitigated by his "virtù-Ideal" (p. 39 ff.). There is no reason to question this thesis, but one must recognize that the ideal which Machiavelli held up for statesmen was quite unconnected with the ideals of the balance of power.

[25] C. G. Koch, *Histoire abrégé des traités de paix, entre les puissances de l'Europe, depuis la paix de Westphalie* (re-ed. by F. Schoell, Paris, 1817–18), I, 3; quoted by Von Laue, "History of the Balance of Power," 62.

contributions to the theory. The peninsular framework was dealt its deathblow in the 1490's, however, and Machiavelli, writing in 1513, seems to have absorbed the pessimism of those later circumstances.[26] He accepted the contemporary international anarchy as a situation incapable of mitigation, whereas the inchoate theory of balance of power was to move one step in the direction of order and organization and assert that a mitigation of existing international disorder was possible. Its remedies may have been far from perfect, but they did represent a step toward an ordered and stable Europe.

Idealization

Justification of an established practice is all too familiar. In the medieval period the universal church found protagonists ready to justify universal monarchy. At a later date and in connection with the institution of absolute monarchy, the concept of the divine right of kings justified, and for many years exacted, the loyalty of subjects to the throne. In more recent history capitalism, even in its more crudely exploitative phase in the nineteenth century, built up a vigorous and resilient myth around the freedom of the individual, labor as a commodity to be bought in the open market, and the infallibility of both the price mechanism and the law of supply and demand. In the eighteenth century an elaborate justification and idealization of the social order appeared in the form of the Great Chain of Being, a successful means of making the hierarchical character of social life appear inherent in the nature of things. Every form of life, according to this rationalization, was asserted to exist in echelon, beginning with the primitive at the lower end of the chain and moving, link by link, up through the more sophisticated forms of life to the apes, the savages, the lower classes, up past the middle classes, to aristocracy and royalty. A servant fulfilled his destiny by being a servant and by not breaking the

[26] See, for example, his remark: "This may have been well enough in those times when Italy was in a way balanced, but I do not believe that it can be accepted . . . today" (*The Prince*, 169).

chain with aspirations toward a link higher up. A static society, honeycombed with compartments, bred this complex justification of the existing order.

A doctrine as important and pervasive as the balance of power was sure to find its propagandists, and it did. Prominent writers and thinkers, particularly those who were interested in politics, government, and international law, made their various contributions. These writers accepted the basic fact of the irrevocable presence of a state system and identified a continuance of the state system with the sovereignty and independence of the individual state. But at this point they began to gild their lily by assuming the state system to be both desirable and good and by making spectacular claims on its behalf for liberty, order, and tranquillity. Some of these assertions were the products of amateur enthusiasts, others came from practicing statesmen, and still others from serious theorists.

Among the writers on government and politics, Lord Brougham is a stirring example of the idealizer. He worked out a detailed code of maxims for balance-of-power statesmen and held all nations, no matter how remote, morally and actually responsible for the functioning of the complicated system of international checks and balances, because "whatever weakens the security of one country, and encourages another in its attacks, tends to lessen the general reprobation of injustice, and give encouragement to usurpers and invaders all over the civilized world." [27] No nation must be allowed to violate the system and go unpunished, since "the impunity of the wrong-doers . . . [gives] a blow to the political morality of all nations, and . . . [lowers] the tone of public principle." [28] He held that war must be localized so far as possible, and to this end neutrality should be encouraged, "both because we thus narrow the evil operation of war, because we mitigate its sufferings, and because we better preserve one material chance of restoring peace when we retain as many neutrals as possible." [29]

[27] Brougham, *Works*, VIII, 76.　　[28] *Ibid.*, 76.　　[29] *Ibid.*, 88.

He vigorously denounced infringements and made no attempt to slide over gross violations which were perpetrated in the name of balance of power. The partitions of Poland are an illustration, and he excoriated the obliteration of that country's national existence. He held that the evils of western international life were due to a failure to live up to the demands of balance of power.

That the system [balance of power] which we are now considering has often-times been abused no one can deny. . . . But many of the evils which are ascribed to the principle in question, have been owing only to an erroneous conception of its nature. Many of them have arisen, from failing to carry the line of policy recommended by it, to the lengths which it enjoins.[30]

Friedrich Gentz's attitude shared common ground with Brougham's but was somewhat blunter and less idealistic. Even so, we find his *Fragments* interlarded with flattering references to the balance of power, an example of which is the phrase "those great enlightened principles." [31] He, like Brougham, condemned the partition of Poland as a "wicked project," the result of the "detestable discovery" by rulers that equilibrist techniques could be used for evil, as well as good, purposes; [32] the virtues of the balance of power, however, far outweighed its disadvantages:

[30] *Ibid.,* 4.

[31] Gentz, *Fragments,* 68–69. See also David Hume's "so necessary and so just a cause" in his *Essays: Moral, Political, and Literary,* I, 353; and Comte d'Hauterive, *De l'état de la France à la fin de l'an VIII* (Paris, 1800), 51: "The general equilibrium which moderates some, tranquillizes others and assures the rights of all." D'Hauterive was head of the archives of the French Foreign Office from 1807 until his death in 1830. During that period he drew up his "Conseils à un élève du ministère des rélations extérieures," a valuable, equilibrist document which contained advice and an extensive bibliography, the latter embracing the works which would presumably train a good balance-of-power statesman—works on diplomacy, on international law, memoirs, letters, and geographies, with comments by the author. The "Conseils" was first published in 1901, when it appeared in *Revue d'histoire diplomatique,* XV, 161–224.

[32] Gentz, *Fragments,* 72, 77.

Two great results were obtained, in the midst of a tumultuous assemblage of the most decisive events. The one was, that no person succeeded in prescribing laws to Europe, and, (until our times) all apprehension, even of the return of a universal dominion, was gradually banished from every mind. The other, that the political constitution, as it was framed in the 16th century, remained so entire in all its members until the end of the 18th (when all ancient ordinances were abolished,) that none of the independent powers which originally belonged to the confederacy, had lost their political existence.[33]

Much of the literature on the balance of power is simply enthusiastic, without the leaven of critical analysis which characterizes the work of both Brougham and Gentz. Examples of this type of idealization are to be found throughout the eighteenth century. The following selections from one author are illustrative:

If there was a Principle which our Forefathers adopted as the *Paladium* of their Liberty; if there was a Blessing which they courted at the Price of their Ease, and pursued with the Loss of their Blood, it was to preserve the balance of power abroad. . . .

By the *Balance of Power* he (a Briton) understands that happy Temper of Interests abroad, by which the Trade, the Peace, the Liberty, and the Religion of his Country is secur'd.[34]

When one has fed for a time on the eighteenth-century enthusiasts for the balance of power, the criticisms of Cobden, John Bright, and Woodrow Wilson sound like blasphemies spoken loudly in a church.

Fénelon, writing early in the eighteenth century, put into one paragraph a good deal about the balance of power—the necessity and justification of it, the immediate aim, and the idealism which in his opinion ennobled it:

[33] *Ibid.*, 64–65.
[34] *The Conduct of the Government with Regard to Peace and War* (London, 1748), 4–5.

It is necessary, therefore, to anticipate . . . that each nation seeks to prevail over all the others which surround it. Each nation is accordingly obliged to take care to prevent the excessive aggrandizement of each neighbor, for its own security. To prevent the neighbor from becoming too powerful is not to do wrong; it is to protect oneself from slavery and to protect one's other neighbors from it; in a word, it is to work for liberty, for tranquillity, for the public safety: because the aggrandizement of one nation beyond a certain limit changes the general system of all the nations which have relation to it.[35]

Similar idealism, although more soberly expressed, to be sure, may be found among the writers on international law. Most of the prominent thinkers on this subject down through the nineteenth century accepted the initial fact of the state system and the desirability of sovereignty and independence for the member states. From these assumptions, they worked out their respective systems, attempting to regularize, channel, and legalize the actions of independent states. With so few available ways to enforce international law, one could not afford to be highly selective; under the circumstances, it was natural and, indeed, inevitable that they should turn to the techniques of the balance of power to enforce their codes. In this way balance-of-power sections crept into these learned treatises on international law. Christian Wolff and Emmerich de Vattel, eminent eighteenth-century writers on international law, both included sections on the balance of power in their major works. Wolff's brief discussion [36] of some of the principles of the balance of power was picked up by Vattel, a Swiss who served the court of Saxony as a diplomatist and who became the translator (from

[35] Fénelon, François de Salignac de la Mothe-, "Supplément" to the "Examen de conscience sur les devoirs de la royauté," in *Oeuvres de Fénelon* (Paris, 1835), III, 361 (translation mine). This essay will be cited hereafter as Fénelon, "Supplément."

[36] Christian Wolff, *Ius Gentium Methodo Scientifica Pertractatum* (Oxford and London, 1934; trans. into English by Joseph H. Drake from the text of 1764), II, 330–335.

Latin to French), modifier, and popularizer of the work of Wolff. Vattel gave substantially more attention than Wolff to his development of the principles of the balance of power and their position in international law.[37] Both of these men illustrate the intimate and fundamental connection between balance of power and the canons of international law in eighteenth-century Europe.[38] Both their works were monuments of idealism, in the sense that they sought a rule of law for international dealings; and they saw balance of power as a necessary and important part of enforcement of the law. These writers dignified and idealized the balance-of-power theory by the bare fact of its inclusion in their monumental works, much as an aristocrat might exalt a tradesman by letting the latter marry his daughter and thereby enter a select circle. Not only was entry permitted in the case of the balance of power but the tradesman sat in the seat of honor. Writers, having found the independent state an unavoidable fact, proceeded in this way to dramatize it as a highly desirable fact.

[37] See Vattel, *Law of Nations,* III, 130, no. 53; 8, no. 22; 251, no. 49, *et passim.*

[38] For further substantiation of this point, see Lassa Oppenheim, *International Law, A Treatise* (4th ed., London, 1928), I, 99. In the present work attention is chiefly directed to those writers and theorists who built up the balance-of-power theory, rather than to those who attempted to tear it down. For a sampling of the latter see the works of Cobden and Wilson (cited above, p. 42). See also the following: Victor Riqueti, Marquis de Mirabeau, *L'ami des hommes, ou traité de la population* (Paris, 1756), II, 398, 399, 400, 500; and Johann G. H. von Justi, *Die Chimäre des Gleichgewichts von Europa* (Altona, 1758), *passim.*

Chapter III

Means

WE CAN now discern the basic assumptions and aims of the balance of power, and we have scraped off some of the obscurities which encrusted it. Given the assumptions and aims, it is possible to enumerate the means and show their proper relationship to the foregoing, much as a Euclidian geometrist, having made assumptions with regard to points, lines, planes, and numbers can build with corollaries an entire theoretical system, self-consistent and demonstrable. One of the difficulties under which the student of balance of power must work is the failure of any theorist to carry out what now seems a fairly obvious philosophical exercise. No one, as far as the present author can discover, has attempted to work out the corollaries of the balance of power—all the more surprising because the assumptions of balance of power were widely accepted in the eighteenth century, an age interested in philosophy and statecraft. The explanation of this curious gap in our historical literature may be comparable to that of the long-standing failure in the same period to see mercantilism as a system. Europe went through a period of wide application of mercantilist theory. Nevertheless, in spite of the abundance of writers who discussed it, attacked it, or championed it, no one writer possessed either sufficient interest or grasp to see its general unity as a system of thought and action. This work was left for later generations of historians, just as the same appears to be true of the balance of power.

Some writers have shown awareness of the intrinsic unity of balance-of-power theory—how means may be derived from assumptions and aims, and in this connection the palm goes to that violent and challenging Britisher, Lord Brougham, whose work on the balance comes closer to such systematizing than any other. Nevertheless, Brougham's stature as a writer and thinker, although not undistinguished, is hardly of the first order. His work is not to be compared, for example, to Machiavelli's comprehensive and penetrating contributions to the study of power politics. Where Brougham was able, Machiavelli was brilliant; where the Scot dumped ore into his readers' laps, Machiavelli pressed his metal into hard, ringing aphorisms. Brougham's work on the balance of power is not really adequate to latter-day needs. The ore is useful, and one is grateful for it, but it needs much refinement and shaping. It is desirable, therefore, to scan balance-of-power literature and to bring together in systematic form the means which are the standard devices of translating balance-of-power theory into practice and which may be derived from the already formulated assumptions and aims.

VIGILANCE

Lord Brougham put his finger on the first corollary of the balance of power when he spoke of "the prevalence of that national jealousy, and anxious attention to the affairs of other states, which is the master principle of the modern balance of power system." [1] That system, consecrated to the independence of the members of the state system, must necessarily employ vigilance as one of its primary means. An equilibrist statesman could never direct policy toward a desired end without having some real understanding of the problems at hand. And since his problems often relate to the expansion of neighboring powers, he must at all times "be instructed in all that passes outside of his kingdom which has relation to him, to his allies, [and] to his enemies." [2] The foreign ministry and its officers have to be watchful of foreign developments, of army and navy increases, of important economic gains and losses, and many other aspects of foreign life.

Watchfulness is not, of course, peculiar to the balance-of-power system. It is just as essential to the preservation of any system. Democracy is by no means self-perpetuating, and its continued existence clearly depends upon the constant vigilance of those citizens who cherish it. The same is true of the members of a state system where watchfulness has been of such singular importance to the balance of power that theorists have taken pains to emphasize it. Lord Bacon, writing in the seventeenth century on this problem, used a fine catch phrase when he wrote of a "general rule . . . which ever holdeth; which is that princes do keep due sentinel, that none of their neighbours do overgrow." [3] Brougham also spoke of the necessity of "constantly watching over the state of public affairs, even in profound peace." [4] By this he meant an intimate scrutiny of all relevant domestic problems in the member states of the system. He

[1] Brougham, *Works*, VIII, 8. See also the comment of Sir James Mackintosh on "that mutual jealousy which made every great Power the opponent of the dangerous ambition of every other" (House of Commons, April 27, 1815; text in C. K. Webster [ed.], *British Diplomacy, 1813–15* [London, 1921], 409). This work will be cited hereafter as Webster, *Brit. Dipl.*

[2] Réal, *Science du gouvernement*, VI, 341–342 (translation mine).

[3] Francis Bacon, "Essay on Empire"; quoted by Cobden, *Political Writings*, I, 266–267.

[4] Brougham, *Works*, VIII, 17.

argued that "no one power should view with indifference the domestic affairs of the rest, more particularly those affairs which have a reference to the increase or consolidation of national resources." [5] Vattel, Gentz, Fénelon, de Réal, and others all urged the necessity of constant watchfulness. There can be no question of either the logical validity of their point or of the vast extent to which it has been practiced in the conduct of balance-of-power policies.

So much for the theoretical aspects of vigilance. We may find evidence of the practical importance of princes keeping "due sentinel," as Bacon admonished them, if we examine the development of two major institutions in modern European history—the diplomatist and the system of permanent foreign missions, both of them closely related historically to the balance of power. With the emergence of the modern state in the Renaissance from the disintegrating fabric of the medieval universal state, there occurred a profound change in ideals from that of universal monarchy to that of the independent state. The new emphasis was upon freedom for separate states and also upon secularism. There arose a need for men within the individual states to handle relations with other states and a need for men to represent their own states at other courts. Out of this need emerged the diplomatist, an institution which was taken over by the Italians from the Byzantine Empire.[6]

Gradually the idea of maintaining regular diplomatic contact through permanent missions was built up, until by the end of the eighteenth century there obtained the complicated network of representation throughout Europe described in the above discussion of the "framework." [7] Brougham aptly described these institutions as based upon "the right of mutual inspection, now universally recognized among civilized states, in the appointment of public envoys and residents." [8] He held that the devel-

[5] *Ibid.,* 33–34.
[6] Harold Nicolson, *Diplomacy* (New York, 1930), 24–25, 29–30.
[7] See pp. 16–18.   [8] Brougham, *Works,* VIII, 12–13.

opment of these institutions was a major "refinement" of the balance-of-power system, as indeed it was.

Their relevance here resides in the fact that they were institutions whose function was that of watchfulness. Instead of casual or unorganized sources of information on other states, each European state could avail itself of the privilege of keeping regular observation posts in foreign lands, in return for permitting those foreign states to do the same. Special immunities from law and from search were granted on a mutual basis to these representatives and to the property of their residences. For someone running away from a policeman, it is useful to remember that by entering the grounds of a foreign embassy one passes onto foreign soil and cannot be arrested without the elaborate raveling of red tape.

In addition to such observation posts, the mutual exchange of consuls and of military and naval attachés has made easier the gathering of information by each country about its neighbors. From consuls have come statistics on the economic life of foreign powers; from the military and naval observers have come details of the strength, discipline, morale, and weapons of foreign armies and navies. It is here that authors often lapse into a discreet silence about still another important way of keeping "due sentinel," namely by using spies.

We have good documentation on the operations of the Hapsburg spy system in the late eighteenth and early nineteenth centuries, especially during the Congress of Vienna. Indeed, one of our important sources of information today on the activities of congress statesmen in 1814–1815 is the published record of the Austrian spies who busily eavesdropped, intercepted dispatches, and rifled wastebaskets. These spies, showing a generous impartiality, collected information on friend and former foe alike. We also know the details of an earlier episode of successful British spying against Benjamin Franklin and other American representatives before and during the peace conference with Great Britain at the end of the war of the American Revolution.

In this remarkable story, Franklin's secretary, one Dr. Edward Bancroft, was paid by the British for a flow of confidential information. His activity as a spy was not proven until a century and a half after the event.[9]

In the light of these and other notable cases, we may assume, pending further research, that spying has been one other prominent means of gathering information about one's neighbors in the state system. We guess that it was rather widely practiced before 1815 and that it often involved elaborate networks. Under these circumstances, one wonders what the relationship was between spying and balance-of-power theory. Should we, in short, designate spying as another legitimate way of keeping "due sentinel" in a balance-of-power system?

Arguing deductively from the assumptions and aims of the balance theory without looking further at the historical record, the answer is that there was no reason why spies should not be employed. There was nothing in the theory, as developed up to this point, which made the use of spies inconsistent with the assumptions or aims of the balance-of-power system. Such usage was indeed inconsistent with New Testament standards, but not with the altogether different principles of the balance of power.

It is, of course, possible to argue that spy systems, whether consistent with the first principles of balanced power or not, are simply unrewarding devices to use: they are expensive, they arouse suspicion, which in turn enhances the instability of the state system (when one really wants to stabilize it), and such instability cancels out the advantage of having the additional information which the spies have gathered. Again we are dealing with suppositions, because of our ignorance of the real facts concerning spy systems. We may say, at any rate, that if one argues from the first principles of balance-of-power theory, one finds no real objection to including spies as a legitimate device

[9] For the whole extraordinary story, see Samuel F. Bemis, "British Secret Service and the French-American Alliance," *AHR*, XXIX (1924), 474–495.

of statecraft. On the other hand, the case is not easy beyond that point, because our balance-of-power theorists have been singularly disobliging in this matter. They are not vocal on the use of spies in the eighteenth and early nineteenth centuries, and spy systems, whether legitimate or not, simply do not figure in their discussions of the theory of the balancing system.

THE ALLIANCE

At an earlier point it was shown that balance of power aims to prevent or check preponderance, because "the greatness of one Prince is . . . the ruin or the diminution of the greatness of his neighbor." [10] In a discussion of the means by which this preponderance might be avoided or checked, one recognizes that theoretically it might be accomplished, as has often been asserted, by giving states equal shares of territory. In a witty and anonymous eighteenth-century lampoon of the balance of power, quoted earlier, a catechist drills "Europa" in this doctrine of equal shares:

Catechist: Hold, my pretty Child—one Word more.—You have been ask'd concerning the Ballance of Power.—Tell me what it is?

Europa: It is such an equal Distribution of Power among the Princes of Europe, as makes it impracticable for the one to disturb the Repose of the other.[11]

In another eighteenth-century work, the Abbé de Mably ascribed to Queen Elizabeth of England the assertion that "it is a matter of dividing Europe into states almost equal in order that, their forces being in balance, they will fear to offend one another, and hesitate to plan too great designs." [12] It is of little importance whether or not Queen Elizabeth ever spoke those words; on the other hand, it is important to realize that such a

[10] Réal, *Science du gouvernement*, VI, 442; quoted above p. 34.

[11] *Europe's Catechism* (London, 1741), 11–12.

[12] Abbé de Mably, *Collection complète des oeuvres* (Paris, 1794–95), V, 65 (translation mine).

conception of equal power was an intellectual cliché that was brandished repeatedly by commentators on the balance of power. It had its defenders and its powerful critics. In using the supposed words of Queen Elizabeth, the Abbé de Mably was eager to attack her plan as *"impossible de réaliser."* His attitude was similar to the line adopted later by Gentz, Talleyrand, and others, who pointedly denied the feasibility of such an equality. Gentz spoke of it as an "imaginary principle." [13] Talleyrand held that "an absolute equality of forces among all the States, aside from the fact that it can never exist, is not necessary to the political equilibrium, and would perhaps in some respects be harmful to it." [14] Vattel rejected equal shares as hopeless: "Once this equality were established, how could it be regularly maintained by lawful means? Commerce, industry, the military virtues, would soon put an end to it." [15] Since the idea of a necessary equality has had a perennial virility in balance theory, it is necessary to point out here the justice of the claims of these critics. Their view is sustained by two very important and obvious facts. The first is that, since the fifteenth century and for a variety of reasons, it has never been feasible to redistribute territory among the rulers of Europe in such a way that all would have equal power. Secondly, the ever-present, persistent, and fundamental fact of continuous change in history precludes any equal distribution which could remain equal for any substantial length of time. Even assuming territory to remain the same, internal changes would so alter the power of states as to nullify any original territorial equality.

These two reasons suffice to dispose of the fallacy of necessary equality. For a balance-of-power theorist to insist on equality is for him to admit at the start that balance of power is impossible. Some intelligent theorists who clearly recognize the prob-

[13] Gentz, *Fragments,* 56.

[14] *Mémoires du prince de Talleyrand, publiés par le duc de Broglie* (Paris, 1891–92), II, 237–238 (translation mine). Hereafter cited as Talleyrand, *Mémoires.*

[15] Vattel, *Law of Nations,* III, 251, no. 48.

lem, however, felt that a successful balance of power required that a number, or even a majority, of the *major* states in the equilibrium possess an approximate equality of power. Such a condition is desirable for a balance-of-power system, although not an easy condition to create and sustain. Policy was directed in a limited sense toward an equality of key states in the settlement at Vienna in 1814–1815, when the attempt was made by Talleyrand, Castlereagh, and Metternich to thwart Russian retention of large Polish territories, and again when Prussian power was increased to create an adequate mass to check France on the one hand and Russia on the other. There was, however, never any real question of general equality, for both Russian and Austrian holdings were vastly greater than Prussian, while England's empire gave her a great overseas ascendancy. Moreover, there were still numerous states of insignificant power in Germany and Italy, not to mention the second-rate powers of Sweden, Denmark, Holland, Spain, and Portugal. We may, then, relegate the theory of general equality in power to a position of relative unimportance in a discussion of the means by which the aims of balance of power may be realized.

In our retreat from the idea of "an equal Distribution of Power among the Princes," we dig in at a second line of defense, which prescribes the dexterous use of artificial bonds to create the equality (or more often the defensive preponderance) which is necessary to a balance-of-power system. Vattel indicated the necessary logical step with simplicity and clarity when he wrote the following:

The surest means of preserving this balance of power would be to bring it about that no State should be much superior to the others, that all the States or at least the larger part, should be about equal in strength. This idea has been attributed to Henry IV, but it is one that could not be realized without injustice and violence. . . . It is simpler, easier and more just to have recourse to the method . . . of forming alliances in order to make a stand against a very powerful sovereign and prevent him from dominating.[16]

16 *Ibid.*

In other words, Vattel was arguing for a kind of equality of power, but an equality which was based on blocs of allied power and not on a hoped-for redistribution of land along the lines of equal shares. He willingly accepted the fact that states were unequal in power and could never be made equal like so many red bricks in a wall. He did not, however, give up hope for achieving a balance of power, but argued that the territorial inequality of states might be corrected by alliances. States A and B might each be smaller and weaker than C, but allied they might well be equal to, or greater than, C.

The alliance, then, becomes one of the prominent means of putting balance theory to work. It is at once one of the commonest, as well as one of the most complicated, means of checking preponderance and preserving the state system. Sir Robert Walpole put the relationship most winningly, after the oratorical manner of his period:

The use of alliances, Sir, has in the last age been too much experienced to be contested. It is by leagues, well concerted and strictly observed, that the weak are defended against the strong, that bounds are set to the turbulence of ambition, that the torrent of power is restrained, and empires preserved from those inundations of war that, in former times, laid the world in ruins. By alliances, Sir, the equipoise of power is maintained, and those alarms and apprehensions avoided, which must arise from vicissitudes of empire and the fluctuations of perpetual contest.[17]

[17] Hansard, *Parl. Hist.*, XII, 168–169; quoted by Kovacs, "Development of the Principle of the Balance of Power," App. XX, F. There is abundant evidence on the alliance as an instrument of the balance of power among the theoretical writers. Brougham asserted, "When any one state menaces the independence of any other, . . . that other ought to call in the aid of its allies, or to contract alliances for its protection, if none have already been formed" (*Works*, VIII, 69–70). He even tried to develop a thesis of "natural enmity" and "natural alliances," to enable a statesman to determine the best direction for policy: "The circumstances which are found to constitute a natural enmity between nations are threefold: *proximity* of situation, *similarity* of pursuits, and near *equality* of power. From the opposite causes arise the natural indifference or relative neutrality of states; a reasonable *distance, diversity* of objects and considerable *in-*

For historical occurrences of alliances as balance-of-power devices in the eighteenth century, one may examine the alliances of the Seven Years' War, where Britain and Prussia joined against France and Austria, or the broader system of French alliances which included Sweden, the Ottoman Empire, Spain, and some of the smaller German states—the pattern being carefully devised to supply a whole series of stabilizing checks against aggressive power.

INTERVENTION

Both watchfulness and a concern with checks against preponderance imply a further necessity—intervention. The problem of intervention in the name of the balance of power has been a persistent difficulty for supporters of equilibrist policy. They ride the horns of a dilemma, and the problem is, in fact, a difficult one for the balance-of-power theorist, more especially for an idealist like Lord Brougham. To him the cornerstone of the whole system of equilibrium was independence, and he recognized the ugly illogic of interfering with the independence which was being disregarded.[18] Intervention not only put the cart before the horse but fouled up the harness and elicited unnerving remarks from the bystanders. Brougham attempted to unravel the paradox by emphasizing the expediency and rightness of in-

---

equality of resources; while natural alliance results from the common enmity produced by a concurrence of the three causes first mentioned, in the relations of two or more powers towards the same third power" (*ibid.,* 39–40). Metternich indicated his equilibrist outlook on alliances by assserting, "Any alliance of Austrian forces with those of any other Power, whose exclusive design is the destruction of the present order of affairs, and whose plans are aimed at dominion, would be a war against holy immutable principles, and against Austria's direct interests" (*Memoirs,* II, 485). See also Vattel's statement that "force of arms is not the only means of guarding against a formidable State. There are gentler means, which are always lawful. The most efficacious of these is an alliance of other less powerful sovereigns, who, by uniting their forces, are enabled to counterbalance the sovereign who excites their alarm" (*Law of Nations,* III, 250, no. 46).

18 See Brougham, *Works,* VIII, 81.

violable independence, then made suggestions for avoiding the necessity of intervention, and finally admitted that necessity in the event of "a great and manifest, and also an immediate danger." [19]

He held that to avoid intervention a state should build up its own strength sufficiently to correct the threatened preponderance of a neighbor. He called this "the right of proportional improvement," [20] and he felt that it could be useful in perpetuating the equilibrium. An alliance structure could perhaps solve the problem, which the above policy could not, by the added support of an ally against the unsettling increase of power in an unruly neighbor.

In extreme cases, however, he did reluctantly admit the correctness of intervention:

Whenever a sudden and great change takes place in the internal structure of a State, dangerous in a high degree to all neighbours, they have a right to attempt, by hostile interference, the restoration of an order of things safe to themselves; or, at least, to counterbalance, by active aggression, the new force suddenly acquired.

The right can only be deemed competent in cases of sudden and great aggrandizement, such as that of France in 1790; endangering the safety of the neighbouring powers, so plainly as to make the consideration immaterial of the circumstances from whence the danger has originated.[21]

Brougham was clearly aware of the dilemma in which he found himself. There is no lack of intelligence in his essays on the balance of power, although his opinions on intervention underwent some change. In the essay dated 1803, he was somewhat more willing to permit interference than in the one dated 1843. Doubtless the immediacy of the early nineteenth-century crisis in balance of power influenced his attitude. His awareness of the complexity of the problem and of the wide ramifications of the concept of interference led him to characterize, quite with-

[19] *Ibid.,* 82.   [20] *Ibid.,* 35.   [21] *Ibid.,* 37, 38.

out irony, the whole system of balance of power as "the refined system of interference, which has regulated . . . Europe in foreign affairs." [22]

Other writers have reflected much the same chary attitude toward intervention. Vattel lay similar emphasis upon internal "self-determination," stating it very strictly:

A Nation has full right to draw up for itself its constitution, to uphold it, to perfect it, and to regulate at will all that relates to the government, without interference on the part of anyone.

. . . All such matters [constitutional changes] are of purely national concern, and no foreign power has any right to interfere otherwise than by its good offices, unless it be requested to do so or be led to do so by special reasons.[23]

He did not, of course, ignore the necessity of occasional intervention under some guise, but he was eager to confine it to legal channels. His particular solution was to bring the matter into the open:

Power alone does not constitute a threat of injury; the will to injure must accompany the power. . . . As soon as a State has given evidence of injustice, greed, pride, ambition, or a desire of domineering over its neighbours, it becomes an object of suspicion which they must guard against. They may . . . demand securities of it; and if it hesitates to give these, they may prevent its designs by force of arms.[24]

Friedrich Gentz recognized the problem and admitted the need for intervention, in such matters, under rare and revolutionary conditions: "when by a mortal distemper in the vital parts of this kingdom, by a violent overthrow of its government, by a dissolution of all social ties, a cessation (though perhaps only a momentary one) of political existence ensues." [25]

A statesman did not have to read balance-of-power theory,

[22] *Ibid.,* 14.

[23] Vattel, *Law of Nations,* III, 18, no. 31; 19, no. 37.

[24] *Ibid.,* 249, no. 44.   [25] Gentz, *Fragments,* 112.

such as the above, to feel the necessity of intervention in order to preserve the balance of power. The wars of the French Revolution began with just such a measure on the part of Austrian and Prussian leaders in 1791–1792. Burke, writer on, and respecter of, balance-of-power traditions, categorically urged on the government of Great Britain a policy of intervention in French affairs in 1791, arguing that it was in the best interest of France as well as of Europe and that a merely defensive posture was not enough.[26]

HOLDING THE BALANCE

An anonymous eighteenth-century commentator on the European balance of power spoke of a fourth corollary in the following way: "Experience as well as Reason will enable us to perceive that some one Power or other generally hinders the rest from going wrong, and this Power is said, I think not without cause, to hold the Balance. A most honourable, a most laudable Office surely!" [27] "Holding the balance" is probably the most familiar of all terms in the theory and practice of balance of power. The phrase is used to describe the role of a third party interested in preserving a simple balance between two other powers or two other blocs of powers. When one side threatens the security and survival of the other, the third party steps in on the side of the weaker and sees that a balance between independent powers is restored. Cartoons on the balance of power have often shown a human figure, symbolic of the "balancer" country, with scales in hand, weighing two other countries in order to determine which side was the lighter and therefore more needful of help to "redress the balance." England is the textbook example of the balancer, and historians are fond of quoting the words attributed to Henry VIII: *"Cui adhaereo, prae-est."* Britain's location as an island, separate from the continent and yet close to it, gave her security, aloofness, and flexi-

---

[26] Hoffman and Levack, *Burke's Politics,* 431–434.
[27] *Appendix to the Memoirs of the Duke de Ripperda,* 359.

bility which were only partly compromised by the Hanoverian possessions of her monarchs. Great Britain herself, sharing territorial frontiers with no modern European power and avoiding that type of vulnerability, was yet a kind of immediate neighbor of all, because of her generous development of water communications. These factors all contributed to a strong balance-of-power tradition in British foreign policy and gave particular emphasis to the balancer conception of policy, which has been so important in English history.

This information is widely recognized. Less commonly realized is the fact that the idea of "holding the balance" is a familiar aspect of equilibrist history not at all peculiar to modern England alone. England's geographical position, to be sure, was ideal for such a role, but European states less fortunate in that respect often consciously adopted a policy of "holding the balance." De Réal quite rightly wrote of this policy as a general phenomenon and not as something confined to the British.[28]

As a continental example of "holding the balance" on a small although almost ludicrously ambitious scale, Favier cited the policy of the court of Turin in northwestern Italy, where one of the lesser sovereignties of Europe controlled an important pass through the Alps and tried to utilize "this local advantage to hold the balance between the two Houses of Bourbon and Austria." [29] With regard to a more important matter, the same author spoke of France's holding the balance between England and Holland during part of the reign of Louis XIV: "In the great days of Louis XIV, France profited from the national animosity, and from the commercial jealousy between the English and Dutch to hold the balance between the two maritime powers." [30] As to relations within the Empire, he held that France could exploit the simple balance between Prussia and Russia.[31] Vergennes, in a memoir to Louis XVI, stated the same argu-

---

[28] Réal, *Science du gouvernement*, VI, 443.

[29] Favier, *Politique de tous les cabinets*, III, 48–49. (Translations from this work are mine.)

[30] In his article on England (*ibid.*, II, 165).   [31] *Ibid.*, 92.

ment: France, in need, could count on Prussia and Austria to offset each other's power, thus enabling France to hold the balance between them.[32]

MOBILITY OF ACTION

More broadly, "holding the balance" implies the need for a ready mobility in the direction of policy. Statesmen must be able to act quickly and expertly in cutting encumbering ties or making new ones as balance necessities dictate. In the writing of Ségur, already referred to, one gets a very clear sense of the mobility of French policy, as he conceived it, in its dealings with the Holy Roman Empire. Austria and Prussia were to be kept in balance and France's weight to be thrown on the side of the weaker. The same mobility was necessary to any foreign office which sought to act as a "balancer." The Abbé de Mably assigned this role generally to all powers except the two most powerful. The latter were to be held in a simple balance by the fluctuations of the former, all of whom were balancers on the middle of the seesaw. The very smallest states were treated as exceptions and were advised, because of their impotence, to remain scrupulously neutral.[33] The necessity of mobility is seen in the work of the Abbé de Pradt when he points out that in crises of the balance system "enemies come together for common defense, and allies momentarily separate for the same reason."[34]

The eighteenth century, so abundant in its materials on the balance of power, is typically openhanded in its supply of actual examples of flexibility in foreign policy. Great Britain serves as a ready illustration in her policies toward the continental states in the decade immediately after 1713. At the beginning of this era, Great Britain and Europe were emerging from the long War of the Spanish Succession. British statesmen forestalled a withdrawal into isolation and kept Britain active in the con-

---

[32] *Ibid.*, III, 161.

[33] Abbé de Mably, *Collection complète,* V, 49, 84, 86–91.

[34] Pradt, *La Prusse et sa neutralité,* 85–86.

tinental alliance systems, starting with participation in the Barrier Treaty (1715) with Austria and Holland against France and an alliance with Austria (1716). This system was then paralleled by a triple alliance (1717) of Britain, Holland, and France, which in turn was elaborated by the inclusion of Austria in a well-known quadruple alliance (1718) created to check Spanish aggression. By 1721, however, we find Britain and France, having dropped their earlier alliance structure against Spain, now going into an alliance *with* Spain. By 1725 Britain, France, and Prussia were allies against Austria; in 1725 Britain renewed the earlier triplice with Spain and France; and in the 1730's Britain was back in an Austrian alliance (1731) and later at war (1739ff) with her erstwhile Spanish ally. These details are anything but fascinating when stripped of their historical context, but they do show the rapid fluctuations which were characteristic of balance-of-power policy.

Elaborate documentation is unnecessary to show that mobility is of real importance to balance policies, but there are two important ramifications of this assertion which need comment. One is that the balance of power is best adapted to absolutism and the other that balance of power is basically amoral. The first of these two implications may claim both a theoretical and historical basis. The former lies in the compatibility between absolutism and quick, decisive action; the latter, in the disability with which balance of power has been saddled under democratic procedures. Policy must be continually readjusted to meet changing circumstances if an equilibrium is to be preserved. A state which, by virtue of its institutional make-up is unable to readjust quickly to altered conditions will find itself at a distinct disadvantage in following a balance-of-power policy, especially when other states do not labor under the same difficulties. Historically, this fact has meant that democracy, with its slow-moving processes, has been less well adapted to the pursuit of balanced power than absolutism, which has benefited, in this sense, from more swiftly moving machinery in foreign policy.

It was not a coincidence that balance of power should have reached the zenith of its popularity in the eighteenth century, when absolutism was still one of the basic conditions in the conduct of diplomacy; nor was it a coincidence that equilibrist diplomacy should have been both unpopular and unsuccessful in the third and fourth decades of the twentieth century. There were other contributing causes, but it seems highly probable that democratic procedure was in itself an important cause for failure.

Mobility of action implies that a foreign minister must be ready to make and remake policy as the international planets wheel in their orbits. According to balance theory, a freshly inked treaty, contracted with all apparent good faith and replete with invocations to Deity, may quickly and justifiably be scrapped, if events prove that treaty incompatible with the necessities of preserving the balance of power. Indeed, under the circumstances, no time should be wasted in scrapping it. Bolingbroke put it cleverly: "Pique must have no more a place than affection, in deliberations of this kind." [35]

Balance-of-power writers naturally did not dwell as a rule on the iniquities of the system which they championed, any more than enthusiasts and partisans usually do. They invented certain euphemisms to cover policies which might well have been described in sharper language. Lord Brougham, instead of exhorting equilibrists to break their pledges, scrap treaties, violate their given words, be insincere, and adopt un-Christian conduct, urged a certain "impartiality" on statesmen as they sought to hold an equilibrium—an impartiality which could serve the higher interest of the state system and ignore special cultural affinities and friendships between nations:

All particular interests, prejudices, or partialities must be sacrificed to the higher interest . . . of uniting against oppression or against the measures which appear to place the security of all in jeopardy. No previous quarrel with any given State, no existing

[35] Lord Bolingbroke, *Works*, II, 293; cited by Kovacs, *op. cit.*, App. XI, 3.

condition even of actual hostility, must be suffered to interfere with the imperative claims of the general security.[36]

What his pronouncement did not make clear was that ordinary morality had little or no place in the balance system, when the "higher interest" was at stake. The history of the balance of power is littered with the carcasses of violated pledges, broken treaties, and abortive friendships among nations. Where this has been the result of equilibrist policy, clearly conceived and rigorously executed, the balance theorist must defend it. In short, the balancing system emphasized the urgency of preserving the state system and stressed the conformity of means to that end rather than the conformity of means to a moral standard. Thus, the alienation of liberal opinion from the balance of power in the nineteenth century was no casual estrangement, but a deep-seated antagonism, where one stood for the "higher interest" of the state system and the other could not condone an abandonment of the morality of liberalism.[37]

RECIPROCAL COMPENSATION

The balance-of-power statesman could not always direct his policy in such a way as to prevent aggrandizement by another power. On occasions he had more to lose than to gain by opposition, when opposition might not affect the state system as a whole. Under such circumstances, the equilibrist might fall back on the idea of "reciprocal compensation" or "proportional aggrandizement." [38] This concept stated that aggrandizement by

[36] Brougham, *Works,* VIII, 72.

[37] Attention is called to the paradox of a system, basically amoral, which nevertheless had no lack of enthusiastic and idealistic admirers. See above, pp. 47–51.

[38] Writers' tastes have run to different phraseology in identifying this corollary: "reciprocal compensation" (Geoffrey Bruun, *Europe and the French Imperium, 1799–1814* [New York and London, 1938], 36, 38); "proportional aggrandizement" (Brougham, *Works,* VIII, 8); "proportional mutual aggrandizement" and "reciprocal reduction" (Burke in Hoffman and Levack, *Burke's Politics,* 407, 408); "accroissemens proportionnels" (Pradt, *La Prusse et sa neutralité,* 67).

one power entitled other powers to an equal compensation [39] or, negatively, that the relinquishing of a claim by one power must be followed by a comparable abandonment of a claim by another.

It was not possible to justify this principle in terms of "idealistic" balance of power. What justification it could muster was based on the contention that the balance system was not only run by the big powers but was also run for them. It was clearly impossible for reciprocal compensation to operate on behalf of many members in the state system, unless there was an abnormal situation as in the latter half of the nineteenth century, when many of the European powers could help themselves to overseas territory in Africa, Asia, or the Pacific. If the compensation had to originate within the confines of the state system itself, however, proportional aggrandizement became manifestly impossible for many states, because the European loaf would soon be consumed by slicing.

From the standpoint of balance theory (with emphasis on the word *theory*), such compensation must be regarded as a corrupt practice of the powerful states at the expense of the less powerful, a policy to be justified only as a "realistic" retrenchment when the usual balance techniques fail to solve the problem of aggrandizement. The fact that international law, in its narrow sense, could not and did not provide for the idea of proportional aggrandizement, even when its codifiers were well aware of the intimacy between international law and balance of power, was an indication of the "corruptness" of the practice. On the other hand, the appearance of the principle of proportional aggrandizement in the history of balance of power was no doubt inevitable. Virtually all western diplomacy and international relations have been based fundamentally on the idea of

[39] See, for example, Hardenberg's assertion of the principle of reciprocal compensation in his demand for Prussia of "a strengthening analogous to that which all the allies and so many other States are obtaining" (Hardenberg to Alexander, Dec. 16, 1814, in d'Angeberg, *Congrès de Vienne*, I, 533).

quid pro quo. The theory and practice of balance strategy could not long dissociate itself from an idea to which it bore such obvious affinity, nor did it. The linkage has been strong throughout modern history. Historical examples of reciprocal compensation may be unearthed in the Westphalia settlement in 1648, when many of the small German principalities were parcelled out among the Empire, Sweden, Bavaria, and Brandenburg. The partitions of Poland in 1772, 1793, and 1795 are other and more spectacular illustrations, and the nineteenth century furnishes an even larger canvas whereon the color patterns of various continental flags were painted, as European imperialists moved throughout the world, to a measurable extent governed by this same idea. In the dictum of Ségur on French policy toward the Ottoman Empire: "France has only two parts to take: that of preventing the dismemberment of the Ottoman Empire, or of cooperating in it." [40] In 1808, Metternich, at that time the Austrian ambassador in Paris, urged a similar attitude toward the partition of the Porte then being considered. He counseled his foreign minister: "If we cannot arrive at an agreement with Russia by persuasion, to stop the destructive plans of Napoleon against the Porte, it would be necessary to take an active part in them." [41] He was willing to see Austria "join in the partition only when it is impossible to arrest it." [42] In short, "If the cake could not be saved, it must be fairly divided." [43]

PRESERVATION OF COMPONENTS:
MODERATION

An equilibrium cannot perpetuate itself unless the major components of that equilibrium are preserved. Destroy important makeweights and you destroy the balance; or, in the

[40] Favier, *Politique de tous les cabinets,* III, 156.

[41] Metternich to Stadion, Paris, April 27, 1808, in Metternich, *Memoirs,* II, 208.

[42] Metternich to Stadion, Paris, February 26, 1808, *ibid.,* 194.

[43] Remark of Count Tolstoy, (1769–1844), Russian general, ambassador to Paris during the period of the French alliance (*ibid.,* 197–198).

words of Fénelon to the grandson of Louis XIV early in the eighteenth century: "never . . . destroy a power under pretext of restraining it." [44]

This necessity of preserving the components of the system may be taken as a corollary of the balance of power, and a most important one. Machiavelli once wrote that "men ought either to be well treated or crushed, because they can avenge themselves of lighter injuries, of more serious ones they cannot; therefore the injury that is to be done to a man ought to be of such a kind that one does not stand in fear of revenge." [45] His injunction is at once so well expressed, cynical, and arresting that one is tempted to snip it out of context and graft it, after trimming, onto the branches of balance of power. By paraphrasing his statement and applying it to international relations, one can make it say that if one is not to crush a defeated state, one must treat it well, because it has work to do and a place to fill in the general balance. Montesquieu came much closer than Machiavelli to putting the sentiment into the context of the balance of power in one of the most interesting of all his assertions: the "law of nations is naturally founded on this principle, that different nations ought in time of peace to do one another all the good they can and in time of war as little injury as possible, without prejudicing their real interest." [46] His remark suggests the immediate relevance of moderation to the balance of power. The evidence on this corollary is easily multiplied. Vergennes wrote to Louis XVI in 1784 that all France's influence "ought to be directed toward the maintenance of the public order, and to prevent the different powers which com-

[44] Fénelon, "Supplément, III, 361. Similarly, "the weakening of a power which serves as a counter-weight can be as dangerous as the positive aggrandisement of such another." Quoted in Alexandre de Stieglitz, *De l'équilibre politique, du légitimisme et du principe des nationalités* (Paris, 1893–97), I, 125.

[45] *The Prince*, 19.

[46] *The Spirit of the Laws* (London, 1906; trans. by Thomas Nugent from *L'esprit des lois*, Geneva, 1748), I, 6.

pose the European equilibrium from being destroyed." [47] Ségur, in a comment on Vergennes' letter, spoke of "the importance of conserving Prussian power, without aggrandisement or diminution, in order to maintain the equilibrium in Europe." [48] A similar concern for the preservation of Prussia as a useful component in the European balance was voiced by the Abbé de Pradt, in his analysis of Prussian neutrality:

The preservation and the integrity of Prussia are important not only to the Empire, to Sweden, Denmark, Turkey, England, and above all to France . . . ; but it is further important to the powers which seem to menace it: because each . . . should prefer its actual state to the excessive expansion of the other, and consequently is interested in its preservation. [49]

Ségur, at another point, accused Louis XV of having attempted in the Seven Years' War "to destroy totally the Prussian monarchy; which would have entirely disrupted the balance in Europe." [50] A central Europe, unbuttressed in the north by an independent, effective, and vigorous Prussia, would involve a profound readjustment of French policy toward her eastern neighbors.

Edmund Burke, not an observer given to underestimating the menace of the French Revolution, nevertheless made very clear the basic restraint in his attitude toward France. In 1791 he declared:

It is always the interest of Great Britain that the power of France should be kept within the bounds of moderation. It is not her interest that that power should be wholly annihilated in the system of Europe. Though at one time through France the independence of Europe was endangered, it is, and ever was, through her alone that the common liberty of Germany can be secured against the single or the combined ambition of any other power. [51]

[47] Favier, *Politique de tous les cabinets,* II, 201.
[48] *Ibid.,* 220.   [49] Pradt, *La Prusse et sa neutralité,* 90.
[50] Favier, *Politique de tous les cabinets,* I, 297.
[51] Hoffman and Levack, *Burke's Politics,* 408.

He felt French power, for the security of the European system, had to be maintained at a high level: "As to the power of France as a state, and in its exterior relations, I confess my fears are on the part of its extreme reduction. . . . the liberties of Europe cannot possibly be preserved but by her remaining a very great . . . power." [52]

In stating this he was emphasizing a policy of moderation which he felt to be a necessary accompaniment to a successful balance of power. Ségur urged the same middle course when, in speaking of peace treaties, he wrote that peace "will be solid and become a glorious and lasting monument only as long as it will be sufficiently advantageous to guarantee our security and that of our allies, and sufficiently moderate to permit no reasonable cause of hatred to exist among our enemies." [53]

We might well demand to know what meaning can be applied to "moderation" here. Pursuit of balance-of-power policies has often shown itself most immoderate: coalition wars cannot be called moderate, and the extinction of weak powers under the plea of balance of power surely cannot be termed moderate. The fear, suspicion, and rapid changes of policy which have characterized much of the history of balance of power do not by any stretch of the imagination appear to have been moderate.

There is, however, a limited sense, and a very important sense, in which this term can be applied. Statesmen have often been moderate in their studied attempts to avoid humiliating a defeated power. In a recent period Bismarck offers a classical example of this moderation—in the Prussian war against Austria in 1866, when as principal civilian adviser to the Prussian monarch, he insisted that the war be ended almost as soon as Prussian military victory was indicated. In spite of the storm of objections which this policy evoked, his line was adopted; no victory march in Vienna was permitted the victorious Prussian soldiers, a "soft" treaty was given the defeated Austrians, and at

[52] *Ibid.*, 450.
[53] Favier, *Politique de tous les cabinets*, III, 369–370.

Bismarck's insistence, every attempt was made to avoid humiliating Austria.

The student may find ample precedent for Bismarck's action in the record of earlier European history. Successful equilibrist statesmen have almost invariably recognized the imperative necessity of maintaining the essential weights which comprise an equilibrium, a necessity which has manifested itself, for example, in the restoration of complete sovereignty to defeated powers. European wars in the eighteenth century "were ended . . . by treaties which, more often than not, represented a compromise, and in their forms studiously respected the dignity of the defeated party." [54]

The fact that such a policy of moderation was prescribed as well by self-interest does not make it any the less a balance-of-power policy. Statesmen have been as persistent as they have been in pursuit of balance of power because of its relation to a kind of higher self-interest. We can be sure that any use of the word *moderation* to describe balance of power does not imply an absolute moral standard. Nevertheless, this concept of moderation is useful and meaningful in describing the large policy of statesmen in their search for equilibrium. It is a very roughhewn and inexact usage, to be sure, but it contains a modicum of truth.

If we seek to uncover this kernel of truth, we will find that moderation, when it has been used, has been extended most often to large, and not small, powers, unless the latter have somehow been useful to the former, as in the case of Belgium to Great Britain from 1837 to 1939. The importance of moderation as far as balance of power is concerned lies in the necessity of preserving the significant counterweights in the system of equilibrium. Moderation is probably necessary to successful equilibrist diplomacy, and its absence may mean failure to establish a workable balance.

The spirit of moderation is often one of the keys to a states-

[54] Phillips, *Confederation of Europe*, 7.

man's balance-of-power policy, because only such an attitude can carry with it a willingness to think of the state system as a whole, and not exclusively of one state. As Talleyrand put it, in connection with the creation of an alliance: "It is necessary to exercise great care . . . , for it [the alliance] must be drawn up in the interest of Europe at large, indeed, of everyone." [55]

Moderation has been especially difficult and praiseworthy when shown by statesmen who have been on the victorious side in a bitter war. A case in point is the persistent distinction which allied statesmen, in the period 1813–1815, made between the government and the people of France. Their policy, they were careful to assert, was directed against the government of Napoleon and not against his subjects. And more important than their mere assertion was the stunning willingness of the same men to reduce their policy to practice in the subsequent peace settlement, as though they had taken to heart the wise words of the international jurist:

A treaty of peace can be nothing more than a compromise. . . . Since, however just our cause may be, we must after all look to the restoration of peace and direct our efforts constantly to that salutary object, the only recourse is to compromise the claims and grievances on both sides, and to put an end to all differences by as fair an agreement as can be reached.[56]

THE COALITION

The alliance has been as common as the pox and has made a very usual, peacetime appearance in a balance-of-power system. The coalition, on the other hand, has typically appeared only in the great war crises of the balance of power, at times when the very existence of the state system seemed shaken and in danger. Among the most obvious examples of coalitions, in addi-

[55] The wording is from the translation by Raphaël Ledos de Beaufort, *Memoirs of the Prince de Talleyrand* (New York and London, 1891–92), V, 354.

[56] Vattel, *Law of Nations*, III, 350, no. 18.

tion to those against Louis XIV and Napoleon, are those which were formed against Charles V, the Central Powers in 1914–1918, and the Axis in 1939–1945. It is noteworthy that only five major examples of coalitions are readily cited for a span of four hundred years of modern history, whereas a listing of alliances would sound like someone reading from a telephone book, so bewilderingly abundant are they in the same period.

Care must be taken to distinguish the alliance from the coalition, since they differ in important respects. An alliance, in this context, is taken to mean a bilateral or trilateral agreement for offensive or defensive purposes; and a coalition, to indicate either a similar agreement signed by four or more powers or a conjunction of several alliances directed toward the same end. Thus the critical distinction is one of size, the alliance becoming a coalition when four or more states are included. There are other differences which arise out of the property of size and which will be discussed below.

One of the persistent reasons for the relative rarity of coalitions as opposed to alliances is the difficulty of constructing them and the further problem of holding them together. Coalitions, being larger, are usually harder to create and therefore rarer in occurrence. De Réal, with a Frenchman's preference for images of courtship, remarked that among the members of a coalition the first ardor was soon frozen by mistrust and consequent disunity.[57] Standard examples of suspicion and discord are to be found in the conflicts which took place between the beginning of the wars of the French Revolution in 1792 and the fall of Napoleon in 1815. For twenty long and disheartening years, each of the coalitions against France fell apart. The story is told by numerous "diplomatic revolutions" in the European scene during those two decades. For example, Austria, at war with France off and on between 1792 and 1809, became the ally of Napoleon and assisted his Russian campaign in 1812—against

[57] Réal, *Science du gouvernement,* VI, 354.

her former Russian ally. Prussia, an enemy of France between 1792 and 1795 and again in 1806, began the same Russian campaign in 1812 as an ally of Napoleon, later to change sides again and fight the French as Austria did. Russia herself, an enemy of France in the second and third coalitions, became a French ally by the Treaty of Tilsit in 1807, later reversing herself again. Vacillation of the small states was just as pronounced, the German states aiding France at one time and later entering the enemy camp against her.

The necessity of forming coalitions is a clear one, according to the rationale of the balance of power: "Confederations would be a sure means of preserving the balance of power and thus maintaining the liberty of Nations, if all sovereigns were constantly aware of their true interests, and if they regarded their policy according to the welfare of the State." [58] Among neighboring states there was a "mutual duty of defense of the common safety against a neighboring state which became too powerful." [59] Or, as expressed in *Europe's Catechism:* [60]

Catechist: When any Potentate hath arriv'd to an exorbitant Share of Power ought not the Rest to league together in order to reduce him to his due Proportion of it?

Europa: Yes, certainly.—Otherwise there is but one Potentate, and the others are only a kind of Vassals to him.

Brougham urged that "leagues or alliances of a defensive kind ought to be formed among States which, from their position, are exposed in common to the hazard of being attacked by any powerful neighbour." [61]

From these statements, it is clear that the motivation behind the formation of coalitions and alliances was approximately the same for both—i.e., the need to check the growth of preponderant power—although there was often a greater sense of ur-

[58] Vattel, *Law of Nations*, III, 251, no. 49.
[59] Fénelon, "Supplément," III, 362 (translation mine).
[60] See above, p. 2.   [61] Brougham, *Works*, VIII, 70.

gency in the case of the coalitions. The chief surface difference between the alliance and the coalition remains a matter of size, and the importance of pressing what looks like a simple numerical distinction lies in what may be argued from the property of size.

Size in this case does not reduce itself to simplicity and to the assertion that an alliance is no more than a small coalition, or a coalition merely a large alliance. In spite of the superficial similarity of the alliance and the coalition and of a certain overlapping in their functions, a qualitative difference emerges with numerical expansion, and the coalition becomes utterly different from the alliance in implication and effect, much as a clipper ship is different from a catboat. We are, indeed, in a position to point out an important distinction between two types of balance of power, both of which lie within the compass of the material which has already been presented. These types may be described as two general approaches to the balancing problems of a state system—an approach through the alliance and another through the coalition.

The difference is most clearly indicated when we ask how the state system is enforced. The answer is that there are numerous means, already discussed, by which statesmen attempt to maintain the balance. Yet there is a more specific answer: if we shear away all superficialities, we come down to the alliance and the coalition, which are at bottom the most significant means of enforcement. Taking the alliance first, one will find assertions in equilibrist literature like the following:

Experience has shown that most wars arose from the excessive overweight that one power or another knew how to create for itself under favorable conditions. From this experience statecraft came to the conclusion that if appropriate alliances, dexterous negotiations, or (when necessary) force, could stop the rise of such overweight—or neutralize it, in case it already had arisen—the peace and security of all must necessarily be materially benefited. . . . The aim was to organize the federative constitution of Europe so

skillfully that every weight in the political mass would find somewhere a counterweight.[62]

This question serves to bring into focus the particular type
of equilibrist strategy which was prevalent throughout most of
the history of the balance of power and which concerns us here.
For lack of a better name, we may call it "alliance balance," in
order to distinguish it from the different strategic conception of
the "coalition equilibrium," to be discussed below. The alliance
balance was a structure of alliances, usually bilateral, which
aimed to organize the state system "so skillfully that every
weight in the political mass would find somewhere a counterweight." This idea was so fundamental to the thinking of Gentz
that he tucked it into his definition of the balance.

A balance of power is that constitution subsisting among neighbouring states, more or less connected with one another, by virtue
of which no one among them can injure the independence or essential rights of another without meeting with effectual resistance
on some side, and consequently exposing itself to danger.[63]

An excellent example of the conception of the alliance balance may be found in that remarkable book already quoted,
Politique de tous les cabinets de l'Europe, by Siour Favier,
edited and annotated by M. Ségur during the last decade of the
eighteenth century.[64] Here one may get an intimate glimpse of
the thinking of Turgot, Vergennes, Favier, Broglie, and Ségur
on the balance of power in Europe and on the details of French
policy as it participated in the general equilibrium. The book,
originally published in 1773, contains numerous memoranda

[62] Friedrich von Gentz in *Historisches Journal*, III (1800), 757–758;
quoted by Paul R. Sweet, *Friedrich von Gentz* (Madison, Wis., 1941), 55.

[63] Gentz, *Fragments*, 55; quoted by Cobden, *Political Writings*, I, 258.

[64] The publication of the third edition of this unusual and influential
work precipitated one of the most stimulating of contemporary articles on
the balance of power, a long review of Favier's book by Brougham. The review appeared in the *Edinburgh Review*, I, Art. IX, and was later published
in Brougham's collected *Works*, VIII, 1–50.

and letters dealing with French policy, as well as an extensive survey of the European scene of that day, with an article on each country, an assessment of the power and treaty structure of the country concerned, and a statement and appraisal of its relations with France. The picture of the European balance which emerges from this work is chiefly one of an alliance balance composed of the copartitioners (Austria, Prussia, and Russia) of Poland in the east, drawn together by their reciprocal compensation in the first partition; Spain and France linked by the *Pacte de Famille,* chiefly directed at Great Britain; Austria and Prussia offsetting each other's weight inside Germany; Great Britain entrenched in Hanover, interested in the Low Countries and in Denmark, where its influence was offset by similar Russian interest and power; France allied with Austria, concerned over the mutual bond among the three eastern powers, uneasy over the great increase in Russian power, and acting as keystone in an arch of alliances and understandings which included Sweden, various German states (Saxony, the Palatinate, Hesse, Württemberg, and others), Spain, Naples-Sicily, certain of the other Italian states, and the Ottoman Empire.[65]

Such was the pattern of the diplomatic ties of the era, a pattern which was consciously directed toward an organization of Europe into a "system of counterweights." [66] The thorough acceptance of this aim by the various men whose works were collected in the handbook is illustrated by the insignificance of their differences, which concerned merely the details of application of this strategic conception of French policy. For example, Favier disliked the *Pacte de Famille* and the Austrian alliance; Ségur tended to approve of both. Favier believed in geographical determination of alliances, while Ségur thought this approach both dangerous and oversimplified. Both agreed that

[65] For an interesting contemporary analysis of the system of "weights and counter-weights," see Burke's "Thoughts on French Affairs" (Dec., 1791) in Hoffman and Levack, *Burke's Politics,* 402 ff., particularly 406–414.

[66] The phrase comes from Stieglitz, *De l'équilibre politique,* I, 136.

Russia needed to be checked by Franco-Swedish and Franco-Ottoman agreements and by an alliance with either Austria or Prussia. Neither questioned the basic necessity of this type of balance strategy.

The Comte de Broglie, in a statement which summarized a "general system of policy," conforming to "true principles, and according to the interests of France," indicated his acceptance of the alliance balance type of policy. French policy, he wrote,

consisted of guarding the equilibrium established in Europe by the treaties of Westphalia; of protecting the liberties of the Germanic body, of which France was the guarantor by her treaties; of binding by another perpetual treaty Turkey, Poland, Sweden and Prussia under the mediation . . . of France; and finally of separating by this means the House of Austria from that of Russia, while throwing the latter back into her vast deserts and relegating her, as far as affairs went, beyond the limits of Europe.[67]

French statesmen were often immersed in the negotiation or renegotiation of alliances which would serve as wings of the

[67] Favier, *Politique de tous les cabinets*, I, 55–56. A description of the alliance balance demands at least a brief comment on the local balance, called variously the "inferiour Balance," "partial equilibrium," and other titles. In the eighteenth century Italy and Germany were commonly regarded as examples of this political localism, as was also the group of Baltic states. One theorist wrote that the balance of power "may authorize the powers of a certain part of Europe to oppose the immoderate aggrandisement of any state among them. Hence the system for maintaining a balance of power among the Eastern powers of Europe, among those of the West, or those of the North; among the states of Germany, those of Italy; among the Europeans in America" (Martens, *Summary of the Law of Nations*, 126–127). D'Hauterive, in an attempt to show the relationship of the partial equilibria to each other, wrote that there was a general equilibrium for all of Europe and smaller "équilibres partiels" which persisted within the larger framework. He wrote of the equilibria of the North, of Germany, of Italy, and of southern Europe (*De l'état de la France*, 109–110). See also *Appendix to the Memoirs of the Duke de Ripperda*, 357–359, for a comment of the "inferiour Balances" of Europe. The local balances were merely a part of the larger picture of counterweighting each weight in the political equilibrium.

rambling mansion of the French alliance system. At the same time British statesmen went ahead, busy with their own plans for a separate system which would counterweight the French at many points. Statesmen of other powers likewise worked on their own systems, repairing this tie and rebuilding that, trusting to ingenuity and the fineness of their calculations to create a workable general equilibrium.

Rousseau, probably the most brilliant of all the writers on what we are now describing as the alliance balance, wrote of the European state system as a group of similar and civilized communities living, so far as their relations with each other were concerned, in a state of nature.[68] He was impressed by the elements of a common European culture, by the brilliance of that culture, and by the bitter paradox of unending hostility and cruelty among these states in their political contacts with each other.[69] "The system of Europe has precisely the degree of solidity which can maintain it in perpetual agitation without destroying it entirely." [70] He found that competition among these states was so universal that there had emerged a state of affairs which he referred to as an equilibrium which can "re-establish itself" [71] and which a twentieth-century naturalist

[68] This and the following references are to a remarkable eighteenth-century work, written originally in rather crabbed French by the Abbé de Saint-Pierre (1658–1743); published in three volumes in 1712, 1713, and 1717; later revised by Rousseau between 1754 and 1756; and finally published in 1761 as "Extrait du projet de paix perpetuelle de M. l'Abbé de Saint-Pierre," in which form it is used here. Professor C. E. Vaughan in his great edition of *The Political Writings of Jean Jacques Rousseau*, I, 360, writes the following: "In the *Projet de Paix perpetuelle* Rousseau has treated his materials with the freest hand. The long introduction (pp. 365–374), itself a brilliant historical essay, is all his own; even in the Articles of Confederation, and the number of states to be admitted, he has made considerable changes . . . ; and throughout he has translated the barren details and endless repetition of Saint-Pierre into broad principles of political prudence. In a word, except as regards the mere kernel of the Project, there is much more of Rousseau than of Saint-Pierre in the whole statement."

[69] *Ibid.*, 368.   [70] *Ibid.*   [71] *Ibid.*

would call a balance of nature. Rousseau assigned to individual equilibrists merely a marginal control over the system; nevertheless, he held that a type of pressure equilibrium emerged from the competition. His balance of power was a product of raw competition within the state system and not due to the beneficence of any theoretically minded statesmen. It existed because the fires of survival and competition burned so fiercely that any monarch who, by possessing "more ambition than genius," was foolish enough to aspire to universal monarchy was destined to fail.[72] Rousseau believed in the efficacy of action and reaction, in the tendency of negotiations to "balance themselves mutually," [73] in the strength of many small checks and many obstacles to conquest of any sizeable amount of foreign territory in Europe,[74] and in the security which the German constitution gave to Europe by its defensive strength and offensive weakness. His deduction that the European state system would perpetuate itself indefinitely was wrong, but many of his insights were unusual and penetrating. One emerges from his essay wiser in the strengths and weaknesses of the balance-of-power system in the eighteenth century.

If the central problem of a state system is the problem of enforcement of an approximate *status quo,* the alliance balance of the eighteenth century was a rather haphazard solution of the problem. Success depended on the emergence of an equilibrium out of the un-co-ordinated and largely un-co-operative efforts of competitors representing different states. There was no European executive who could suggest that, since Prussia, for example, was inadequately checked in the south, Austria should strengthen her Silesian frontier as a counterweight to Prussian weight at that point. Any such Austrian action was strictly a matter for Austrian statesmen, and the erection of an appropriate counterweight, upon which the future security of Europe itself might depend, remained a decision for Austria and not for Europe. Seen in this light, the eighteenth-century system of

[72] *Ibid.,* 370–371.   [73] *Ibid.,* 372.   [74] *Ibid.,* 371.

alliance balance looks immature and unwise to a high degree, like a house built by a host of jealous carpenters with no boss and with many different plans for the design of the building.

Writers on the balance of power were aware of the complexities and weaknesses of the system of alliance balance, where enforcement of the balance depended to such an extent upon this intricate system of alliance and counteralliance. And some writers turned to the coalition as a more enlightened means of enforcement of the balance of power. They saw in it an improvement upon the older and more un-co-ordinated system of alliance balance. For example, Fénelon held that when "one power may increase to a point where all the other neighboring powers together cannot resist it, all these others are right in joining to prevent this increase, after the completion of which there would no longer be any time to defend the common liberty." [75] Brougham expressed a similar argument in the following significant passage:

When any one state menaces the independence of any other, not only that other ought to call in the aid of its allies, or to contract alliances for its protection, if none have already been formed, but . . . other states, though not either attacked or threatened, ought to make common cause with the one which is placed in more immediate jeopardy; and for this plain reason, that its overthrow will further increase the power of the aggressor, and expose them to the risk of afterwards being assailed and conquered.[76]

Vattel supported the same type of enforcement by coalition:

If this formidable sovereign should betray unjust and ambitious dispositions by doing the smallest wrong to another State, all Nations may profit by the opportunity, and together join forces with the injured State in order to put down the ambitious Prince and disable him from so easily oppressing his neighbors, or from giving them constant cause for fear.[77]

[75] Fénelon, "Supplément," III, 361 (translation mine).
[76] Brougham, *Works*, VIII, 69–70.
[77] Vattel, *The Law of Nations*, III, 250, no. 45.

An anonymous eighteenth-century writer described the same necessity when he characterized the balance of power as "the Art requisite for preserving the *European* States independent, by forming Confederacies"; [78] and the Abbé de Pradt declared rather optimistically that "one would no more endure in Europe the destruction of one state by its neighbor than one would tolerate in Germany the invasion of one member of the association by another. The whole body would rise against the usurper. . . . It is the same in the great diet of Europe." [79] And finally, in an unusually interesting paragraph, Brougham argued:

The European powers have formed a species of general law, which supersedes, in most instances, an appeal to the sword, by rendering such an appeal fatal to any power that may infringe upon the code; by uniting the forces of the rest inevitably against each delinquent; by agreeing, that any project of violating a neighbour's integrity shall be prevented or avenged, not according to the resources of this neighbour, but according to the full resources of all the other members of the European community; and by constantly watching over the state of public affairs, even in profound peace. Such, at least, would be the balancing system, carried to its full extent; and such is the state of refinement towards which it is constantly tending.[80]

These selections are important here because they state the theory of the coalition equilibrium.[81] All three authors argue, in

[78] *Appendix to the Memoirs of the Duke de Ripperda*, 356–357.

[79] Pradt, *La Prusse et sa neutralité*, 86–87.

[80] Brougham, *Works*, VIII, 17. See also Vaughan, *The Political Writings of . . . Rousseau*, I, 365 ff., for a relevant argument on the necessity of confederating Europe.

[81] Definitions of the balance of power rarely distinguish alliance balance from coalition equilibrium. For an example of one which does, see J. B. Scott in E. A. Walsh (ed.), *History and Nature of International Relations* (New York, 1922), 98–99. Nevertheless, both are implicit in most definitions. That the alliance balance is implicit in such definitions is obvious. That the same definitions embrace the alternative system of coalition equilibrium becomes evident upon re-examination of a sample definition. See for example that of Gentz (above, p. 81). See also *Appendix to the Memoirs*

effect, that formidable expansion must be met by a coalition of all states, regardless of previous affiliations. To them, this maxim was the ideal of the balance of power, an ideal which could boast only a limited application in the principal crises in international relations in the three preceding centuries; nevertheless, an ideal which held some promise of future realization.

The significance of coalitions to the theory and practice of the balance of power is considerable, because they mark, when fully developed, a radical departure from the strategy of the alliance balance. There is a breaking of party lines, so to speak, as countries which may normally be allied to the aggressor nation join the opposition in order to thrust down an attempt toward preponderance. The coalition, therefore, aside from being larger than the usual alliance, is also characterized by a qualitative difference demanding a radical revision of the roster of enemies and allies. For example, the last coalition against Napoleon came to include not only those countries which might have been regarded by contemporaries as "natural" enemies of France—Great Britain, Austria, and Russia, to mention only three, but also most of the countries which were usually linked to the French treaty structure—Sweden, Prussia, Spain, and certain of the German and Italian states. In other words, there was a conscious use against France of a preponderance of power which included many of the first-, second-, and third-rate states

---

of the Duke de Ripperda, 356–357. With regard to Gentz a further comment is necessary, because he later distinguished balance of power from "the principle of a general union," i.e., from the post–1815 concert of Europe (Anton von Prokesch-Osten [ed.], *Dépêches inédites du chevalier de Gentz aux Hospodars de Valachie* . . . , [Paris, 1876–77], I, 354; cited by Hanns Frederich, *Die Idee des politischen Gleichgewichts* [Würzburg, 1914], 42). Frederich went on to point out Gentz's mistake in such a rigid distinction, and to show that the "general union" was merely a different appearance of the balance of power, "a means the better to realize it" (*ibid.*). Gentz's earlier work shows clearly enough that the coalition equilibrium was a species of balance of power rather than a new principle. See, in addition to the above, Gentz, *Fragments,* 61–62.

of Europe. This achievement was the realization of the real aim of the coalition equilibrium, i.e., the breaking of traditional alignments by the formation of a large coalition to reduce a preponderant power and restore the general equilibrium.

A coalition equilibrium could not supersede a system of alliance balance without establishing its superior workability. The former was a theoretical improvement over the latter, but its development as an accomplished fact in the world of diplomacy was quite a different thing from its existence on paper. As a rule, institutional improvements come with painful slowness in any area of the life of a state, but progress seems to be even slower in the conduct of relations between states. The coalition equilibrium could get its opportunity for development only in a great international crisis when the continued existence of the state system was in danger and when states were driven by that danger into coalitions. Moreover, its success in superseding the older system of alliance balance depended upon the development of an automatic coalition which became operative when any state threatened to "injure the independence or the essential rights of another." [82] Only such a device could inspire sufficient confidence among states to render obsolete the less efficient and more complicated system of alliance and counter-alliance.

WAR

It would be difficult to study the stated assumptions, aims, and means and still be unaware of the connection between balance of power and that most disheartening of all human institutions —warfare. As mentioned, the ablest theorists universally accepted the connection and thought of war as one more corollary of the balance of power. Vattel was typical of these in his assertion that governments, when faced with danger from a powerful neighbor, "may prevent its designs by force of arms." [83] War

[82] Gentz's phrase; see above, p. 81.   [83] See above, p. 64.

was an instrument to be used when other devices failed and to be used relatively deftly and sparely. One of the pleasanter things to recall about the seventeenth and eighteenth centuries is the fact that European warfare was appreciably different in that era from its more catastrophic descendant in ours.[84] Armies were smaller and more apt to be personal than national. A colonel losing his regiment was not apt to get another; strategy reflected this fact and tended to create a war of maneuver rather than a war of decisive battles. In a prenational period, generally devoid of fierce loyalties to the state, the ranks were often filled by professional soldiers and mercenaries whose loyalties were fluid and whose disciplining was harsh in the extreme. The officers, like the Duke of Plaza Toro, marched behind their men to keep a watchful eye on them; and tactical deployment was unwise under the circumstances, because the men might desert. These points help to explain the old prints which embrace in single plates entire battlefields, usually an impossibility for a comparable twentieth-century battle.

The limited war of the eighteenth century meant limited objectives, the reliance on fortresses, and a consequent emphasis on the science of siege warfare. Limited war also made possible a workable distinction between soldier and civilian. The numerous and important advantages of eighteenth-century warfare over its twentieth-century counterpart were unfortunately balanced by the utterly inadequate medical care which resulted in the loss of many more soldiers from disease than from battle. In glancing back at earlier methods of fighting, one of the points that commands attention is the relative appropriateness of the balance-of-power theory to an era of limited warfare and its relative inappropriateness to the more modern era. With the 1790's warfare began to change profoundly. The *levée en masse*, the mass army, the development of a new and fanatical concept of loyalty to the nation-state, the emergence of a new discipline, changes in supply, the greater strategic reliance on wars of de-

[84] See the Montesquieu quotation above, p. 73.

cisive battles, the ultimate marriage of warfare to the industrial revolution—all these elements altered the facts of war. In passing, they took a screw driver from the hands of the equili-brist, replacing it with a sledge hammer. In the twentieth cen-tury tinkering became impossible, and when the machine was out of repair it was likely to be pounded.

PART 2 ❦ APPLICATION

Chapter IV

Defending the Balance of Power:
Formation of the Last Coalition

IN 1802 the European state system was considered by many observers to be out of joint. Composed of several hundred states of varying sizes, it was dominated by a group of large powers—Great Britain, France, Austria, Russia, and Prussia, among whom France was by far the most powerful. France in 1789, at the time of the outbreak of the French Revolution, had been bounded substantially by the frontiers which Louis XIV had left her at the time of his death in 1715. The additions between 1715 and 1789, consisting chiefly of Corsica and the not-very-large Duchy of Lorraine, were of no overwhelming importance, and the country continued to enjoy the confines of salt water (the Mediterranean, the Bay of Biscay, the English Channel) and mountains (the Pyrenees and the Alps) on all but her northeastern frontier, where French territory fell shy of the fresh water of the Rhine by fifty to one hundred and fifty miles. In the years of bursting energy between 1789 and 1802, France had added to her pre-Revolutionary frontiers most of the areas on the left bank of the Rhine, Piedmont, and the neighboring Ligurian Republic, which embraced Genoa. To the more-or-less outright annexation of these territories, we should add the satellite states whose destinies Napoleon manipulated—the Italian Republic of northern Italy (Napoleon became president of this in 1802); the Kingdom of Etruria in central Italy; the Helvetic Republic, comprising the Swiss cantons; and the Batavian Republic, which covered much of the Low Countries. In 1802 the situation was more obscure than it appears to our eyes today, when we recognize at a glance that Europe was in a critical condition, with an expanded France and a French leader certain to exploit her satellite system to the disadvantage of Europe. To Europeans in 1802 the situation was debatable: with regard to annexations, France could be said merely to have compensated herself for the earlier partitioning of Poland by the eastern monarchies; and with regard to the satellite states, Napoleon of course denied that they were controlled by France. No observer could have been finally sure that their linkage to France was more than an amiable connection or would develop a dangerous cancer in Europe. The French connection with the satellites was not unlike the extension in the 1940's of the Soviet system into eastern Europe through the device of sister socialist republics, although the parallel connection was perhaps more puzzling and ambiguous in the early nineteenth century. In addition to the ambiguities arising out of the French system of puppets, there were other points that obscured the scene: for example, Napoleon was a new and untried ruler, busy with internal problems, eager to make a new government work, and not yet committed either publicly or privately to a policy of imperial expansion.

OVERBALANCE OF THE NAPOLEONIC EMPIRE

Whatever dispute there might have been in 1802 about the disproportionate power of France, disagreement was dispelled in the following decade, when, under Napoleonic leadership, French control was extended eastward and westward. In the spring of 1812, no one who believed in the balance-of-power system could have denied the dangerous overbalance of the Napoleonic Empire. France, the core of this empire, had dropped her subterfuge and had swept up by further annexation Tuscany and the Illyrian Provinces in the southeast, all territory west of the Rhine, and a generous portion of the Low Countries. By indirection French control now extended over the Confederation of the Rhine, which cut a wide, north-south swathe in western Germany, the Kingdom of Italy (successor to the earlier Italian Republic), the Kingdom of Naples, the Grand Duchy of Warsaw, and Spain, although here rebellion was overt and the hand of France increasingly uncertain. In short, Napoleon's dominion extended from the Atlantic to the Vistula and from the Baltic to the Mediterranean, and the extensive military dominion of Napoleon was reinforced in the sphere of economic warfare by the vast economic pretensions of the Continental System.

Moreover, France itself possessed extravagant resources of power: her homeland was compact and centralized; her leadership, able and militant; her military spirit, fathered partly by a degeneration of fiery revolutionary principles, was the most threatening in Europe; her army, more than 600,000 strong in April, 1812, the most imposing to be seen on the Continent.[1]

The continental cake grew no larger with renewed slicing; as the Napoleonic share increased, the non-Napoleonic diminished. It was inevitable that the extension of French power over

[1] A. W. Ward, G. W. Prothero, and Stanley Leathes (eds.), *Cambridge Modern History* (Cambridge, Eng., 1902–12), IX (1906), 488.

Europe should mean a loss in power, directly or indirectly, for every other major state, since "the greatness of one Prince is . . . only the ruin or the diminution of the greatness of his neighbor." [2] Austria and Prussia, among the major powers, lost territory outright to France: Austria had been shorn of much influence and many possessions in Italy, Illyria, and Germany; Prussia had lost heavily in north Germany. Spain, Holland, and Italy had French kings.

Control of so much of Europe was palpably dangerous to the state system itself. Gentz had warned in 1806 that "no [state] . . . must ever become so powerful as to be able to coerce all the rest put together." [3] The condition most dreaded by balance-of-power exponents had been created by Napoleon, and Europe now had ample opportunity to savor the wisdom of Fénelon's observation that "the aggrandizement of one nation beyond a certain limit changes the general system of all the nations which have relation to it." [4] It was predictable that a continuation and consolidation of French control would sooner or later prove fatal to the sovereignty and independence of all.

NAPOLEON'S RUSSIAN CAMPAIGN

Sweden, the Russian Campaign, and the Collapse of the Grand Army

In early 1812 Great Britain, the perennial opponent, was still at war with France. Napoleon's Continental System, almost six years old, gigantic in conception and calculated to weaken England by depriving her of important European markets, lay like a disabling fog over continental commerce. Britain's answers, the blockade and the development of new markets and channels of trade, were not only tiding her over years of great commercial crisis but inflicting extensive harm upon the Napoleonic Empire.[5] Russia, a signatory of the Continental System since

---

[2] See above, p. 34.   [3] See above, p. 34.

[4] See above, p. 50.

[5] This complicated economic warfare may best be studied in Eli F.

1807 and one of its greatest violators since late 1810, was one of the principal channels by which a flood of British goods entered eastern Europe, thereby destroying the effect of Napoleon's system of economic warfare in that area. "By the apostasy of Russia, . . . the Continental System had lost one of its retaining walls." [6] This important irritant lay at the bottom of the deterioration of Franco-Russian relations in 1810–1812 and was to prove the principal reason for Napoleon's most egregious blunder, his Russian campaign of 1812.

The approach of war between Napoleon and Alexander was not hard to discern in 1811–1812. It resulted, among other things, in temporarily increasing the diplomatic importance of Sweden. Lying next to the Skagerrak, the Kattegat, and the Sound, together forming one of the chief navigational bottlenecks in European waters and one of the principal British trade channels, Sweden had been important to Napoleon in his attempt to cut off British trade outlets and similarly important to the British, who were eager to wreck Napoleon's Continental System. A Napoleonic blunder and much diplomatic maneuvering by Sweden, Russia, and Great Britain, resulted in the reorientation of Swedish policy, then under the direction of Bernadotte, crown prince of Sweden.[7] Napoleon's blunder was

Heckscher, *The Continental System, An Economic Interpretation* (Oxford, 1922), although the work is not definitive. Great Britain developed important new trade channels in the Mediterranean, Baltic, and northern Europe (*ibid.,* 230 ff.); and new markets in South America, the Mediterranean area, northern Europe, and Russia (*ibid.,* 175–177, 181–182). For the effects of the struggle on France, see 266–294; for the "continuous dislocation" (321) of commerce in the rest of the continent, see 295–323; and for the effects on the United Kingdom, see 324–363.

[6] *Ibid.,* 153; for the customs ukase which signalized Alexander's "apostasy," see *ibid.,* 152–153, 235.

[7] Jean Baptiste Bernadotte (1763–1844), former French soldier and one of the eighteen marshals of France under Napoleon. He was active in France until 1810, when he was chosen to be crown prince of Sweden as a substitute for the deceased prince; he later became King Charles XIV John. Soon after his election as crown prince he became chiefly responsible

his occupation of Swedish Pomerania in January, 1812, an event which drove Sweden into the arms of Russia. The period of April–May, 1812, was one of feverish diplomatic activity in Stockholm. War appeared imminent, and both sides were interested in Swedish support. Lying just to the north of the principal axis of the impending war between France and Russia, Sweden occupied a favored position in the balance structure of Europe. Given a military situation in which events might hang in delicate balance, the weight of Swedish soldiery thrown into one scale or the other might tip the scales decisively. The balance was never delicate enough, nor was Sweden powerful enough, to make her the balancer. Nevertheless, it was a situation which, on a small scale, prefigured the "flank" position of Austria in 1813, which Metternich tried to utilize for purposes of "holding the balance." [8]

The rapprochement between Sweden and Russia developed into the treaty of April, 1812, by the terms of which Sweden could look forward to the ultimate acquisition of Norway,[9] her price for risking participation in warfare against the formidable French emperor. In July, 1812, Great Britain signed treaties with both Sweden and Russia, thereby ending the technical state of war among those countries which had arisen earlier when Sweden and Russia were allies of France. Thus Sweden was detached from Napoleon and a beginning was made on the groundwork for the union of Sweden and Norway, an aim later strengthened by another compromising bit of diplomatic parch-

---

for the direction of foreign affairs in Sweden. The relation of Bernadotte to the European balance of power was of rather minor importance and cannot be explored here. It is interesting, however, because it illustrates how entangled balance of power and blackmail can become. Bernadotte was primarily interested in the addition of Norway to Sweden. His diplomacy in this period may be followed in F. D. Scott, *Bernadotte and the Fall of Napoleon* (Cambridge, Mass., 1935), 15–46.

[8] See below, pp. 111 ff.

[9] Great Britain, Foreign Office, *British and Foreign State Papers* (London, 1832–), I, 306 ff.

ment—the Anglo-Swedish treaty of March, 1813, wherein Great Britain promised support of Sweden's western aim in return for Swedish military participation in the war against Napoleon.[10] The British promise later provided its sponsors with the embarrassment of close and hostile questioning in the House of Commons. Like so many war promises, redolent of lost dynasties and human dead, it attracted harsh criticism.

On June 24, 1812, Napoleon crossed the Niemen and began his advance into Russia with an international army of 450,000 troops.[11] Both Prussia and Austria had been drawn into reluctant alliance with France—Prussia in February and Austria in March of 1812. In addition to 20,000 Prussian and 30,000 Austrian troops, extracted by the terms of the alliances, Napoleon had a solid French core of some 200,000, many of them veterans, and the military gleanings of Italy, western Germany, and Poland. The story of this most spectacular and decisive campaign of nineteenth-century Europe is well-known, and need not be rehearsed in detail here. Napoleon advanced, his main central thrust carrying from Kovno to Vitebsk, to Smolensk and Borodino, and finally to Moscow on September 14th, 1812.

The Russian retreat, partly the result of a plan which had been worked out in 1811 by Colonel Clausewitz and General Pfühl, two Prussian officers in Russian service, proved disastrous for Napoleon. His occupation of Moscow, which soon became a bed of ashes, was followed by hesitation and failure to initiate any profitable line of negotiation with Tsar Alexander. The order for retreat on October 19th and the descent of winter began the real destruction of the French army. Harried by Cossack bands, unable to transport its wounded, butchered at the crossing of the Beresina, the army dragged its way back to Ger-

[10] For the text of the Anglo-Swedish Treaty of Alliance of March 3, 1813, see Martens, *Nouveau recueil,* I, 558–563; also d'Angeberg, *Congrès de Vienne,* I, 2–5.

[11] The numbers of reinforcements and baggage-train personnel which also crossed into Russia before the end of the campaign brought the figure to 610,000 (*Camb. Mod. Hist.,* IX, 488).

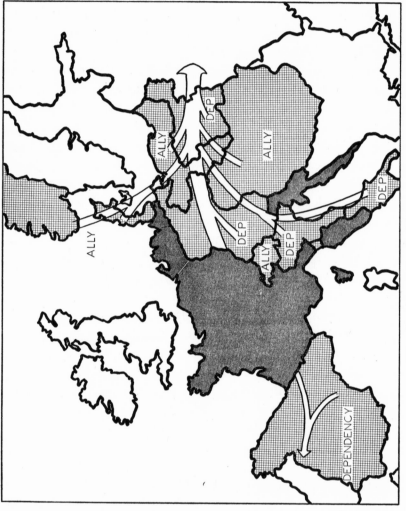

Napoleon's massive coalition of 1812.

many in a retreat which lasted into the spring of 1813. Napoleon's belated and celebrated twenty-ninth bulletin, verifying the general outlines of the catastrophe, echoed throughout Europe.

Napoleon preceded his army to Warsaw and dashed on to Dresden, whence he sent letters to Francis I of Austria and Frederick William of Prussia, asking for more troops—Austria to raise her quota from 30,000 to 60,000 and Prussia to raise hers from 20,000 to 30,000. Meanwhile, three different policies of far-reaching importance were taking initial shape in Russia, Austria, and Prussia: the Russian decision to pursue Napoleon across Europe was assuming form, attempts were being made to detach the Prussian auxiliary corps from Napoleon, and Metternich was speculating on balance-of-power opportunities for Austria in a new Europe in which French power might be receding.

Alexander Becomes Temporary Arbiter of Europe

It is unlikely that a workable balance of power would have been restored as early as 1815 if these three streams of policy had not combined in 1813 to carry Napoleon back to the Rhine. Certainly it could not have been done without the Russian decision to invade Europe; further, it is unlikely that Alexander could have sustained this decision in the face of opposition at home if Prussia had not opportunely joined Russia early in 1813; [12] and, lastly, the ultimate adherence to these allies by Austria, so strategically located on the southern flank of the proposed westward drive against Napoleon, consummated the necessary coalition which was to defeat Napoleon in the important central German campaigns of 1813.

The year 1812 had been a hideous one for Russia, and the time for harrowing decisions had not yet passed. The retreat of Napoleon's Grand Army by no means removed the Napoleonic menace from Europe, and Alexander still had to determine his country's European policy. He had a theoretical choice of three

---

[12] By the treaty of Kalisch; see below, pp. 109–110.

plans: [13] he could keep his armies on Russian soil after the French had been driven out, a policy supported by Kutuzov, the victorious, ailing, and conservative commander in chief; he could pursue Napoleon across Europe as a purely Russian policy independent of European help, as advised by Rumiantsev, chancellor and former minister of foreign affairs; he could thrust at Napoleon across Europe with the help of Austria and Prussia, the plan suggested by Nesselrode, a young secretary of state. The last-named aristocrat was just in this period coming into prominence as an adviser to the tsar on foreign policy and was displacing Rumiantsev, who had been in the ascendant during the years of the tsar's "Tilsit" (pro-French) policy.[14] Nesselrode, a balance-of-power statesman himself,[15] was an admirer, friend, and correspondent of Friedrich Gentz, an outstanding exponent of the balance of power in the Napoleonic era. He received backing for his proposed line in foreign policy from Baron Stein, the great German reform statesman who had been forced out of Prussia by Napoleon and had subsequently, in the spring of 1812, become special adviser to Alexander. Nesselrode, supported by Stein,[16] argued that Russia could not successfully play

[13] For a brief discussion of the alternative plans, see Albert Sorel, *L'Europe et la révolution française* (Paris, 1895–1904), VIII, 9–11; hereafter cited as Sorel, *L'Europe*. For material on the men who wanted the Russian army to remain in Russia, see K. Waliszewski, *La Russie il y a cent ans: Le règne d'Alexandre Ier* (Paris, 1923–25), II, 147–148.

[14] See Karl Robert, Graf von Nesselrode, *Lettres et papiers* (Paris, 1904–12), II, 89 ff. and Grand Duke Nicolas Mikhailovitch, *Le tsar Alexandre Ier* (Paris, 1931), 165.

[15] See Nesselrode, *Lettres et papiers,* II, 33 ff.; V, 12. See II, 78 ff., concerning Nesselrode's strong commitment against Napoleon.

[16] Stein was preoccupied with a restoration of a balance of power in Europe. To achieve this end, he urged upon Alexander the necessity of converting his defensive position into an offensive, of getting rid of Chancellor Rumiantsev, and of making common cause with Austria and Prussia. See his memoir of Nov. 17, 1812, in Erich Botzenhart (ed.), *Freiherr vom Stein: Briefwechsel, Denkschriften und Aufzeichnungen* (Berlin, 1931–37), IV, 155–160. In the reconstructed balance of power in Europe he envisaged a united Germany taking its place among the Great Powers and

a solitary hand; the aim must be to defeat Napoleon and reduce France to her natural frontiers; and to do this Russia must not only have help from both Prussia and Austria but must separate Napoleon from his own people. Nesselrode was developing a line of reasoning which Alexander himself had used with Pitt in 1804, as will be explained. Nesselrode was successful, and, given the preconceptions of balance of power, he was strikingly correct. He was helping Alexander formulate policy which was to last through the defeat of Napoleon, and, in part, to outlast his own lifetime.

Alexander's attitude toward the balance of power had been markedly inconsistent. At one time the ardent and willing supporter of balance-of-power policies, indeed the exponent of improving the balancing system, Alexander could later be found using his influence to corrupt the same system. In 1804 he had proposed to Napoleon that the French withdraw behind the Rhine and the Alps. When Bonaparte refused, the tsar sent his friend Novossiltsov to London with a project for an Anglo-Russian alliance which, if realized, would have resulted in a decisive improvement and "refinement" of the balance-of-power system.[17] The secret instructions to Novossiltsov enjoined him

---

serving as a central barrier against aggression from east or west. For his attitude toward the balance of power, see *ibid.,* II, 39, 90, 107, 232; III, 109, 125, 233, 252, 505; IV, 72 ff.; V, 82 ff.

[17] A. Gielgud (ed.), *Memoirs of Prince Adam Czartoryski* (London, 1888), II, 41 ff. (secret instructions for Novossiltsov); 52 ff. (memorandum of Czartoryski); 56 ff. (letters concerning the mission); 59 ff. (report by Novossiltsov on the interview with Pitt). These are all interesting and significant documents; the last one is especially interesting, because it virtually epitomizes the transitional nature of the balance-of-power system in the early nineteenth century, containing equilibrist terminology, equilibrist statement of war aims, and the idea of using a coalition for re-establishing the balance and for preserving it. This collection of papers will be cited hereafter as Czartoryski, *Memoirs.* For further information on the Novossiltsov mission, see Webster, *The Foreign Policy of Castlereagh, 1812–15* (London, 1931), 54 ff. This work will be cited hereafter as Webster, *Castlereagh.*

to propose to Pitt nothing less than the creation of an automatic coalition: Alexander proposed a "new code of international law which, being sanctioned by the greater part of the European states, would, if violated by any one of them, bind the others to turn against the offender and make good the evil he has committed." [18] The impulse died within the next three years, however, and Napoleon's defeat of Austria and Prussia in 1805–1806 led up to the Conference at Tilsit, in which Alexander joined Napoleon in alliance and effectually put aside his equilibrist tendencies for several more years. At Erfurt in 1808, in a series of dressy meetings with his French ally who was then seeking further partitions of the Continent, he performed a belated service to the European balance by not supporting Napoleon in his design to crush Austrian power. In 1809, with the outbreak of a Franco-Austrian conflict, he failed to avail himself of the opportunity to "hold the balance" between the antagonists, with the result that France once more defeated Austria, added more territory to her already bulging empire, and threw the European system still further out of balance. In late 1810 the tsar canceled his adherence to the Continental System and began a pendulum movement back toward equilibrist strategy, a return which was accentuated by Napoleon's invasion of Russia and crowned by Alexander's decision to carry the struggle back across Europe.

It is sufficient to note here that in spite of previous wild fluctuations of attitude toward the continental equilibrium, Alexander acted in the winter of 1812–1813 in conformity with the needs of the European balance. He was acting on the advice of two outstanding exponents of balance strategy, Stein and Nesselrode, and his action in this instance was impeccably equilibrist in nature: it was calculated to overthrow the preponderant power of France which threatened the survival of the state system; it was directed toward a reduction of that power to a size compatible with the safety of neighboring states; and it was

[18] Czartoryski, *Memoirs*, II, 48.

based, consciously or unconsciously, on a concern with the preservation of the state system as a means toward achieving a balance of power in Europe.[19]

While the tsar was wrestling with his problems of statesmanship, the military situation in the Baltic Provinces was ripening in most favorable fashion. During Napoleon's advance into Russia in the preceding summer, the 20,000 troops which he had extracted in his treaty of alliance with Prussia were assigned the task of advancing through the Baltic Provinces toward St. Petersburg. These troops were a reluctant portion of the left wing of his army, reluctant because the real enemy of Prussia in that era was Napoleon himself and not Alexander, against whose soldiers the Prussians were compelled to fight. Nevertheless they participated in a successful advance as far as the environs of Riga, for the most part avoiding costly engagements with the retreating Russians and preserving their corps virtually intact. When the tide turned in the fall of 1812 and French might receded from Russia, General Yorck, the commander of the Prussian corps and a harsh and austere patriot, carefully maintained his corps by withdrawing southward, toward East Prussia, before the right wing of the Russian advance. His position was a difficult one, because he was subordinate to Macdonald, the French marshal, who was aware of Yorck's motives and conduct and recognized them for what they were—in French eyes, treason. Yorck's position was rendered even more complex because he received no help in his dilemma from top Prussian sources. As early as mid-October, 1812, he had been urged to go over to the Russians. By December the possibility of defection was strong, but he had no clear instructions from Berlin, and circumstances were singularly importunate. On Christmas Day Prussian leaders took important steps, but their meeting was unknown to Yorck.

[19] Anstett, Alexander's armistice envoy to Schwarzenberg, the Austrian general, declared to the latter that Russia wanted a "revival of the balance of power in Europe" (Wilhelm Oncken, *Oesterreich und Preussen im Befreiungskriege* [Berlin, 1876–79], I, 213).

On that day, Hardenberg, chancellor of Prussia, met with two advisers, Knesebeck and Ancillon,[20] and agreed that the time for rebellion against Napoleon was at hand, although they must continue to act with great circumspection as well as sound out Austria regarding joint action against France.[21] Knesebeck left to see Metternich, who was then the chief architect of Austrian policy. Yorck did not know of Knesebeck's mission; even if he had known of it, it would have been small comfort, since Metternich was the most cautious and devious of statesmen. Next day, Yorck received a letter from Tsar Alexander offering an alliance and the reconstruction of Prussia, which since 1807 had been a "partitioned" state, having lost considerable territory at Napoleon's hands. The offer to Yorck was very tempting, and after deliberation, he decided to accept it. It was a dazzling decision. Consummation of this first step toward a new continental coalition was affected on December 30, 1812, at Tauroggen, just northeast of Tilsit; the agreement specified a secret armistice and the neutrality of the Prussian troops. Yorck had done the proper thing, but it was still too early and too dangerous for his king and chancellor to acknowledge it publicly, because of the presence of French troops in Prussia.

Alexander's decision to pursue Napoleon across Europe was not irrevocable early in January, 1813,[22] because the main army

----

[20] Karl Friedrich von dem Knesebeck (1768–1848) had been active in various German armies since boyhood and in many campaigns, among them Valmy and Jena; from 1812 on, he was used by the king of Prussia for diplomatic missions, and he was prominent in Prussian counsels in the summer of 1815. Johann Peter Friedrich Ancillon (1766–1837) was a minor Prussian historian and statesman, author of *Tableau des révolutions du système politique de l'Europe depuis le XVᵉ siècle* (4v., Berlin, 1803), a prominent work in its day.

[21] Oncken, *Oesterreich und Preussen*, I, 45.

[22] The tsar's original decision to advance into central Europe was probably made by Dec. 1, 1812. Kutuzov ordered a halt at Vilna on Dec. 7, and Alexander countermanded the order on Dec. 14, 1812, with instructions for a limited advance (Max Lehmann, *Freiherr vom Stein* [Leipzig, 1905],

which he then threw against the French garrisons in Poland consisted of not much over 100,000 troops and because Prussian policy was as yet uncertain. Thus far Prussia and Russia had merely agreed on a secret armistice; they were not yet allies, nor could anyone have been sure they would become allies. Moreover, opposition to the tsar's decision was current in powerful quarters at home. General Yorck was not the only cat walking on hot coals.

An alliance with Prussia against Napoleon would give the tsar sufficient weight to carry his country with him.[23] Alexander could then point out that Russian arms were not alone in the fight. Moreover, the tsar could probably draw Prussia into such an alliance if his army advanced rapidly toward East Prussia itself. In this sense he was dependent upon Prussia, and, at the same time, arbiter of Europe. He needed the Prussian alliance, but he could create the conditions under which Prussia could scarcely refuse it. He would carry off a winning hand by forcing Prussia into discards—the discard of her French ally and of any dream of neutrality which her statesmen might have held.

By letter he urged the alliance upon Frederick William of Prussia. Simultaneously, Russian divisions totaling 50,000 troops flanked East Prussia, after neutralizing Yorck's Prussian corps, and arrived in Pomerania. After a torment of indecision

---

III, 197–201). Alexander had left St. Petersburg on Dec. 18 and arrived at Vilna on Dec. 23, where he took upon himself the responsibilities of commander-in-chief. Remaining at Vilna for more than two weeks, Alexander was busy with the military plans for the new campaign against Napoleon (Mikhailovitch, *Le tsar Alexandre Ier*, 139–140).

[23] During Alexander's stay at Vilna (Dec. 23 on) the argument over the tsar's decision to march into central Europe reached its height. Stein, Arndt, and Clausewitz, all present in Vilna, were eager for the advance. Kutuzov and others were still heartily opposed to it. The news of Tauroggen reached Vilna during the first week of January, 1813, and effectively undercut the opposition to the tsar. Alexander left Vilna on Jan. 9, 1813, to join the troops, which had been assembling near the Niemen (Waliszewski, *La Russie il y a cent ans*, II, 152 ff.).

lasting a month, Frederick William sent General Knesebeck to Alexander with specific terms of alliance which demanded for Prussia pre-1806 boundaries, a territorial increase in north Germany, no separate peace, return of her Polish lands, and an agreement to supply 80,000 troops to Russia's 150,000.[24] Alexander, furious over Prussia's haggling terms, had Nesselrode counter with a draft treaty which granted Prussia her pre-1806 *proportions* but deleted the clauses on Poland. Knesebeck refused to sign, but an appeal to Hardenberg assured the Russian draft of approval, and the Treaty of Kalisch was signed at Breslau and Kalisch on February 27–28, 1813; [25] it was destined to become the cornerstone of a new and successful coalition against Napoleon.

The treaty was a working agreement, rather hastily thrown together to fit the circumstances of the immediate future. No mention was made of the balance of power. The document provided chiefly for matters which demanded immediate attention, such as numbers of troops, close military co-operation, no separate negotiations, exchange of information, and regulation of Russian soldiers in Prussia. The treaty was to be secret from everyone except three potential allies—England, Sweden, and Austria. Two secret articles were appended, the first of which was the most important in the treaty: Nesselrode's compromise formula for the restoration of Prussia to pre-1806 *"proportions statistiques, géographiques et financières."* [26] The omission of any guarantee of Polish land to Prussia was ominous. This subject was the core of future problems which were nearly to destroy the coalition during the peace settlement; during the war they were allowed to slumber.

[24] The evolution of the Prussian demands may be followed in Oncken, *Oesterreich und Preussen,* I, 183 ff. For painstaking details on the Treaty of Kalisch, see *ibid.,* I, 234 ff.

[25] Text in Martens, *Nouveau recueil,* III, 234–238.

[26] Text of the secret articles in d'Angeberg, *Congrès de Vienne,* I, 1–2.

METTERNICH EXPLOITS AUSTRIA'S FLANK POSITION

Metternich's Design

Great Britain and Austria occupied similar positions with regard to the great latitudinal axis of the 1812 struggle between Napoleon and Russia: England held a flank position on the north, Austria on the south; England was involved in the struggle on one side, Austria, on the other; and the foreign offices of both countries were run by men who believed in balancing power. There were, however, important differences in their diplomatic positions, especially with regard to their potential influence on affairs in central and eastern Europe and the depth of their present commitments to the struggle.

Austria, herself the most important central European power of the day, obviously carried great weight in that area. On the other hand, direct British influence on eastern and central European affairs was negligible at the end of 1812 and the beginning of 1813. Great Britain and Russia, the two principal sources of opposition to Napoleon at that time, were, after all, separated by hundreds of miles, and Britain had no troops on the eastern front. To be sure, Britain's influence on the other fronts was substantial, through her blockade of the shores of the Napoleonic Empire, her blockade-breaking trade with Russia, and the peninsular campaign under Wellington. But, although supreme at sea and although she was engaging Napoleon in Spain, Britain did not have direct and immediate influence on Austrian, Prussian, and Russian decisions which were being made in the winter of 1812–1813. Her power there was potential rather than actual.

With regard to the depth of commitment to the war—Britain to an anti-Napoleonic stand and Austria to an anti-Russian position—there was substantial difference. Britain was profoundly committed, Austria only superficially, after the manner of Napoleon's reluctant Prussian ally. Thus, Austrian importance was magnified by her geographical position, by the absence of British influence in the central European area at that time, and by a relatively superficial tie to France. Metternich was in an excellent position to flex Austrian policy and attempt to hold the balance in central Europe, and he was thoroughly and happily aware of it. His analysis of the scene is interesting and instructive; it is also a classic of equilibrist reasoning, beautifully illustrative of the thought process of a balance-of-power statesman who was recasting policy in the midst of the swift flow of great military and diplomatic events. The analysis [27] may be summarized as follows: Austria held a "flank" position which should be exploited, but Austria was also encumbered by three important ties to France—the marriage of Austrian Archduchess Marie-Louise to Napoleon; the French alliance of March, 1812, whereby Napoleon had the disposal of 30,000 Austrian troops; and the treaty of 1809, wherein the Austrian army was limited to 150,000. Austria therefore had to regain the disposal of her 30,-000, remove the ceiling on her army, and get out from under the French alliance—all without bringing down upon her the wrath and arms of France until Austrian arms were adequate for defense. This strategy would give Austria her mobility of action and enable her to exploit the role of balancer. Moreover, a westward Russian advance into Europe was to be feared as much as the earlier eastward expansion by France; Russian arms should be checked at the Galician frontier, else they would be posted threateningly along the northern frontier of the Austrian Empire. To achieve this objective, Prussia could be given the Duchy

[27] See Metternich to Hardenberg, Oct. 5, 1813, and Metternich to M. de Floret, Dec. 9, 1812, printed in Oncken, *Oesterreich und Preussen*, I, 378 ff. See also extracts from the letters of Ernst Hardenberg, Hanoverian minister in Vienna, also *ibid.*, II, 95 ff. There is a good summary of Metternich's grand design in Sorel, *L'Europe*, VIII, 30 ff. Metternich laid down his axiom at least as early as 1810 in a report to the Austrian emperor on the results of his observation in France in 1810: "In a war between France and Russia, Austria must take a position on the flank which will ensure a decisive importance for her opinions during the war, and at the end of it" (Metternich, *Memoirs*, I, 140).

of Warsaw, thereby strengthening her sufficiently against Russia and turning her energies eastward against the latter instead of westward into Germany and against Austria. Prussia should be encouraged to revolt and bear the brunt of French arms. Europe ought to be prepared for Austrian mediation: Metternich could use the 30,000 troops and the possibility of an alliance with Austria as instruments to keep the balance between east and west; and Austria should build up the Austrian army by gaining time from Napoleon and money from England.

Whether one likes Metternich or not, one might as well admit at the outset that his analysis was brilliant. It was an extraordinary adjustment of equilibrist thought to the special strengths and weaknesses of the Austrian position at that time. There are few other analyses in equilibrist literature which show so clearly the insights, the thought processes, the clarity, and the terrible hard headedness of an able balance-of-power statesman with difficult decisions to make. The core of this design was his desire to get a free hand for Austria and exploit her southern flank position for balancing purposes. The working out of the plan covered a period of eight months from December, 1812, to August, 1813, and may be dissected into three processes which overlapped in point of time, but which have some claim to treatment as different stages in the negotiations. The first was Metternich's cutting of ties with France; the second was his attempt to "hold the balance"; the third was the gradual Austrian approach to the anti-Napoleonic forces, ending with Austrian entry into the last coalition against Napoleon and the Austrian declaration of war against Napoleon on August 10, 1813.

Metternich Gradually Cuts Ties with France

The first of these processes extended over a period of six months.[28] Metternich began cutting ties with France by sending

---

[28] The details of Metternich's separation of Austria from France may be followed in Oncken, *Oesterreich und Preussen*, I, 57 ff., 101 ff.; II, 189 ff., 395 ff. See also Heinrich Ritter von Srbik, *Metternich: Der Staatsmann und der Mensch* (Munich, 1925), I, 146 ff.

an emissary to Napoleon in December, 1812, to listen to the
Emperor and hint at Austrian mediation, which of course implied that Napoleon's Austrian ally was meditating disloyalty to
her alliance. Then, by the Armistice of Zeycs, January 30, 1813,
between Austria and Russia, he took another step toward freedom of action: the Austrian corps of 30,000, relatively useless
to Napoleon in the campaign of 1812, now by secret agreement
fell back systematically before the Russian left wing, much as
the Prussians had done on the Russian right, to the Galician
frontier, at which point Metternich wanted to check the Russian advance.[29] By February 15 Metternich had achieved his
mobility of action with the receipt of a letter of questionable
wisdom from Napoleon, urging Austrian army preparations.
Napoleon had in no way rescinded his earlier treaty restriction
on the size of the Austrian army, but Metternich lifted out of
context Napoleon's eagerness to have Austria strengthen herself
and interpreted it to mean a removal of the ceiling.

Although Napoleon was aware of the dubious loyalty of Austria, he was under the necessity of humoring her, to a certain
extent. He needed her support, and his willingness in February to allow Austrian rearmament was based on the hope that
Austria, when rearmed, would add her weight to the French
cause. On the other side of the fence, Metternich exploited for
his own ends Napoleon's need for a strengthened Austria and
did not by any means contemplate giving automatic support to
France against Russia.

There existed in Vienna a situation of considerable delicacy
which made exacting demands on Narbonne, the new French
ambassador to Austria, whose job it was to observe the shifts in
the light and variable diplomatic winds there. In an April interview with Metternich, Narbonne finally discerned much of
the structure of the former's plan for Europe—Prussia strengthened by a new Kingdom of Poland as a barrier in the east;

<hr />

[29] Feodor F. Martens, *Recueil des traités et conventions conclus par la
Russie avec les puissances étrangères* (St. Petersburg, 1874–1909), III, 90–91.

Illyria returned to Austria; dissolution of the Confederation of the Rhine; the French out of the Hanse cities; the future of Holland and Spain to be referred to Great Britain; the Franco-Austrian alliance dead and Austrian obligations under the Continental System similarly dead. Metternich soon confirmed the latter's impression. The Austrian felt that, by a timely revelation to France of his own attitude, he had taken a further important step in his *"marche oblique,"* as he described his cautious, and almost tedious, separation of Austria from France. Narbonne, angered at Austrian infidelity to the French alliance, mistakenly went over Metternich's head in an appeal to Francis I, Emperor of Austria, only to be rebuffed.[30] The gulf between France and Austria was perceptibly widened. It was further widened by Metternich's contact with Prussia and Russia during the same months, as will shortly be shown. His commitments to the allies increased in this period, that increase overlapping and helping the leisurely Austrian dissociation from the Napoleonic alliance. Metternich was not one to jar the harmony of the cosmos by unseemly haste, and it was not until the end of June that Napoleon agreed to a written release of Austria from the terms of the alliance.

Metternich's Attempt to Hold the Balance

While this process of dissociation was going on, a reverse process of association was in progress between Metternich and the allies. Metternich had been in occasional contact with Hardenberg and Alexander since January, 1813, and had indicated to them that, if not interested in an immediate *rapprochement,* he was at least moving away from France toward a position of neutrality. He wanted to mediate the European conflict. Ernst Hardenberg, friend of Metternich and representative from Hanover to Vienna, has described a February interview with the Austrian, in which the latter sketched his plan to see 200,000 Russians and Prussians on the Oder, 30,000 Swedish troops supporting them, Denmark neutral, and Austria neutral with 100,000

[30] Sorel, *L'Europe,* VIII, 92–93.

effectives, but giving secret guarantees not to employ them against Russia or Prussia.[31] These conditions would establish the basis for mediation, and Austria would go to war against France if Napoleon refused a peaceful settlement. This plan is an early form of the design which Metternich was later to follow. It indicated a weighting of the mediation in favor of the eastern powers.

During the early months of 1813, Metternich chiefly wanted to secure for Austria a position of neutrality by severing connections with France and avoiding commitments to Prussia and Russia. Once having secured Austrian neutrality, he could then hold the balance between France on the one hand and Prussia and Russia on the other. He hoped to mediate in the conflict between east and west and thereby enhance the power and prestige of Austria. This plan was thoroughly equilibrist in nature and serves as a refutation of the common idea that Great Britain was the only power which followed a policy of holding the balance.

Metternich did not succeed in this diplomatic maneuver.[32] His plan was a hothouse plant and demanded special conditions for fruition. It depended on the acquiescence of several neighboring powers, who were stubbornly suspicious of Austrian policy, and the advance of spring saw the gradual withering of Metternich's plan for mediation.[33] On the one hand, the Treaty of Kalisch, which bound Russia and Prussia together in

[31] Oncken, *Oesterreich und Preussen*, II, 105 ff. See *ibid.*, I, 137 ff., for an earlier form of this plan.

[32] For the details of his plans of mediation, see Oncken, *Oesterreich und Preussen*, II, 189 ff., 298 ff.

[33] Metternich's envoy arrived in London in late March. His position was difficult because of the dubious nature of Austrian foreign policy. His proposal of Austrian intervention, his later proposal of Austrian mediation, and his request for subsidies fell on deaf ears. Castlereagh later accepted Austrian mediation (end of June) but refused subsidies as long as Austria was not at war with France. The first subsidies were given Austria in August, 1813 (Webster, *Castlereagh*, 147, 150; see also C. S. B. Buckland, *Metternich and the British Government from 1809 to 1813* (London, 1932), 523 ff.

late February, 1813, created a power bloc on Austria's northern frontier which was able, in conjunction with other events, to force Metternich's hand. On the other hand, his offer of intervention to Great Britain in the early spring was immediately brushed aside, and Metternich saw that active participation of Austria in an anti-French coalition would be the price of a British subsidy. Moreover, indirect pressure was put on Austria by Britain by the fact that, while Austria was not promised any British gold, Prussia and Russia were both to receive subsidies which would enable them to increase their armed forces. This situation presented Austria with certain disadvantages which Metternich was not eager to perpetuate. He clung to vestiges of the idea of mediation into August, but the substance had gone out of it. In June he utilized the occasion of Prussian and Russian military reverses, a period when they were somewhat desperate, to gain acceptance of Austrian mediation, but Austria could no longer claim neutrality, and the mediation degenerated into a mere technical formula, bereft of meaning.

Formation of the Last Coalition (May–June, 1813)

Throughout the period when he was both separating Austria from France and attempting to erect a condition of neutrality for Austria to hold the balance, Metternich was also flirting with the inevitable idea of joining a new coalition against Napoleon. He was nothing if not flexible, and he never rested content with but one iron in the fire. As early as the first week in March, 1813, Metternich had sent an envoy to Alexander to find out, under the cover of talk of intervention, what the Tsar would offer in return for an alliance with Austria. By the end of the month, both Austria and Russia were signatories to a convention of secondary importance which at least indicated the direction of Austrian policy and further committed her to the allies. In retrospect Sorel found this convention to be the foundation of the new coalition.[34]

That was in March, and, although it was an indication of

[34] Sorel, *L'Europe*, VIII, 72–73.

things to come, things were to come slowly. Metternich's approach to the allies was performed with as carefully graduated steps (*"nuances intermédiares"* in his own phrase) [35] as his termination of the French alliance. On April 2 he indicated that if Napoleon refused Austrian mediation, Austria would cooperate fully with the allies in order to arrive at an arrangement suitable for Austria and Europe. A guarded indication, suffused with caution, it showed that his drift toward the allies was not to be rushed. Because they had not yet consented to Austrian mediation, which Metternich still wanted, he made no "hasty" commitment to their cause and refused as premature the Prussian invitation in April to join Nesselrode and Hardenberg in a conference. Then Austrian fortunes improved during the next weeks, and May, 1813, was a good month for Metternich: Napoleon's victory of May 2 at Lützen in western Saxony gave Metternich his opportunity to gain acceptance from Prussia and Russia for Austrian mediation. He needed time for Austrian rearmament and for preventing Napoleon from attacking Bohemia before that rearming could be well advanced. Napoleon was expected to reject the terms of mediation, but meanwhile a valuable delay would have been gained by slow and meaningless negotiations, and Metternich would have created for Austria a safe and plausible form of entry into the coalition.

Early in May, 1813, he sent Alexander his terms for armed mediation. This move initiated an exchange of notes and a series of conferences which extended through May and into June [36] and which witnessed the forging of a group of terms to be presented to Napoleon. Metternich's plans were subtle and intricate; he wanted Napoleon to accept Austrian mediation, but to refuse the proposed European settlement. He wanted him to accept the time-consuming device of a "peace" conference,

[35] *Ibid.,* 33.
[36] *Ibid.,* 112. For the May and June notes and conferences of 1813, see *ibid.,* 116, 136, 138, and 141, n.1.

but after sufficient delay to reject the terms which would be proposed by Austria at that conference. He therefore asked that the terms be split into two categories, minimum and maximum —the first to be used to get Napoleon to accept mediation or a conference, the second for later rejection by Napoleon at the conference, a rejection which would provide the excuse for Austrian entry into the allied coalition. The sport was not one for participants without steady nerves. A fisherman who used this type of bait ran the risk—when Napoleon was the prey— of having the line torn from his hands.

Metternich's minimum terms comprised renunciation of French annexations in Germany, abandonment of the Duchy of Warsaw, and the return of Illyria to Austria. These were not extreme terms: both the Duchy and Illyria were remote from France. The Austrian ambassador, Bubna, presented these to Napoleon, who refused armed mediation but accepted the suggestion for a conference, just as the others wanted. He had been maneuvered into the position where a refusal would have placed upon his shoulders the onus for a renewal of the war. Nesselrode, after a conference with Stadion on May 13, redrafted what he believed to be the basic Austrian terms, added three more concerning Holland, Spain, and Italy, gained Hardenberg's approval, and sent them to Metternich in his important note of May 16.[37] These terms he regarded as invariable and absolute for the preliminary peace, and he expected Napoleon to reject them.

Napoleon's acceptance of the invitation to a conference was followed by the agreement upon the Armistice of Pläswitz, to last from June 4 to July 20. June 12 saw Hardenberg, Nesselrode, and Stadion in conference, working further on the final set of terms which would go to Napoleon. [38] Four stipulations were regarded as *sine qua non:* (1) dissolution of the Duchy of Warsaw, (2) enlargement of Prussia, (3) the return of Illyria to

---

[37] *Ibid.,* 116.　　　　　　　　[38] *Ibid.,* 135–136.

Austria, and (4) the renunciation by France of the Hanseatic cities and the thirty-second military district.[39] Two others were included: (5) dissolution of the Confederation of the Rhine, and (6) reconstruction of Prussia in its 1805 proportions. Stadion assured the others that Napoleon would reject the terms. Metternich also, five days later at Reichenbach, assured Alexander that if Napoleon refused, Austria would aid the allies; that if Napoleon accepted, the subsequent negotiations would be distasteful to him, he would then refuse, and the result would be the same.

Alexander was nevertheless uneasy about the possibility of Napoleon accepting their terms. He thought the Austrian minimum unacceptable now and wanted some assurance of adequate protection against France. The Russian note of June 19 voiced the urgency of this desire for *"barrières puissantes"* against France [40] and became an important document in the correspondence of this period of preparation of terms. In it the Tsar expressed one of the special needs of the European balance of power—containment of a preponderant power. The note recognized a concern which had haunted equilibrist statesmen in various circumstances for generations, a concern which was repeatedly to vex these architects of a new balance structure in the next two years. Nevertheless, the terms of June 12 stood and were the basis of the abortive bargaining at Prague, where the peace conference convened. The note of May 16 remained in the background, ready for use if Napoleon showed signs of accepting the minimum terms of June 12.

[39] A word of identification may be helpful here: in 1810 Napoleon, eager to tighten up his Continental System, had annexed to France both the Kingdom of Holland, and the German area which ran from Holland to Hamburg. This latter area bordered the North Sea, lay just north of the Confederation of the Rhine, and was described as the Hanse cities and the 32nd military district. Napoleon divided it into seven *departements*. The area was of great importance because it included the mouths of the Ems, Weser, and Elbe Rivers. Annexation of Holland and of this area meant that Napoleon controlled German access to the North Sea.

[40] Sorel, *L'Europe*, VIII, 138–139.

The terms, once they are untangled, are interesting to a student of the balance of power, because they indicate the effortless return of the eastern powers to the basic assumptions of a balanced state system. When the time came to discuss preliminary plans for peace, the statesmen flew as straight as bees towards the hive of balance of power. The state system was to be restored; Prussia was to be increased in order to stabilize north-central Europe; and France was to be reduced to a size compatible with the secure independence of other states. The evolution of policies from May 7 to June 12 gives us a panorama of the body of terms which the three eastern powers held important for a restoration of a Europe in balance. The terms also indicate, by contrast with later and less favorable offers to France, the essentially inexact nature of the balance-of-power system. The phrase balance of power is quite specific in designating a *system;* it does not, however, specify the details of that system or the details of policy whereby that system can be maintained. "Among the members of the coalition, agreement on the necessity of the equilibrium did not eliminate differences on the manner of reestablishing it." [41]

In the midst of the preparations for the peace conference at Prague, the new coalition assumed tangible form in the treaties signed at Reichenbach, a small town in south-central Silesia, not far from the border of Bohemia. Great Britain, having been sounded out earlier by Prussia and Russia regarding new treaties of alliance, here became a member of the coalition in June, joining both of these powers in separate treaties. Here shortly afterward, Metternich secretly joined the eastern allies, thereby completing the essential, inner structure of the last coalition against Napoleon, which can be dated from this month—June, 1813. The Anglo-Prussian Treaty of Alliance was signed on June 14.[42] From Prussia, Britain extracted agreement to re-

[41] Charles Dupuis, *Le principe d'équilibre et le concert européen* (Paris, 1909), 47.

[42] Martens, *Nouveau recueil*, I, 571–573; d'Angeberg, *Congrès de Vienne*, I, 9–10.

store Hanover, which had been Britain's outpost on the continent for a century, and to put 80,000 troops in the field against Napoleon; in return, England agreed to support a re-creation of Prussia's 1806 proportions, to guarantee the paper money of the allies, and to subsidize the Prussian arms with £666,666 for 1813. No separate peace would be permissible. On the following day substantially the same terms were signed by Britain and Russia,[43] with a doubled subsidy for twice as many men, plus £500,000 in payment for the Russian navy, then in use by Britain. Separate negotiations with the enemy were forbidden.

At this point, Metternich was invited to visit Napoleon, who still thought Austria might support France. Before going, Metternich arranged for Austrian participation in a Reichenbach treaty (with Prussia and Russia), although he ordered the actual signing to be delayed until after his interview with Napoleon. This technicality would enable him to say, if necessary, that Austria was yet uncommitted. Signed on June 27, however, this document finally added Austrian power to the coalition.[44] It brought to a focus the earlier search for preliminary peace terms, enumerated them, and designated the note of May 16 as an accepted part of Austrian policy. By this treaty of alliance, Austria undertook to put 150,000 troops in the field and agreed not to make a separate peace with the French. The three signatories agreed to partition the Duchy of Warsaw among themselves. This last touch is hard to explain, because it ran exactly counter to Russian plans, and yet it was accepted by the Russians. Alexander had forgotten it by the fall of 1814 and refused to grant its validity. There was still no Anglo-Austrian subsidy treaty nor any treaty of alliance between Britain and Austria. In spite of obvious inadequacies, however, the coalition had taken shape

[43] Martens, *Nouveau recueil,* I, 568–571; d'Angeberg, *Congrès de Vienne,* I, 10–12.

[44] For the text see Martens, *Recueil des traités . . . conclus par la Russie,* III, 105 ff. This was a preliminary treaty. For mention of the balance of power, see Article I; for analysis of the treaty see Oncken, *Oesterreich und Preussen,* II, 364 ff.

among the big powers; the treaties of Kalisch and Reichenbach witnessed its appearance in concrete form. It was not embodied in a general instrument to which all members were signatory, but was merely a cluster of bilateral arrangements, rather loose in structure.

Austria was now a covert member of the new coalition, but Metternich still had to complete his masquerade by cutting the last ties with Napoleon, joining the coalition openly, and declaring war on France. So elaborate were his maneuvers that it took six weeks to encompass this ritual, and his stage properties included both an armistice and a peace conference. The interview with Napoleon at the Marcolini Palace in Dresden on June 26 lasted many hours, during which the emperor did most of the talking. Metternich, with typical caution, revealed very little of his intentions. He did secure a formal abrogation of the Franco-Austrian alliance, an extension of the armistice to August 10 (the date by which Austrian arms would be ready), and considerable insight into the workings of Napoleon's active mind. He withheld from Napoleon the terms of preliminary peace which had been drafted by the eastern powers in May and June, apparently because Napoleon would have rejected them out of hand and frustrated any further delay.

The conference at Prague dragged on from mid-July to mid-August, 1813.[45] It was politically useful only to Metternich, for whom it supplied a relatively graceful entry into war against France. According to the terms of the Treaty of Kalisch, Prussia could not negotiate without Russia. Moreover, Alexander's representatives were empowered to treat only *ad referendum* every point of any consequence if Napoleon accepted the preliminary terms; in addition, according to the stipulations of the Anglo-Russian Treaty of Reichenbach, Russia could not negotiate a separate accord without her ally, England. The assembly at Prague was therefore doomed even before it began by the absence of uninvited England. Napoleon for his part, did

[45] Sorel, *L'Europe,* VIII, 154–160.

nothing to make the conference meaningful. He delayed designating and sending his plenipotentiaries. When he finally chose Caulaincourt and Narbonne, they were instructed, like the Russians, to negotiate only *ad referendum*. They were to try to split the allies so that Napoleon could make peace with Russia and smash the influence of Austria, toward which his earlier feeling of suspicion had now changed into a desire for revenge.

Nothing was done in the conference at Prague, and virtually nothing was even attempted. On July 28 Metternich indicated to Caulaincourt that Austria would declare war on France unless a treaty were signed by August 10. He still had not given France the terms, which had been ready for six weeks. Finally, on August 7, he submitted terms to Caulaincourt, who was now very short of time, then promptly adjourned the conference at midnight of August 10, before a reply could be returned, and signalized the entry of Austria into war against France. The counterproposals which were submitted the next morning were not even considered.

The conference at Prague was stillborn. It is moderately interesting today for two relatively unimportant reasons: it served to crystallize allied plans, showing us what the conception of the new Europe was; and it was the rounding out of Metternich's extraordinary diplomatic tour de force, which lasted from December of 1812 to August 10, 1813. He had guessed shrewdly at eventualities, selected the best of alternative balancing possibilities, and, aided by external events and his own good timing, maneuvered Austria out from under France and into the coalition against France, inviting but not incurring disaster from French armies before Austria was ready. Although this maneuver will remain as one of the masterpieces of the classical equilibrist diplomacy, it was neither wholly of Metternich's own creation nor entirely desired by him. He had first sought to cut the ties with France, and in that phase of his master design, he was eminently successful. In his attempt to hold the balance between east and west, however, he was unsuccessful because of the unwillingness of the powers to submit to effective mediation by Austria. The third phase, his gradual approach to the coalition, was an outgrowth of his failure to hold the balance, and as such it was not a policy which recommended itself to him as perfectly desirable. It was rather the kind of alternative which is so common in diplomatic history—where a statesman does not have a choice between a good and a bad policy, but rather between two which he dislikes.

The amorality of balance-of-power theory and practice is evident from a study of Metternich's design in 1813. It is no less present in the equilibrist policies of other statesmen, and one would be wrong in ascribing it to Metternich alone, but he does us the service of making it perfectly clear. His fundamental aim was a Europe in balance, not a Christian commonwealth nor a utopian brotherhood embracing all peoples of the continent. He hoped to end war through Austrian mediation, but he was prepared to follow the alternative policy of smashing Napoleonic power through battle and, if necessary, an immense amount of bloodshed and human tragedy. In his policy toward his potential Prussian ally, although he did not want to see Prussia eliminated as a power in the balance, he was not averse to withholding Austrian support until Prussia should have borne the brunt of Napoleonic wrath.

The Metternichian cycle was complete, much to the relief of Prussian and Russian statesmen. The armistice had served its unequal purpose, benefiting the allies much more than Napoleon. French armies in Germany at the end of April had totaled 226,000 [46] in the Elbe and Weser valleys, in addition to strong garrisons, secure lines of communication, and a steady flow of reinforcements. At that time Great Britain was not a military power in Germany, Napoleon was at peace with Austria, Prussia had only recently begun her fierce military resurgence, and the Russian field army did not comprise much over 100,000 men,

[46] Figures in this and the following paragraphs come from the *Camb. Mod. Hist.*, IX, 507–510, 522.

with reserves slow in coming up. Thus Napoleon had a definite advantage in the spring.

In August the picture was utterly different. Napoleon had been able to bring up vast numbers of reinforcements which raised his total troops in Germany to nearly 700,000. On the other hand, many of Napoleon's troops were untrained recruits; the Russian field army had been increased to 185,000, and the Russian reserves had arrived from the east. The decisive diplomatic event of the summer of 1813, the entry of Austria into the coalition, brought against Napoleon an Austrian field army of 130,000, exclusive of reserves and troops in Italy. Moreover, the Prussian promise at Kalisch to put 80,000 effectives in the field had been spectacularly doubled by August, with an enormous backlog of reserves in addition. There were also some 40,000 effectives made up of Swedish troops, Anglo-Germans, and troops of Mecklenburg. Thus allied armies totaled 515,000 in field armies alone, with an estimated 350,000 more in reserves and Austrian troops in Italy. The comparative totals in August were Napoleon, 700,000; allies, 865,000.

TOEPLITZ AND THE BALANCE OF POWER

The first test of strength between Napoleon and the new coalition came in the latter part of August, a short two weeks after the expiration of the armistice of Pläswitz. In five days four battles were fought—Dresden, Kulm, Katzbach, and Grossbeeren, the first of which was undoubtedly a Napoleonic victory, the last three just as assuredly French losses. After six weeks of less decisive campaigning, the battle of Leipzig focused in combat nearly 500,000 troops between October 16 and 18, 1813. Napoleon's indecision, desertions to the allies, and superior numbers, all conspired to grant victory to the coalition. A battered French remnant of no more than 40,000 survived the westward retreat, the crossing of the Rhine, and the toll of typhus. "Within little more than a year, two French armies, amounting together to nearly a million of men, had perished." [47]

[47] *Ibid.,* 541.

On the diplomatic front, the coalition had been tightened slightly by the signing of the treaties of Toeplitz on September 9 and October 3, 1813. The September 9 treaties, contracted by Austria, Russia, and Prussia, served as a reinforcement of the new ties of the coalition and, through their more important secret terms, repeated the main lines of the agreements on Central Europe of May–June, 1813.[48] One noteworthy exception was that the Reichenbach formula for a repartition of the Duchy of Warsaw was watered down at Toeplitz to an agreement to settle the matter amicably, a phrasing which was less out of line with real Russian intentions than the earlier, and rather puzzling, agreement to redivide the Duchy.

On October 3 the earlier Toeplitz treaties were supplemented by the belated appearance of an Anglo-Austrian preliminary treaty of alliance, plus a subsidy treaty by which the echoing vaults of the Austrian treasury would receive £1,000,000.[49] These Anglo-Austrian treaties of alliance and subsidy filled an important gap in the coalition; theretofore, Great Britain and Austria had been allies of both Prussia and Russia but had not been allied to each other, just as the tracks of two railway lines might lead to the same towns, yet remain unlinked to each other. On October 3 those connections were completed. By this Anglo-Austrian treaty of alliance the balance of power became the unanimous, official aim of the coalition. At an earlier date, in preliminary discussions at Zeycs, it had been declared to be the Russian aim in carrying the war to Napoleon. Mention of the

[48] The secret terms of Toeplitz specified: (1) the reconstruction of Prussia and Austria to their 1805 strength; (2) the dissolution of the Confederation of the Rhine and the independence of intermediary German states; (3) the reconstruction of Hanover; (4) the intention to come to an amicable understanding on the lands in the Duchy of Warsaw; (5) the restoration of the 32nd military district; and (6) the restoration of other French holdings in Germany. For the texts of the treaties of Toeplitz of Sept. 9, see Martens, *Nouveau recueil,* I, 596–599; and d'Angeberg, *Congrès de Vienne,* I, 50–52. The secret articles will be found in F. Martens, *Recueil des traités . . . conclus par la Russie,* III, 122 ff.

[49] Martens, *Nouveau recueil,* I, 607–609. Half of the subsidy had been advanced to Austria in August, after her declaration of war.

balance had been omitted from Kalisch,[50] however, and from the first two treaties of Reichenbach (the Anglo-Prussian and Anglo-Russian treaties).[51] Its first official use as an aim of the new coalition came at the end of June, in the first article of the third treaty of Reichenbach (among Austria, Prussia, and Russia), with the phrase "the re-establishment of a state of equilibrium and lasting peace in Europe." [52] It was reaffirmed in the Toeplitz treaties among these same eastern powers in September; then it made its first appearance in an Anglo-Austrian agreement at Toeplitz on October 3. Thus it had been sporadically used before the fall of 1813, but by early October all the four big allies had signed treaties confirming it as their general aim. The Austro-Russian treaty of September 9, 1813, had declared the intention of the signers to be to end Europe's troubles and "assure its future peace by the re-establishment of a just equilibrium of the powers." [53] The Austro-Prussian treaty had echoed this with the expressed desire "to put an end to Europe's sorrows and secure its future peace through the restoration of a just balance of power." [54] Furthermore, the preamble to the secret article had declared as its aim "the re-establishment of the equilibrium of the European states and a redivision of their respective forces suitable to assure this equilibrium." [55] And finally the Anglo-Austrian preliminary treaty of alliance of October 3 had declared its aim "to speed the time . . . of a general peace, which, by the re-establishment of a just equilibrium among the powers, will assure the peace . . . of Europe." [56]

It is likely that the aim was expressed in these words at the suggestion of Metternich, with whose entry into the coalition they first appeared. Whatever their origin, with Toeplitz they became the official aim of the coalition and thereafter they ran like a bright thread through the fabric of the coalition's treaties. This usage is revealing because it illustrates an attitude toward

---

[50] See above, p. 110.   [51] See above, p. 122.   [52] See above, p. 122.
[53] Martens, *Nouveau recueil,* I, 596.   [54] *Ibid.,* 600.
[55] *Ibid.,* III, 295.   [56] *Ibid.,* I, 607.

the balance of power which is utterly at variance with the later, widespread abuse of balancing conceptions. In drafting war aims in 1813, statesmen were drawing up statements which were to be published in whole or in part and which were intended to elicit enthusiasm and support. No statesman has ever consciously drafted public war aims with the intention of offending his own people. One seeks rather to coat the bitter pill of war, and such coating in 1813 involved using balance-of-power terminology and aims. Thus we have one other evidence that balance-of-power attitudes in that period were an available vehicle for idealism. Later in the nineteenth century, support of balance-of-power theory was more likely to be interpreted as evidence of cynicism or a harsh "realism."

The treaties of Toeplitz had a further significance: their secret articles gave the first official indication of the future outlines of a German state system. The earlier treaties had tended to avoid specific commitment on the future nature of Germany, except for matters like the restoration of Prussia and the elimination of the Confederation of the Rhine, Napoleon's much-hated "holding company" for central and west Germany. Metternich, deeply interested in blocking any attempt at the unification of Germany, quickly followed up the Toeplitz treaties with a further series of treaties between Austria and willing German princes, with the idea of restoring enough of the *status quo* to block those planners, such as Stein, who sought the unification of Germany. The Austro-Bavarian Treaty of Ried [57] of October 8, 1813, set the pattern for this line of policy. Its declared purpose was "the re-establishment of an equilibrium among the powers, calculated to guarantee to Europe a state of true peace. . . ." It provided for Bavaria's break with the Confederation of the Rhine and for her future sovereignty. Metternich regarded it as important; it was indeed a cornerstone of his policy toward Germany. He hoped to attract other German states by this agreement with Bavaria, and he was generally successful in

[57] For the text see *ibid.*, 610–614.

drawing other states into the Austrian fold: Württemberg, Baden, Hesse-Darmstadt, Nassau, and Saxe-Coburg all signed treaties similar to the Bavarian agreement within the next six weeks.[58]

Stein, one of the ablest Germans of this period and still a prominent adviser of Alexander I, was in direct disagreement with Metternichian policy regarding the immediate future of Germany. Both were balance-of-power statesmen, both knew a great deal about Germany, both possessed great intelligence, and yet each urged antipodal policies toward Germany. Here we find a wholly typical situation in the history of balance-of-power ideas: two men using the same frame of reference in international affairs and accepting the same general assumptions, aims, and means to arrive at widely divergent conclusions on how to carry out their specific policies. Where Stein sought a united Germany (exclusive of Austria) to take its place as an equal among the major powers, Metternich wanted the more usual state system within a state system—i.e., he wanted to retain the framework of German political disunity within the larger framework of European disunity.

It has been customary to extend heartfelt sympathy to men like Stein for their early vision of a united Germany, a vision which they saw frustrated by the conservatism of Austria, but caution is recommended in this attitude. A state system is difficult enough to maintain in a semblance of equipoise without adding to the difficulties by taking the supports from under it. One of the substantial props of the European balance was, oddly enough, the political disunity of Germany, because the division of sovereignty in that area gave to the state system itself a surprisingly stable center. The German atoms could not easily be pressed into an explosive molecule, so to speak; and Europe could count on the German center to be relatively incapable of offensive warfare. On the other hand, the atoms did tend to coalesce into a resistant molecule whenever outside powers

[58] Sorel, *L'Europe*, VIII, 197, n.2.

sought to move into or through Germany. A disunited Germany not only did not threaten to conquer Europe—a negative virtue —but stood positively as a potential bulwark against the conquest of central Europe by a non-German power. When viewed from the point of view of a European statesman who was deeply motivated by balance-of-power concepts, German disunity was better for the security and duration of the state system than German unity, however sympathetically one may feel toward German patriots in the nineteenth century who struggled for unification. Such unification, although granting fulfillment to those patriots, would at the same time dangerously revolutionize the state system.

Chapter V

Refining the Balance of Power:

The First Great Treaty

DURING the fall of 1813, Britain's voice in central European affairs was still ignored, as noted. Britain was active and victorious in Spain, had been successful in sweeping the seas of French shipping, and was by now financing the new coalition. Nevertheless, she had not participated in the conference at Prague in midsummer; had been excluded from the secret Toeplitz treaties of September 9, among the eastern powers; and was largely disregarded throughout the remainder of 1813. The reasons for this continued low tide of British influence apparently lay in several conditions not previously mentioned. Contact was poor; while Metternich, Hardenberg, and Nesselrode could meet relatively quickly, Castlereagh could not easily join them. Moreover, there was marked confusion in British representation on the Continent. Britain was represented by three ambassadors of inconspicuous ability, one to each of the major powers, with no clear delineation of authority among them, and with resulting conflicts in their dealings with each other.[1] Such a division of authority was not unprofitable to the eastern powers in the autumn of 1813, and they exploited it.

There were two other basic reasons for continental neglect of Britain's influence. She was a maritime power and had not yet assumed a military role in Germany. Russian, Prussian, and Austrian armies, unaided by British troops or mercenaries, fought the bloody campaigns of 1813 and early 1814. Castlereagh was sensitive to the importance of this factor and later made a great point of Britain's assumption of a military role of equal numerical importance with Austria and Russia—150,000 troops. The other reason was the unwillingness of Castlereagh at first to link British subsidies directly and intimately to specific elements of his foreign policy. He was soon to learn better. After a series of frustrations in 1813 with headstrong partners, he recognized the necessity of such a tie-up on a rather strict *quid pro quo* basis; henceforth British subsidies would become available when British policy was taken seriously by European recipients.

CASTLEREAGH URGES A CONSOLIDATING ALLIANCE

Although England had joined the coalition in June, 1813, Castlereagh's active penetration of the central European scene did not begin until he attempted in the autumn to alter the structure of the coalition. He was impressed by the haphazard and ramshackle character of the coalition, which consisted of no less than nine separate treaties of alliance.[2] There was ob-

---

[1] For insight into their work on the Continent see Webster, *Brit. Dipl.*, 1–120, where a sampling of their correspondence is printed.

[2] Russia-Sweden (April, 1812), Russia-Prussia (Feb., 1812), Great Britain-Sweden (March, 1813), Great Britain-Russia (June, 1813), Great Britain-Prussia (June, 1813), Austria-Prussia-Russia (June, 1813), Austria-Russia

viously a real need for one comprehensive and unifying instrument, especially since the nine treaties differed appreciably in their provisions and phraseology. He began working toward this objective in September, hoping to get an alliance against Napoleon of all the important powers as soon as possible and thinking it not difficult to secure. He drafted a project of a treaty of alliance against France, a project of secret articles, and a long dispatch to his ambassador to Tsar Alexander, Cathcart, who was to handle the negotiations for the alliance.[3] These documents show us very clearly the state of his plans for Europe at that time. They have been carefully analyzed by C. K. Webster, an outstanding British scholar, although their importance to the theory and practice of the balance of power has not been fully indicated by him.

The "Project of a Treaty of Alliance Offensive and Defensive against France" contained articles specifying co-operation in the war, no separate peace, mutual communications in negotiations, "a perpetual defensive Alliance," co-operation in case of future French attack, and validity of prior treaties. Castlereagh hoped it would be signed at once by Russia, Prussia, Austria, Sweden, and Great Britain, and that Spain, Portugal, and Sicily would be asked to accede later. The document was calculated to strengthen the bonds of the coalition by creating "one comprehensive instrument, which should place the coalition beyond the reach of dissolution by Napoleon's diplomacy."

His conception went further than mere consolidation. He wanted a permanent coalition which would automatically act against any future French aggression. In this connection, the fourth and fifth articles are especially noteworthy. In the fourth, he specified a postwar continuance of "a perpetual defensive Alliance for the maintenance of . . . peace, and for the mutual

---

(Sept., 1813), Austria-Prussia (Sept., 1813), and Austria-Great Britain (Oct., 1813).

[3] The text of these documents is in Castlereagh to Cathcart, two letters, Sept. 18, 1813, in Webster, *Brit. Dipl.*, 19–29.

protection of their [i.e., the signatories] respective States"; [4] and in the fifth, "in the case of attack hereafter by France on any one of the . . . Parties, the several Powers will support the party so attacked with all their forces." [5] The importance of this conception to the balance of power is obvious; Castlereagh was in search of an instrument which would create an effective coalition equilibrium.

In order to avoid the impression of being too vague and theoretical, Castlereagh also drafted the "Project of Secret Articles," by which he indicated his desired outlines for the new Europe: dissolution of the Duchy of Warsaw and the Confederation of the Rhine; a barrier for Holland against France; re-establishment of the Spanish Bourbons; restoration of Hanover and Naples; freedom of Italy from France; the turning over of Norway to Sweden; restoration of German independence; and restoration of Austria, Prussia, Spain, and Portugal "as barriers without which no equilibrium can be established in Europe." The equilibrist outlook of Britain's foreign minister is clearly demonstrated by such a group of documents.

Although written in mid-September, the documents were delayed on the water leg of their journey to the Continent, and Cathcart was unable to approach Alexander with regard to the consolidating alliance until the end of October, 1813, when both men were at Frankfurt. The Tsar was not unreceptive, but he mentioned several points which he felt should be included in any such treaty, such as subsidies and maritime rights. He desired the exclusion of Sweden and a limitation of the new treaty to a four-power arrangement.[6] In addition to these changes, he later asked for inclusion of the details of Britain's proposed colonial cessions.[7]

There were objections from other sources. Lord Aberdeen,

[4] Webster, *Brit. Dipl.*, 24.   [5] *Ibid.*, 25.
[6] Cathcart to Castlereagh, Oct. 30, 1813, and Dec. 5, 1813, *ibid.*, 35–36, 48–49. See also Webster, *Castlereagh*, 167–168.
[7] Cathcart to Castlereagh, Nov. 11, 1813, in Webster, *Brit. Dipl.*, 37–38.

the British ambassador to Vienna, approached Metternich, to be told that while the latter approved the treaty, it really depended upon the tsar.[8] On the other hand, Stewart, Castlereagh's eccentric half brother and British minister to Berlin, reported that Prussia was receptive and was prepared to go ahead without Austria or Russia.[9] Such an Anglo-Prussian arrangement was of no use to Castlereagh, for had it been completed, it would merely have increased the number of alliances to a total of ten instead of reducing them to one.

When it became evident that both Metternich [10] and Alexander desired a four-power arrangement as opposed to an eight-power treaty, Castlereagh accepted their amendment.[11] Nevertheless, he could not have yielded to their desires for a statement of subsidy policy in the treaty, since he felt that Parliament would never agree to such a general statement. In this fashion, progress was so trifling that in December Castlereagh, having watched his idea founder on the rocks of delay, was prepared to put the whole discussion aside for the time.[12] The allies were treating his proposed consolidation of the coalition as a specifically English aim, something to be granted to Castlereagh only after wringing some concession from him. The disappointed British foreign secretary, still convinced of the importance of the alliance, wrote Cathcart in December that his only object with regard to the alliance was to create "permanent counterpoise to the powers of France, in peace as well as in war." [13] "Nothing . . . but a defensive League is likely to deter France from returning to the old system of progressive encroachment." [14]

On December 8 the continental allies pursued their line of

---

[8] Webster, *Castlereagh,* 174.
[9] Stewart to Castlereagh, Nov. 24, 1813, in Webster, *Brit. Dipl.,* 88.
[10] Cathcart to Castlereagh, Dec. 5, 1813, *ibid.,* 50.
[11] Webster, *Castlereagh,* 186.
[12] Castlereagh to Cathcart, Nov. 30, 1813, in Webster, *Brit. Dipl.,* 45.
[13] Castlereagh to Cathcart, Dec. 18, 1813, *ibid.,* 62.
[14] *Ibid.,* 59.

negotiation by sending Pozzo di Borgo to Castlereagh. This man was one of the most interesting of the statesmen of lesser rank. A Russian diplomatist born in Corsica half a decade before Napoleon, and an archenemy of the latter, he had been in Russian service, 1804–1807, had later re-entered that service in 1812, and in 1814 became Russian ambassador to France. In December of 1813 he was instructed to get Castlereagh to include in his project specified colonial cessions and subsidies and to request that one representative instead of three be empowered to represent Great Britain at headquarters. At about the same time, the eastern allies had their ambassadors in London supply Castlereagh with a counterproject which embodied their criticisms of the original British project of alliance.[15] The draft included clauses on colonies and subsidies and restricted the alliance to the war then in progress. It is possible that the treaty might have been negotiated in London at that time if the British cabinet had not decided to send Castlereagh to the Continent to supply the urgent need of England for better, less confused, and less confusing representation. Castlereagh declined discussion with Pozzo and planned to take up the whole matter himself at headquarters on the Continent.

PLANS FOR A NEGOTIATED PEACE

One of the difficulties which prevented Castlereagh's project from achieving an early success was Metternich's excursion into psychological warfare against France—his "Frankfurt proposals" in November, 1813. During the late autumn, after the front had receded toward France, Frankfurt became a gathering place of allied royalty, statesmen, and generals. It was full of the great men of the day, among them Alexander, Francis I, Hardenberg, Knesebeck, Humboldt, Stein, Nesselrode, Pozzo di Borgo, Aberdeen, Stewart, Schwarzenberg, Gneisenau, and Metternich. Metternich wanted to satisfy Austrian war aims by negotiation if it were possible to do so; and neither he nor his

[15] Webster, *Castlereagh*, 187.

monarch had any idea of continuing the war simply to dethrone Napoleon.

Among the diplomatists at Frankfurt was Saint-Aignan, Napoleon's minister to Weimar, and Metternich took this occasion to utilize him as bearer of a message to Napoleon, before whom Metternich wanted to dangle the prospect of a negotiated peace.[16] In discussions with Saint-Aignan,[17] Metternich declared that Napoleon could have peace on the basis of the natural frontiers of France and that Great Britain was disposed to make colonial sacrifices. Nesselrode, present with Aberdeen at one of these interviews, declared that both he and Hardenberg agreed with Metternich. Aberdeen, with only a poor knowledge of French, was duped into lending his support to the conversations, and the French diplomat went off to Paris with this oral message for Napoleon.[18]

Aberdeen's approval of the offer was virtually unheard-of for a British representative and has often been castigated. The offer of the left bank of the Rhine to France meant the violation of one of the sacred cows of British diplomatic practice. The Rhine reaches the North Sea after bisecting the Low Countries into southwestern and northeastern halves. French possession of the left bank would have meant that the southwestern half, along

[16] The background of this return to negotiations with France was briefly as follows: after the adjournment of the Congress of Prague in August, 1813, Maret, then foreign minister, wrote Metternich (Aug. 18) asking for another conference, even though an armistice might be unobtainable. Metternich replied on Aug. 21 that he would bring the matter to the attention of the allies, which he did. Britain had replied with guarded approval by the end of September, and Metternich went ahead with his idea in early November (Webster, *Brit. Dipl.*, 80, 98, 107; d'Angeberg, *Congrès de Vienne*, I, 47–49).

[17] For brief, firsthand descriptions see Aberdeen to Castlereagh, Nov. 8, 9, 1813 (Webster, *Brit. Dipl.*, 107–111) and "Report of Baron de Saint-Aignan" (d'Angeberg, *Congrès de Vienne*, 73–75). For analyses of the Frankfurt Proposals, see Sorel, *L'Europe*, VIII, 199–224; and Webster, *Castlereagh*, 169–173.

[18] Saint-Aignan reduced the offer to writing in the presence of Metternich, but Metternich did not sign it (d'Angeberg, *Congrès de Vienne*, 76–77).

with Antwerp on the Scheldt, would have been in Napoleon's hands.

Saint-Aignan was a fortunate selection for Metternich, because he was a brother-in-law of Caulaincourt, who was soon to become foreign minister of France, and because he was under the influence of Talleyrand, who was both a critic of Napoleon and a confirmed equilibrist himself. Sorel has shown how the Frankfurt overtures made a great impression on Paris, where many prominent men were eager for Napoleon to accept.[19] Napoleon himself was very skeptical of the worth of an oral message of this nature, but he was unable to disregard its effect on his capital. Caulaincourt, who possessed evident devotion both to the Emperor and to a policy of moderation, was moved to the foreign office after the first, cautious French reply had been dispatched. Caulaincourt was not successful in keeping the offer alive or in nursing it into usefulness to France. It soon died during the exchange of letters [20] between Metternich and Napoleon and may indeed never have been meant as more than a trick to sow discord in the French camp. There are still some obscurities surrounding this offer. It did serve to elicit from the French an acceptance in principle of the balance of power, the French note of December 2 agreeing to a peace "based on the equilibrium of Europe, on the recognition of the integrity of all nations within their natural boundaries, and on the recognition of the absolute independence of all States, so that none can assume . . . supremacy . . . over any other." [21]

It would be a mistake to read into this more than it deserves. There is no evidence to indicate that Napoleon had changed his character and now thought cordially of a balanced European state system. He was a continental imperialist, and no amount of talk could change that fact. His imperialism could not, and can-

[19] Sorel, *L'Europe*, VIII, 222–223.
[20] D'Angeberg, *Congrès de Vienne*, 77–81.
[21] *Ibid.*, 79–80; quoted in August Fournier, *Der Congress von Châtillon* (Vienna and Prague, 1900), 33.

not, be reconciled with the concepts and practice of the balance of power. His lip service to this principle, however, is interesting and possibly meaningful. For one thing, the example of December 2 was not merely an isolated tactic employed in that one note, but was a change in line on Napoleon's part, a change which persisted through the remaining months of his waning power. The French notes of February and March, 1814, were garnished with the same sprigs. It is possible therefore to deal with the change as a piece of evidence which is worth interpreting. For our purposes, it indicates that Napoleon now had to talk the language of the coalition and that the language of the coalition was equilibrist in character. The allied declaration of Frankfurt [22] on December 1, 1813, just the day before the signature of Napoleon's note, showed clearly once again what that language was. In their statement of policy toward France, the allies asserted that they did not make war on France, but on French preponderance outside France; that they wanted France to be strong because French power was one of the *"bases fondamentales"* of European life; that other powers, however, must in their turn be free and strong, a condition to be achieved by "a just equilibrium." This allied statement may be taken even more seriously than Napoleon's because we know that it expressed a genuine and effective policy which was later put into practice.

CASTLEREAGH GOES TO THE CONTINENT

The upshot of the Frankfurt overtures was a peace conference to be held without any suspension of military operations. During the subsequent lapse of time before the conference, which was to be convened at Châtillon-sur-Seine in eastern France,

[22] Written by Metternich; see Srbik, *Metternich,* I, 166. The text of the declaration is in F. von Demelitsch, *Aktenstücke zur Geschichte der Koalition von Juni, 1814* (Vienne, 1899), 231 ff., and d'Angeberg, Congrès de Vienne, 78–79.

Castlereagh arrived on the Continent and was soon at head-quarters. Prior to his departure he had discussed with the cabinet various aspects of Britain's continental policy. Since he was the only member of the cabinet who was deeply and broadly interested in continental affairs beyond the purely military matters which interested all Englishmen, he was in the curious position of drawing up a directive which was formally addressed to himself.

These cabinet instructions which he carried with him form an interesting and important equilibrist document in this period.[23] During the preceding year, in spite of the series of treaties and their parade of secret articles concerning the shape of the Europe to come, there had been scarcely any recognition of British interest in the Low Countries. Accordingly, the most important points which Castlereagh made in the cabinet instructions were aimed at achieving an adequate recognition of Britain's vital interests. He sought first to exclude France "from any naval establishment on the Scheldt, and especially at Antwerp" and to strengthen Holland against France by augmenting Dutch territory with as much of Belgium as could be secured. Some of the extensive colonial empire which Britain had swept into her arms during the war years could be used as bargaining for this primary aim, the cessions "to be contingent upon equivalent securities to result from the continental arrangements." He here illustrated the lesson of *quid pro quo* which had just been drilled into him by the hard-boiled diplomacy of the continent. The second principal aim should be the creation of the consolidating alliance which had been his chief concern during the fall of 1813:

The Treaty of Alliance *not to terminate with the war,* but to contain defensive engagements with mutual obligations to support the powers attacked by France with a certain extent of stipulated suc-

[23] The text of the instructions is in Webster, *Brit. Dipl.,* 123–126; see also Webster, *Castlereagh,* 194–195.

cours. The *Casus Foederis* to be an attack by France on the European dominions of any one of the contracting parties.[24]

Spain and Holland should be included, but not Sweden. Colonial cessions, again, were available as bargaining power.

At various points in the instructions, Castlereagh sketched some of the desired outlines for a European balance of power: Holland, Spain, Portugal, and Italy to be established "in security and independence"; Sardinia to be restored and possibly augmented by Genoa; the Pope to be restored. The sum of £5,000,-000 was to be available for subsidies. In a "Memorandum on the Maritime Peace," [25] further details on the colonial cessions were given. Its declared aim was "to see a maritime as well as a military balance of power established amongst the Powers of Europe." Spain and Holland should be "effectually provided for," and French maritime power was to be limited.

In a search for the essentials of British foreign policy in the 1812–1815 period, it is particularly rewarding to study the details of Castlereagh's analyses, because he *was* British foreign policy. This eminent Irish lord found himself, as has been mentioned, the one member of the Liverpool cabinet who was interested in foreign affairs and the only one who followed them closely. Liverpool, aside from an ardent desire to see the Bourbons restored, made scant effort to influence foreign policy and was content to let Castlereagh have free rein within certain basic limits. As long as Castlereagh protected Britain's most valuable colonial gains, as long as he cherished her maritime rights and naval supremacy, he could go ahead on his own.

Castlereagh's foreign policy itself, however, cannot be under-

[24] Webster, *Brit. Dipl.*, 126.

[25] There is some question about the date of this memorandum. Its content indicates that it must have been drafted about the same time as the cabinet instructions of Dec. 26, 1813. Webster dates it after Jan. 14, 1814, but finds that it is closely related to the earlier instructions of Dec. 26 (*Castlereagh,* 196, n.1). For the text, see Webster, *Brit. Dipl.,* 126–128. It will be obvious that Great Britain was less interested in a real maritime balance of power than in British predominance.

stood without reference to his legacy from Pitt, for it was from Pitt's plans and hopes that he derived much of his own outlook as foreign minister.[26] Pitt had led England in war to restore the balance of power, and from what we know of his plans in 1798 and 1805, we can observe many of the details of his hopes for the postwar balance of power.[27] He made his outline for Europe especially clear in negotiations with the tsar in 1804–1805, when the third coalition was taking shape. Alexander had sent Novossiltsov to London in 1804 to negotiate an Anglo-Russian treaty of alliance. His proposals to Pitt, unusual in themselves, elicited an extraordinary answer, dated January 19, 1805.[28] In this answer, Pitt laid down the essentials of his European policy: he wanted to defeat France, reduce her territory, erect barriers against her to prevent future aggression, provide for the "security and happiness" of Europe, and contract a general alliance to guarantee the balance of power and safeguard the peace. Specifically, he wanted France returned to her old boundaries, Holland strengthened, Prussia brought forward in western Germany to act as the main rampart in the barrier against France, and a general strengthening of Austria and Prussia in order to equip them to serve as a solid core in the center of the continent, able to resist aggression from east or west.

Pitt argued that all these territorial provisions, even if en-

[26] Castlereagh's self-confessed indebtedness to Pitt is shown by his letter to Cathcart, April 8, 1813, in Charles William Stewart (ed.), *Memoirs and Correspondence of Viscount Castlereagh* (London, 1848–53), VIII, 356; cited by Webster, *Castlereagh*, 125.

[27] See Nov. 16, 1798, dispatch in J. Holland Rose, *William Pitt and the Great War* (London, 1911), 371; and Rose, *Napoleonic Studies* (3d ed., London, 1914), 54–58. See also Mulgrove to Gower, Jan. 21, 1805, in J. Holland Rose, *Select Despatches . . . relating to the Third Coalition against France, 1804–05* (London, 1904), 94.

[28] For Pitt's Memorandum on the Deliverance and Security of Europe, Jan. 19, 1805, usually referred to as the "Draft to Vorontsov," see Harold Temperley and L. M. Penson (eds.), *Foundations of British Foreign Policy from Pitt (1792) to Salisbury (1902); or, Documents, Old and New* (Cambridge, Eng., 1938), 9–21. The complete text may also be found in Webster, *Brit. Dipl.*, App. I, 389–394. See above, pp. 105–106.

acted, would still be incomplete and "imperfect, if the restoration of peace were not accompanied by the most effectual measures for giving solidity and permanence to the system." [29] To
render it secure, he proposed that Alexander's earlier and less
specific suggestion of an automatic coalition of European states
be converted into a "general agreement and Guarantee for the
mutual protection and securing of different Powers, and for re-
establishing a general system of public law in Europe." [30] He
called for a treaty among the major powers by which "their respective rights and possessions" should be determined and by
which they would agree "to protect and support each other,
against any attempt to infringe" those rights and possessions.[31]
The alliance so visualized by Pitt would automatically come
into operation when any member state committed an act of
aggression. This bold suggestion called for a much-needed refinement of the classical balance of power, where reliance was
placed on a haphazard weighting and counterweighting by bilateral alliances. Here Pitt expressed hope for a treaty including
all European powers which would act in concert against aggression. The proposal has a very modern ring to it.

Pitt considered the balance-of-power system capable of adjusting to the movement of history; further, he considered that the
balance-of-power approach had to admit of judicious territorial
change of the *status quo,* even to the point of the occasional sacrifice of the independence of some states. He insisted, for example, that there were former states whose independence, if
restored to them after the war, "would be merely nominal and
alike inconsistent with the security for the country itself, or for
Europe." [32] He cited Genoa, the Italian Republic, Parma,
Placentia, the Austrian Netherlands, and the states on the left
bank of the Rhine. These would "never again have any solid
existence in themselves," and should be disposed in a manner

[29] Webster, *Brit. Dipl.,* 393.   [30] *Ibid.,* 390.   [31] *Ibid.,* 393.
[32] *Ibid.,* 391.

"as may be most conducive to the general interests," because "there is evidently no other mode of accomplishing the great and beneficent object of re-establishing . . . the safety and repose of Europe on a solid and permanent basis." [33]

Castlereagh may have assisted Pitt in drawing up this "Draft to Vorontsov"; he was, at any rate, familiar with it and deeply impressed by it.[34] It served as the inspiration of his "Project of a Treaty of Alliance Offensive and Defensive . . ." in the fall of 1813, by which he sought to tighten and strengthen the bonds of the coalition. It was the model upon which he based that part of the "Cabinet Instructions of Dec. 26, 1813" which dealt with his projected consolidating alliance, and the model, in part, for the final coalition at Chaumont. It was the model for most of Castlereagh's general plan for the reconstruction of Europe and the source of many of the details of that plan. When Castlereagh had to face parliamentary criticism in 1815 over the peace settlement, he produced Pitt's January 19, 1805, document as a kind of scriptural justification for his own policy and action. It must have been comforting to Castlereagh, as he undertook his arduous midwinter quest for continental headquarters, to know that his country had abundant bargaining power (subsidies and colonies) and a simple, explicit, well-thought-out program sanctified by the authority of his great predecessor.

CHÂTILLON: ALLIES OUTLINE THE NEW EQUILIBRIUM

After Castlereagh's arrival in eastern France, where headquarters had been located since late December, his preliminary conversations with Metternich, Hardenberg, and Alexander were all satisfactory.[35] He was soon able to report to Liverpool that Metternich and Hardenberg had both agreed to the cession

[33] *Ibid.*   [34] Webster, *Castlereagh,* 57.
[35] Castlereagh to Liverpool, Jan. 22, 1814, in Webster, *Brit. Dipl.,* 135–136.

of Antwerp to Holland; moreover, that he had suggested to them an extension of Prussian influence in western Germany,[36] since Austria did not contemplate a return to the Netherlands and her withdrawal would leave that area unprotected; and that he had convinced Metternich of the desirability of a Bourbon restoration.[37] Clearly Castlereagh had not been idle, nor had his labors been unproductive.

There was still some uncertainty about the impending congress at Châtillon. Metternich was especially eager that the congress be called, since he wanted to exhaust any remaining possibility of a negotiated peace with Napoleon. Alexander, on the other hand, skeptical of the value of such a conference, gave way to the Austrian plan only when Metternich implied that Austria might withdraw from the coalition if there were no conference.[38] Alexander apparently felt confident that he could sabotage the congress when it was in session and that its convening would make little difference. He was correct, although this attitude of mistrust and merely nominal co-operation complicated his relations with Metternich, which fluctuated between bad and worse.

Statesmen of the "big four" met on January 29 at Langres, not far from Châtillon, to consider common action for the impending conference.[39] Castlereagh took the opportunity to correct Aberdeen's mistaken commitment of England to grant colonial sacrifices and concessions in the Low Countries made in the Frankfurt overtures; he went on to suggest that the allies offer the boundaries of 1792 to France and expressed the hope

[36] His indebtedness to Pitt on this point is noteworthy; cf. Pitt's "Draft to Vorontsov," Jan. 19, 1805, where he speaks of "the importance . . . of rendering it [Prussia] a powerful and effectual Barrier for the defense not only of Holland but of the North of Germany against France" (*Ibid.*, 392).

[37] Castlereagh to Liverpool, Jan. 22, 1814, *ibid.*, 137–138.

[38] Sorel, *L'Europe*, VIII, 254–255.

[39] Castlereagh to Liverpool, Jan. 29, 1814 (in Webster, *Brit. Dipl.*, 141–144), gives some of the details of this meeting. See also Sorel, *L'Europe*, VIII, 256–257.

that none would oppose a Bourbon restoration if the French seemed to want it. Metternich was delegated to draft a common instruction for the delegates who would be sent to meet with the French at Châtillon.

The common instruction, when drafted, stipulated the *"anciennes limites"* (i.e., those of 1792) for France and indicated that France would have no part in the reconstruction of Europe. In general outline, the instruction called for a Germany composed of sovereign and confederate states; a confederated Switzerland; Italy to be divided into independent states; Spain to be restored to the Bourbons; Holland to be independent and enlarged. With these terms, the plenipotentiaries left for the small, deserted village of Châtillon on the upper Seine, where on February 5 the congress was convened.[40] Alexander's disinclination to support the congress led him temporarily to withhold instructions from his representative; Humboldt, representing Prussia, likewise had no instructions,[41] and the work of the conferees could not begin at once. Finally, on February 7, the conference was in full session, and Caulaincourt, now basing the French case on the Frankfurt proposals, found to his dismay that France would be offered nothing beyond her *"anciennes limites."* [42] The difference was appreciable, since the Frankfurt offer had gone up to the left bank of the Rhine, whereas the new, February offer of the French frontiers of 1792 fell shy of the Rhine by several thousand square miles of territory.

There was no armistice and the conference suffered from the fluctuations of military operations which were then in progress. Blücher had defeated Napoleon at La Rothière on February 1,

[40] Sorel, *L'Europe,* VIII, 258 ff. Castlereagh revealed certain of the details of the British colonial cessions (Castlereagh to Liverpool, Feb. 6, 1814, in Webster, *Brit. Dipl.,* 146).

[41] When the Prussian instructions came, they committed Humboldt to returning France to "boundaries compatible with a system of independence and political equilibrium" (Fournier, *Der Congress von Châtillon,* 306).

[42] See the protocol of the meeting of Feb. 7, 1814 (d'Angeberg, *Congrès de Vienne,* I, 107). See also Sorel, *L'Europe,* VIII, 263.

strengthening the hand of the allies at the opening of the congress. Napoleon, rather panicky at one point, gave Caulaincourt carte blanche to get whatever terms he could and then quickly revoked it when his own military position had improved. Meanwhile, the French plenipotentiary had written Metternich to discover whether or not France could have an armistice if she accepted the formula of *"anciennes limites."* [43] Then, between February 10 and February 12, Napoleon won unquestioned victories at Champeaubert, Montmirail, and Château-Thierry, and the diplomatic picture changed once again, this time with the allies under the necessity of adjusting to a temporary ebb of their military fortunes.

The news of Napoleon's successful battles precipitated a meeting of allied ministers at Troyes,[44] where the majority opinion did not yield to panic and was both against the granting of an armistice and in favor of continuing to treat with Napoleon as long as the negotiations showed any signs of success. On February 14 Metternich suggested to Alexander that a preliminary treaty be drafted and offered to Caulaincourt. Such a treaty was written by the ministers and is usually referred to by historians as the *bases de Troyes*. The text stipulated the boundaries of 1792 for France; a solemn assertion of the principle of sovereignty and independence for all states; re-creation of the state system (Germany to be confederated, Italy to be composed of independent states, Holland to be expanded and placed under the House of Orange, Switzerland to be freed and placed under a guarantee by the great powers, Spain to be restored to the Bourbons); most of her captured overseas possessions to be restored to France; and certain conditions concerning the disposition of French troops.[45] The treaty was sent to Châtillon and given to the French on February 17.

If Napoleon had accepted the treaty, he would have retained the leadership of the territories of historic France; he would also

[43] Sorel, *L'Europe*, VIII, 263.   [44] *Ibid.*, 276–278.
[45] For the text see d'Angeberg, *Congrès de Vienne*, I, 110–113.

have secured for his son the right of succession to the imperial French throne, an assurance which lay close to his innermost impulses. On the other hand, peace on the terms offered would have meant a very great sacrifice, perhaps too great for Napoleon to consider. He would have had to confine his influence to the boundaries of the France of 1792; renounce the titles of King of Rome, King of Italy, Protector of the Confederation of the Rhine, and Mediator of the Swiss Confederation; evacuate specified fortresses; witness the rebirth of the European state system without any voice in the details of its re-creation; and give up all right to part of France's captured overseas possessions —all this, after he had changed the flow of life in Europe and controlled the continent from the crashing swells of the Atlantic to Warsaw and beyond. For someone who was primarily a military figure (and a great one), and for someone who was a newcomer to the ranks of royalty (and therefore particularly eager to justify his position by making obvious gains for his country), it may have seemed unthinkable to accept a treaty which stood for French military defeat and which, by taking from France the gains of the 1790's on the left bank of the Rhine, would have left her smaller than when Napoleon had become First Consul in 1799.

Before the French reply, internal troubles nearly visited disaster upon the coalition. Disagreements almost became breaches. Alexander, ever skeptical of Austrian loyalty to the coalition, and Metternich, suspicious of Russian motives and fearful of Russian preponderance in European affairs, were continually at loggerheads.[46] Their daily inability to agree on policy almost brought the Austrian to the point of bolting the coalition and the Russian to the point where he might have been glad to see him go.[47] The effectiveness of the coalition was seriously damaged by these quarrels, and Castlereagh hastened to take this opportunity in mid-February to reopen the question of his long-sought consolidating alliance, in order to weave together the

[46] Sorel, *L'Europe*, VIII, 278.   [47] *Camb. Mod. Hist.*, IX, 550.

flying strands of the coalition fabric. His timing was apparently excellent, and he at once received "satisfactory assurances from the respective ministers that their Courts are favorably inclined to the principle of the measure." [48] Although at the end of the month he was describing the conflicts among the allies as still "very embarrasing, if not alarming," [49] his suggestion had fallen on fertile ground and promised fruition within the near future.

Meanwhile, the French reply took shape in a long memoir [50] drafted by la Besnardière,[51] able counselor of state to Caulaincourt, and read to the allies by the latter at the session of March 10 amid some embarrassment. There was a certain pathos, recognized by the others, in the figure of Caulaincourt, loyal to Napoleon but never given sufficient latitude by his master to achieve the aims which he sought, reading with emotion a careful document whose words were wholly ineffective in blunting the purpose of the allies. The document itself was very closely reasoned, as were the other papers by the same author. Its argument was based on the professed allied aim of re-establishing a balance of power in Europe and was carefully built upon that position, with plenty of historical material for support. For example, it began with observations on the allied gains during the previous two generations—gains for Prussia, Russia, and Austria in the partitions of Poland; gains for Russia at the expense of

[48] Castlereagh to Liverpool, Feb. 18, 1814, in Webster, *Brit. Dipl.,* 157.

[49] "The criminations and recriminations between the Austrians and the Russians are at their height, and my patience is worn out combatting both" (Castlereagh to Liverpool, Feb. 26, 1814, *ibid.,* 160; see also 161).

[50] Sorel, *L'Europe,* VIII, 292–293, discusses it. It is quoted in part in Léonce, Donnadieu, *Essai sur la théorie de l'équilibre* (Paris, 1900), 113–114; the full text is in d'Angeberg, *Congrès de Vienne,* 121–126.

[51] Jean-Baptiste de Gouey, comte de la Besnardière (1765–1843), a prominent, hard-working, permanent official in the French Foreign Office. After 1807 he was director of the first political division of that office; he was an adviser on foreign affairs to Napoleon and Talleyrand, and he assisted Caulaincourt at Châtillon and Talleyrand at the Congress of Vienne.

Finland and in the treaties of Yassy and Tilsit. The allies talked of equilibrium, but how could they then offer France her *"anciennes limites"* on the Continent, take away many of her colonies, and at the same time keep their own swollen gains? They talked of equilibrium; yet they reduced the power of France and increased their own.

It was a clever argument based on the equilibrist principle of reciprocal compensation, but after twenty years of French aggression, it was a contention which fell on unlistening ears. The French Revolution and the Napoleonic despotism had unleashed new energies within the French state, with the result that France, even without reciprocal compensation, was much more powerful in 1814 than in 1789. On this basis the allies were justified in offering France her boundaries of 1792 while they helped themselves to liberal compensations. The Caulaincourt argument took no account of these facts.[52]

CHAUMONT: THE NEW COALITION EQUILIBRIUM

On March 9, 1814, the allied ministers met at Chaumont, a town on the upper Marne about halfway between the Rhine and Paris, and signed one of the outstanding documents of diplomatic history since the Renaissance—the Treaty of Chaumont.[53] They sought through this unusual document "to draw closer the ties which unite them for the vigorous prosecution of . . . [the] war." [54] The aims of the coalition were once again affirmed: "putting an end to the miseries of Europe, of securing its future repose, by re-establishing a just balance of Power, and . . . maintaining against every attempt the order of things which

[52] For a further discussion of them, see below, pp. 171–172.

[53] For the French and English texts of the Treaty of Chaumont, see *British and Foreign State Papers*, I, pt. I, 121–129; also Martens, *Nouveau recueil*, I, 683–688; and J. L. Klüber, *Acten des Wiener Kongresses in den Jahren 1814–1815* (Erlangen, 1815–1819), I, 1–8.

[54] Martens, *Nouveau recueil*, I, 683.

shall have been the happy consequence of their efforts." [55] All these verbal gestures were part of the preliminary ritual of a treaty in this period, and the phraseology, particularly "the re-establishment of a just equilibrium," sounds in its context much like a Wagnerian leitmotif announcing the arrival of the hero onstage. The alliance consisted of six bilateral treaties, one between each possible pair of the Big Four. These six were signed by the principals—Metternich, Nesselrode, Hardenberg, and Castlereagh. They contained a preamble, seventeen regular articles, and several secret articles. Structurally, the main section of seventeen regular articles fell into easy subdivisions: the first four provided for matters relating to the pursuit of the war, which was the most pressing business; the next twelve (5–16), for a new scheme of permanent coalition against France; and the last, for the customary ratifications.

With regard to the pursuit of the war, it was decided that each power would put 150,000 troops on the field, that Great Britain would supply £5,000,000 in subsidies for their support, and that attachés would be exchanged. In the secret articles, the allies confirmed their prior agreements with regard to Holland, Spain, Switzerland, Germany, and Italy; invited Spain, Portugal, Sweden, and Holland to sign the treaty; and agreed to maintain their forces for a year after the defeat of France.[56] Thus far the treaty was little more than a consolidation of the subsidy treaties of 1813. It summarized and confirmed previous agreements, wove them into one standard fabric, and decorated it with recent decisions regarding the future peace. Castlereagh had sought the benefits of uniformity for months, and by this treaty he secured them. These articles represented no departure from conventional diplomacy, except in the fact that the agree-

[55] *Ibid.,* 683–684; see also the first secret article: "The re-establishment of an equilibrium of the Powers and a just division of forces among them being the aim of the present war . . ." (Martens, *Recueil des traités . . . conclus par la Russie,* III, 163).

[56] Text of secret articles in d'Angeberg, *Congrès de Vienne,* I, 120; Martens, *Recueil des traités . . . conclus par la Russie,* III, 163–165.

ment was a four-power treaty instead of the more typical two-power instrument. As such, it was not new anyway; it was merely rather unusual.

With the fifth article, however, an important new line of thought was introduced:

V. The High Contracting Parties, reserving to themselves to concert together, on the conclusion of a Peace with France, as to the means best adapted to guarantee to Europe, and to themselves reciprocally, the continuance of the Peace, have also determined to enter, without delay, into defensive engagements for the protection of their respective States in Europe against every attempt which France might make to infringe the order of things resulting from such Pacification.

VI. To effect this, they agree that in the event of one of the High Contracting Parties being threatened with an attack on the part of France, the others shall employ their most strenuous efforts to prevent it, by friendly interposition.

VII. In the case of these endeavours proving ineffectual, the High Contracting Parties promise to come to the immediate assistance of the Power attacked, each with a body of 60,000 men.

VIII. Such Auxiliary Corps shall respectively consist of 50,000 Infantry and 10,000 Cavalry, with a train of Artillery, and ammunition in proportion to the number of Troops: the Auxiliary Corps shall be ready to take the field in the most effective manner, for the safety of the Power attacked or threatened, within 2 months at latest after the requisition shall have been made.

IX. As the situation of the seat of War, or other circumstances, might render it difficult for Great Britain to furnish the stipulated Succours in English Troops within the term prescribed, and to maintain the same on a War establishment, His Britannic Majesty reserves the right of furnishing his Contingent to the requiring Power in Foreign Troops in his pay, or to pay annually to that Power a sum of money, at the rate of £20 per each man for Infantry, and of £30 for Cavalry, until the stipulated Succour shall be complete.

The mode of furnishing this Succour by Great Britain shall be settled amicably, in each particular case, between His Britannic Majesty and the Power threatened or attacked, as soon as the requisition shall be made: the same principle shall be adopted with regard to the Forces which His Britannic Majesty engages to furnish by the 1st Article of the present Treaty.

X. The Auxiliary Army shall be under the orders of the Commander-in-Chief of the Army of the requiring Power; it shall be commanded by its own General, and employed in all military operations according to the rules of War. The pay of the Auxiliary Army shall be defrayed by the requiring Power; the rations and portions of provisions and forage, &c., as well as quarters, shall be furnished by the requiring Power as soon as the Auxiliary Army shall have passed its own Frontier; and that upon the same footing as the said Power maintains, or shall maintain, its own Troops in the field or in quarters.

XI. The discipline and administration of the Troops shall solely depend upon their own Commander; they shall not be separated. The trophies and booty taken from the Enemy shall belong to the Troops who take them.

XII. Whenever the amount of the stipulated Succours shall be found inadequate to the exigency of the case, the High Contracting Parties reserve to themselves to make, without loss of time, an ulterior arrangement as to the additional Succours which it may be deemed necessary to furnish.

XIII. The High Contracting Parties mutually promise, that in case they shall be reciprocally engaged in Hostilities, in consequence of furnishing the stipulated Succours, the Party requiring and the Parties called upon, and acting as Auxiliaries in the War, shall not make Peace but by common consent.

XIV. The Engagements contracted by the present Treaty, shall not prejudice those which the High Contracting Parties may have entered into with other Powers, nor prevent them from forming new engagements with other States, with a view of obtaining the same salutary results.

XV. In order to render more effectual the Defensive Engagements above stipulated, by uniting for their common defence the Powers the most exposed to a French invasion, the High Contracting Parties engage to invite those Powers to accede to the present Treaty of Defensive Alliance.

XVI. The present Treaty of Defensive Alliance having for its object to maintain the equilibrium of Europe, to secure the repose and independence of its States, and to prevent the invasions which during so many years have desolated the World, the High Contracting Parties have agreed to extend the duration of it to 20 years, to take date from the day of its Signature; and they reserve to themselves, to concert upon its ulterior prolongation, 3 years before its expiration, should circumstances require it.

This section of the treaty is especially striking because it marks very clearly the appearance in European statecraft of a new and improved form of balance-of-power strategy—the coalition equilibrium. It is true that the coalition itself was not new —neither this last coalition against Napoleon, which was almost a year old, nor the idea of several powers uniting in action for the defeat of a common enemy, as was done earlier in European history and repeatedly against Napoleon himself. Nor, indeed, was the idea new. Basically, the treaty called for an automatic peacetime coalition of great powers to preserve the balance of power in the European state system. Such a device was no more than the realization on diplomatic parchment of the ideal toward which balance-of-power theorists had been pointing for more than a century. Fénelon, the Abbé de Saint Pierre, de Réal, Ségur, Vattel, and Wolff had all described it in the eighteenth century. More recently, Brougham, Koch, Vogt, and Gentz had discussed it in their books. In short, the idea had been alive for a century. Nevertheless, its practical application was new. While there are earlier expressions of the theory of an automatic peacetime coalition to preserve the balance of power, there are no earlier treaties in European history which embody it, and in detail. Indeed, one of the vivid aspects of this remarkable document is its specific provisions, wherein practical statesmen are not content to blaze a new trail without doing it carefully.

The Treaty of Chaumont was therefore old in theory but new in practice. If one keeps that in mind, there is nothing very mysterious about the treaty, but its new aspects have nevertheless bred complications by leading many writers to dissociate the central conception of Chaumont from the balance-of-power tradition and call it by a new name—the Concert of Europe. For example, we find one prominent American writer asserting that "the idea of the Concert of Powers is fundamentally different from the balance of power principle. The Concert aims to secure harmony and cooperation by conciliation and by minimizing the tendency of the powers to group into opposing combinations." [57] While there is no reason for passionate argument over coalition equilibrium as opposed to Concert of Europe, as long as the facts are clear there is good reason to be perfectly sure where Chaumont stands with relation to the balance-of-power tradition.

A careful examination of the treaty text and of its sources reveals that it was written and signed by balance-of-power statesmen and that it contains typical balance-of-power phraseology. With regard to the phraseology of eighteenth-century treaties, it is worth recalling that reference to the "balance of power" or "equilibrium" was often confined to the preambles, where one could take it less seriously, as a piece of happy idealism or immaterial promise. In the Treaty of Chaumont, both the Preamble and Article XVI contain references to "the equilibrium in Europe" as the aim of the treaty, making it doubly evident that the balance-of-power aim was seriously intended.

Scrutiny of the sources of the treaty suggest the same intimate connection between Chaumont and the balance tradition. This derived from the intellectual tradition of Castlereagh, Pitt, Alexander (in 1804), and both the contemporary and early balance-of-power theorists. All of these were concerned with the re-

[57] Sidney B. Fay, "Concert of Powers," *Encycl. of Soc. Sc.*, II, 153–154.

tention or re-creation of a European equilibrium. It also derived out of the recent extensive, and often painful, experience with coalitions against the French overbalance. One need scarcely add that this background was a balance-of-power background. In short, there is nothing in its sources which gives comfort or support to someone seeking to sever the link between Chaumont and the balance-of-power past, and we can only conclude that Chaumont was deeply rooted in the balance-of-power tradition of Europe.

So much for the connection between Chaumont and the past; there remains a question about Chaumont and its future. Did the treaty text or its authors envisage or assume a perpetuation of a balance of power, or did they not? We know that the signers certainly wanted a Europe in balance, where no single power could dictate to the others, and we find in the text that the expressed aims and assumptions, as reflected either in the Preamble, the secret articles, or the body itself, all conform to our earlier examination of balance-of-power theory. Moreover, the text envisaged a type of balance-of-power practice (the use of the coalition) which had often been employed by equilibrist statesmen in crises in the past. While it is surely permissible to call it the Concert of Europe in order to distinguish it from the classical, bilateral jumbles and jungles of earlier decades, one must not divorce this blossom from its stems and roots simply because it looked different. They were all parts of the same plant.

It is questionable how far the allies intended to go in making this a general instrument for preserving the equilibrium of the European state system. During the adult lives of most of the signatory statesmen, France had been the only preponderant power threatening the equilibrium and endangering the future of the state system. The treaty recognized this specific threat by directing most of its provisions against France, and Chaumont was in this sense a coalition with a rather narrow and specific purpose. There are, nevertheless, indications that its conception was broader than might first be inferred from its dominant pre-occupation with the French danger. The Preamble provided for maintaining against "all" attacks the "order of things that shall be the happy outcome of their efforts." In Article V, where provision is made for a later peace conference, it is clearly stated that the allies will "concert together . . . as to the means best adapted to guarantee to Europe, and to themselves reciprocally, the continuance of peace." Webster, one of the most careful students of this period, has gone on record to the effect that Chaumont was designed to guarantee the settlement both against France and against any disturber of the peace.[58]

The treaty was of course never as clear in this matter as was, for example, the Covenant of the League of Nations. Nevertheless, we know that it had overtones suggesting its general use; we recognize that Castlereagh, its chief architect, thought of it as a general weapon; and we can show that it was the key initial document in formulating what actually became for the better part of a decade the definite postwar tendency of the great powers of Europe.

Broadly speaking, the creation of this new coalition equilibrium represented an attempt by Europe to give organization to a relatively new situation. The seventeenth and very early eighteenth centuries witnessed, as far as the balance of power was concerned, a basic dualism, where power resided chiefly in two scales—those of France and the Austrian Hapsburgs, with Great Britain representing a lesser source of power and occupying an unusually suitable position as balancer.[59] The eighteenth century saw the growth of Prussian as well as British power, the modification of French and Austrian power, and the appearance of Russia as a major force in the European framework, particularly after her breaking of the Ottoman monopoly of navigation on the waters of the Black Sea (1774) and her immense acquisi-

[58] Webster, *Castlereagh*, 229.

[59] For a superb, comprehensive essay on the European balance of power in the seventeenth and eighteenth centuries, see Leopold von Ranke, "The Great Powers," in Theodor Von Laue, *Leopold Ranke: The Formative Years* (Princeton, 1950), 181–218 *passim*.

tions of Polish territory in the seventies and nineties. Thus the simple balance of 1700 had been converted into the multiple balance of 1800, and the earlier basic dualism had given way to the dynamic equilibrium of five powers.

The partitions of Poland and the conquests of Napoleon had done much to discredit the new multiple balance as a viable way of life for Europe. Perhaps, as suggested by Dupuis, a French writer on the balance of power, those great challenges to the balance of power had not legitimately discredited the principle but had made it appear more indispensable.[60] Improved, the balancing system would still be effective. Certainly the allied statesmen of 1814 followed that line, and their efforts evoked the coalition equilibrium from the chaos into which Napoleon had thrown the system. This coalition equilibrium, or Concert, became the institutional adjustment of the European state system to the new multiple balance and the inadequacy of the older system of alliance balance.

Meanwhile, the congress at Châtillon was living out its last few days. The Caulaincourt paper on the balance of power did nothing to divert the allies from their proposed action toward France. The counterproposals of Napoleon, [61] submitted to the congress on March 15, likewise had no effect, and the congress was adjourned on March 19. A week later the allies issued a "declaration of the powers at the Rupture of the Negotiations at Châtillon" [62] publicly reiterating the equilibrist aims of their policy. They declared that they had offered France all the terms which were necessary for the "re-establishment of the political equilibrium" [63] and that France persisted in holding out for territorial dimensions "incompatible with the establishment of a system of equilibrium and out of proportion with the other great political bodies of Europe." [64]

The Congress of Châtillon was no world-shaking conference.

---

[60] Dupuis, *Le principe d'équilibre*, 111.
[61] For the text see d'Angeberg, *Congrès de Vienne*, I, 130–135.
[62] For the text see Martens, *Nouveau recueil*, I, 689 ff.
[63] Martens, *Nouveau recueil*, I, 691.   [64] *Ibid.*, 692.

It did, however, help to crystallize allied plans toward France, and it apparently had its pleasanter side too:

To the memory of these interesting days I must add, that the conviviality and harmony that reigned between the ministers made the society and intercourse at Chatillon most agreeable. The diplomatists dined alternately with each other; M. de Caulaincourt liberally passing for all the ministers, through the French advanced posts, convoys of all good cheer, in epicurean wines, &c. that Paris could afford; nor was female society wanting to complete the charm, and banish *ennui* from the Chatillon congress, which I am sure will be long recollected with sensations of pleasure by all the plenipotentiaries there engaged.[65]

[65] Charles William Stewart Vane, Marquess of Londonderry, *Narrative of the War in Germany and France in 1813 and 1814* (Philadelphia, 1831), 200–201.

Chapter VI

Restoring the Balance of Power:
The Second Great Treaty

OVERWHELMING preponderance of power now lay with the allies.[1] Their combined military forces were more than double those of Napoleon, and their political bonds had new structural strength. Time was too short for the emperor to divide them before his own defeat could be accomplished. The wizardry which he had shown in the use of smaller forces with poorer equipment since the Battle of Leipzig in the preceding fall could only delay ultimate defeat, and after Chaumont there was scant opportunity even for delay.

[1] In February, 1814, Castlereagh roughly estimated the coalition strength at 600,000, with 200,000 in France and 100,000 in each of the following: Italy, Spain, Upper Rhine, and Flanders (Castlereagh to Metternich, Feb. 18, 1814, in Webster, *Brit. Dipl.,* 159). For the end of 1813, the *Camb. Mod. Hist.,* IX, 543, estimates the coalition strength at 620,000 men.

DEFEAT OF NAPOLEON

The allied entry into France in late 1813 had been effected through two major crossings of the Rhine, one south of Coblenz, near the mouth of the Moselle, and the other almost two hundred miles to the south in the vicinity of Basel. From the former crossing, the Army of Silesia under Blücher had advanced southwest up the Moselle Valley, crossed over to the Meuse, and then advanced to the line of the Marne, just over one hundred miles from Paris. In the south, the main allied army under Schwarzenberg swung west from Basel and then northwest in a gradual arc which crossed the Saône, a tributary of the Rhone, and brought them into the Seine watershed southeast of Paris and only several days' unobstructed march from it. Napoleon's military genius burned brightly in some of the February and March engagements on French soil, which took place during the work of the Congress of Châtillon, but it was powerless to impede for long the grinding advance of the allies.

By the last week of March, the allies were in a position to by-pass Napoleon and thrust deeply into the vitals of France. With the French forces under Napoleon concentrated in the Saint-Dizier area, roughly one hundred miles east of Paris, Alexander decided to ignore Napoleon and march on Paris itself. He accepted the unusual risk of leaving Napoleon to his rear, between the main allied forces and Germany, in the hope that a quick advance upon Paris and a quick seizure of the capital would mean to Frenchmen the loss of the war. Happily it did. Blücher's Army of Silesia and the main army under Schwarzenberg effected a junction on March 28 at Meaux on the Marne, less than thirty miles east of Paris, and at once advanced with 180,000 troops down the Marne Valley toward the capital; the allies then invested the city on March 31 after a brief engagement at Montmartre and Romainville. The occupation was unattended by any of the bitter house-to-house fighting that had characterized the French campaigns in Spain, and the victors, much to their surprise, found themselves in a rather listless capital, a Paris for once without an obvious partisanship for either its present government or any of the alternative possibilities. "No more striking proof exists of the thoroughness with which Bonaparte had disciplined the Revolution, than the inertia which held them motionless in the face of this national crisis." [2]

THE BOURBON RESTORATION

During the days of flux between the dissolution of order under the Napoleonic regime and the creation of a new order sponsored by the coalition, policy was guided to a large extent by Tsar Alexander and Talleyrand, the one acting as representative of the coalition and the other as the self-styled middleman between the Bourbons and the conquerors. Alexander arrived in Paris on March 31 and took up residence at Talleyrand's town house on the Rue Saint-Florentin, thereby lending weight to the growing power of his French host. The mansion itself, large and magnificent, is close to the Place de la Concorde and near the Hotel Crillon, which housed the American peace delegation in 1919. The tsar, comfortably established on the ground floor, was disposed to grant, although with reservations, the probable desirability of a restoration of the Bourbons. [3] The absence of a clear demonstration by Parisians of the desired

[2] Geoffrey Bruun, *Europe and the French Imperium,* 196.

[3] For an excellent discussion of the Bourbon Restoration, complete with fine bibliographical notes, see E. J. Knapton, "Some Aspects of the Bourbon Restoration of 1814," *JMH,* VI (1934), 405–424. Knapton argues that the Restoration was the result of "a fortunate coincidence of a number of forces" (405), i.e., the ferment of royalist activity after 1812, the suspended judgement of the allies in early 1814, the Bordeaux Declaration of March 12, 1814, in favor of the Bourbons, and the presence in Paris of a group ready to undertake a provisional government. He believes that historians have overemphasized the importance of Parisian intrigue and allowed a legend to grow up concerning Talleyrand's importance. He shows that Talleyrand was considering the idea of a regency as late as the middle of March, just two weeks before the occupation of Paris. For a more enthusiastic reading of Talleyrand's role during the early days of the Restoration, see Crane Brinton, *The Lives of Talleyrand* (New York, 1936), 159 ff.

shape of their future government gave no positive assurance of popular support for the government which the occupation authorities were about to sponsor, but Talleyrand's apparent certainty provided a backlog of confidence.

Talleyrand himself had been much in the public eye since the early days of the Revolution. Foreign minister for Napoleon for a decade, he had been put aside by the emperor after the Congress of Erfurt in 1808, when he had dabbled in treason. Later, on several occasions and especially after the disaster of the Russian campaign of 1812, Bonaparte had asked him to return to office but had been met with refusals. In 1813 Talleyrand had decided that the Bourbons would be the better vehicle for the realization of his aims and had made his home a rallying point for clandestine activity on behalf of the Restoration.[4] When the allies occupied Paris, Talleyrand subverted Napoleon's order to leave by arranging that he be "caught" in the city. He succeeded in establishing quick contact with the Russians, met Nesselrode on the following day, and invited the tsar to be his guest during the occupation.

The next few days finally revealed to Frenchmen the identity of their future monarch, a problem which had been agitating the coalition for several months. This matter was really part of a much larger problem facing the statesmen of the coalition— i.e., how the sources of French aggression might be shut off. No statesman suggested the destruction of France as a means to that end. All accepted the assumption that France, after the war, must take her place in the European state system, the health of which would inevitably depend upon the political soundness of France. In the words of the Declaration of Frankfurt, the allies desired France "great, strong and happy, because French

---

[4] Knapton, "Some Aspects," 417–420, indicates the extreme circumspection of Talleyrand in the early months of 1814 and shows how his support of the Bourbon Restoration was not irrevocable until the occupation of Paris. This is contrary to the *ex post facto* account by Talleyrand himself in *Mémoires,* II, 134, 156; cited by Knapton.

power . . . [was] one of the essential foundations of the social structure" of Europe.[5]

It was assumed that France would continue to govern herself after the war. Accordingly, allied planning for France was chiefly concerned with her territorial extent and with the monarch by whom she would be ruled. With regard to the monarch, there had been several possibilities. For example, Metternich had at various times indicated an interest in a regency for Napoleon's son under Marie-Louise, the Austrian archduchess who had married Napoleon in 1810; Metternich also had intimated that he was not unwilling to see Napoleon himself continue on the throne. In 1812, at the time of the formulation of his *"rêve politique,"* he had felt that peace would be impossible with Napoleon and that a regency under Marie-Louise would be best both for France and for Austria;[6] but in 1813–1814 his insistence upon negotiations with Bonaparte at Prague, Frankfurt, and later Châtillon suggests that the idea of retaining Napoleon on the throne was never very far from his mind. He reasoned that the Revolution was the basic threat to the European balance of power and that Napoleon, by virtue of having "mastered the Revolution," was, if properly checked by other means, the best guarantor of that balance.[7]

A third plan, the projected restoration of the Bourbons, had begun to take shape as a serious possibility in January, 1814, when Castlereagh first went to the Continent, just before the congress of Châtillon. In 1800 Pitt had said, "The restoration of the French monarchy I consider as a most desirable object, because I think it would afford the strongest and best security to this country and to Europe."[8] Castlereagh, accepting this thesis,

[5] Text in d'Angeberg, *Congrès de Vienne,* I, 79.

[6] Sorel, *L'Europe,* VIII, 35.

[7] Metternich, *Memoirs,* I, 227. See Pierre Rain, *L'Europe et la restoration des Bourbons, 1814–18* (Paris, 1908), 31 ff., regarding Russian, Prussian, and Austrian policy toward the Restoration. See also Charles Dupuis, *Le ministère de Talleyrand en 1814* (Paris, 1919–20), I, 236 ff.

[8] Webster, *Castlereagh,* 234.

went to headquarters early in 1814 as an active supporter of the Bourbons—with the reservation that they be acceptable to France. He talked with Metternich on January 22 at Basel, as noted, and felt satisfied that he had persuaded him that the Bourbons were the best of the alternatives, since they were unconnected with any other big power and likely to be too weak to cause trouble.[9]

Comforted by Metternich's willingness to accept the Bourbons, Castlereagh was understandably upset by discovering that Alexander supported still a fourth plan—the elevation to the French monarchy of Bernadotte, prince royal of Sweden. The tsar, indeed, gave this candidacy strong support between October and April of 1813–1814.[10] To the mind of the British secretary, the possible choice of Bernadotte was an unmistakable threat to the balance of power, and for a very obvious reason: the elevation of the adopted prince royal of Sweden to the French throne with the tsar's help would mean, at worst, an extension of Russian influence through Sweden and Norway (which had been promised to Sweden by both Russia and Great Britain) to France. While this was only the worst of several possibilities, a foreign secretary perforce had to plan for the worst; both Castlereagh and Metternich were almost instinctively op-

[9] Castlereagh to Liverpool, Jan. 22, 1814, in Webster, *Brit. Dipl,* 137–138.

[10] Alexander denied that he had any *understanding* with Bernadotte, prince royal of Sweden, concerning his candidacy for the French throne. He did not disclaim *support* of him (Castlereagh to Liverpool, Jan. 29, 1814, *ibid.,* 139). Metternich and Castlereagh were very suspicious of his support of Bernadotte and acted on that basis (Castlereagh to Liverpool, three letters on Jan. 22, 1814, *ibid.,* 133–138). See also Knapton, "Some Aspects," 414, n.39, and Srbik, *Metternich,* 170, n.2. F. D. Scott, "Bernadotte and the Throne of France, 1814," *JMH,* V (1933), 465–478, sums up the details surrounding Bernadotte's candidacy. He shows that Alexander and Bernadotte apparently did have an understanding in the fall of 1813 after the Battle of Leipzig (468) but that Bernadotte weakened his claim on Alexander's support by separating the forces under his own command from those of Alexander, thereby cutting himself off from Alexander at the critical time, March, 1814.

posed to such a possibility and vigorously protested Bernadotte's candidacy. The tsar's persistence led to tensions among the three in February and early March and embittered the relations of the allies.[11] Castlereagh was at least successful in getting Alexander to admit that the Bourbon title "had the advantage of legitimacy" [12] and that the prevailing sentiment among the allies was pro-Bourbon.[13] The tsar also agreed with Metternich and Castlereagh that the question was essentially one for France herself and that no monarch unacceptable to France should be imposed.[14] In this manner, Castlereagh whittled away methodically at the tsar's policy and enjoyed some modest gains. Even so, the specter of Bernadotte as a royal possibility did not dissolve until the last days of March, 1814. Meanwhile, the allies had been waiting for a strong indication from France as to what post-Napoleonic government the French wanted. That indication reached the allies on March 26, 1814, in the form of news that the Bourbons had been enthusiastically proclaimed at Bordeaux on March 12. On March 28 it was evident that Alexander would support the Bourbons if Paris did not reject them.[15] There were indeed some indications that the Bourbon cause was also receiving sporadic support from circles inside Paris. Talleyrand was in touch with both Hartwell House, where Louis

[11] See above, pp. 149–150.

[12] Castlereagh to Liverpool, Jan. 29, 1814, in Webster, *Brit. Dipl.*, 139.

[13] Castlereagh to Liverpool, Feb. 16, 1814, *ibid.*, 149.

[14] Castlereagh to Liverpool, Jan. 22 and Jan 29, and Bathurst to Castlereagh, Feb. 27, 1814, *ibid.*, 138, 139, 162.

[15] Indicated by diplomatic innuendo, when the plenipotentiaries openly toasted the Bourbons at Dijon (Webster, *Castlereagh*, 243). During the last week of March Bernadotte was frantically and unsuccessfully trying to reach headquarters. He was out of touch during the most important days, and meanwhile the decision to restore the Bourbons was made. Alexander referred to Bernadotte as a possible candidate as late as April 4 (Knapton, "Some Aspects," 424), and Bernadotte himself, as late as April 5, momentarily contemplated taking his army to Paris and storming his way to power (Scott, "Bernadotte and the Throne of France," 477).

XVIII held court in Buckinghamshire, and the allies. A secret emissary from his group managed to get through to allied headquarters on March 11 with the assurance that the Bourbons did have support in powerful quarters in the capital.

Thus, when Alexander arrived in Paris and settled into the luxury of Talleyrand's town house, he was the representative of an agreed allied policy and was caught, somewhat against his will, in a Bourbon groundswell. He signed a proclamation, drafted by Talleyrand, Nesselrode, and others, declaring that the allies would no longer treat with Napoleon or his family, that they would respect the integrity of France, and that they would guarantee a new constitution which France might give herself. On the second of April Talleyrand, as brimful of expedients as the wily Odysseus himself, convened a rump Senate and presented it with an immediate program for gaining the confidence of the nation—a program containing both guarantees of civil liberties and guarantees to officers, bondholders, and owners of property. He was himself made a member of the five-man provisional government, whose duties were to carry on the administration and present a draft constitution. Marshal Marmont, well-known to Frenchmen for his loyalty to Napoleon, put his troops at this critical moment under the provisional government. The Senate absolved the nation of loyalty to Napoleon and, on April 6, approved the constitutional charter, which recalled Louis XVIII to the throne. On the twelfth the Comte d'Artois, reactionary younger brother of the new king-elect, arrived to assume titular power pending the arrival, early in May, of the new monarch himself. Thus events had moved with immense swiftness after the occupation of Paris. Talleyrand's role during those days, instead of being decisive in determining the Restoration, as is often recorded in histories of the period, was rather one of allaying Alexander's ready suspicions of its workability. The Restoration was really a matter of agreed policy after March 28, and Talleyrand was more an instrument of its success than a major participant in the decision to attempt it. His importance lay, therefore, in his role as active and adroit executive of policy.[16]

Meanwhile, Napoleon lived out impatient days at Fontainebleau, about forty miles from Paris. Torn with uncertainty and anxious over the future of his son, he wavered between plans for hasty action and abdication. By the fourth of April, his marshals had convinced him of the inevitability of defeat, and he sent Ney, Caulaincourt, Macdonald, and Marmont (who had not yet gone over to the provisional government) to Alexander with an offer of abdication in favor of his wife and son. The offer was too late. The Bourbon Restoration was virtually launched on its uncertain way; and Alexander returned a refusal, saying that Austria opposed Napoleon's compromise. The tsar, intent upon showing Christian forbearance toward his enemy, offered him the island of Elba, a generous financial settlement, and the continued enjoyment of his title, but nothing more. On the sixth Napoleon agreed to abdicate, and, as indicated, the Senate restored the Bourbons. Bonaparte signed the Treaty of Fontainebleau [17] on April 12 and was soon on his way to Elba, near the malarial coast of Tuscany, within one hundred miles of his birthplace at Ajaccio, and disquietingly close to the shores of his onetime empire.

Looking back for a moment at the Restoration, one finds that there is quite an explicit connection between balance-of-power analysis and the policy of restoring the Bourbons. To be sure, one may read the standard histories of the Restoration and be almost unaware of it,[18] but for someone tracing the elements of

[16] This conclusion is clear from Knapton's analysis of Talleyrand's activity ("Some Aspects," 420 ff.).

[17] Text in d'Angeberg, *Congrès de Vienne*, 148–151.

[18] Knapton makes no mention of it; neither do any of the following prominent accounts of the Restoration: H. Houssaye, *1814* (41st ed., Paris, 1903); Dupuis, *Ministère de Talleyrand en 1814;* Rain, *L'Europe et la restauration des Bourbons;* Marie, Marquis de Roux, *La restauration* (Paris, 1930); Gilbert Stenger, *Le retour des Bourbons* (Paris, 1908); Édouard Driault, *Napoléon et l'empire: La chute de l'empire* (Paris, 1927).

balance-of-power policy the scent is clear and quite possible to follow. It leads particularly to the analyses of Castlereagh and Talleyrand, more faintly to Metternich and the tsar, and largely disappears before it gets as far as Hardenberg.[19]

We can see now from the research of Webster and Knapton that Castlereagh was chiefly responsible for the decision to return the Bourbons to the French throne. It was he, for example, who convinced Metternich of the desirability of the Bourbons, and it was he who, together with Metternich, successfully opposed Alexander's alternative plan. It is also clear that he arrived at his decision by way of equilibrist reasoning and that he influenced Metternich by such reasoning.[20] It can also be shown that Alexander's alternative was alien to the conception of a state system in balance, because it might have given Russia disproportionate power [21] and enabled her to "injure the independence or the essential rights of another." [22]

It is similarly clear that these objections applied to Metternich's earlier ideas about a regency under Marie-Louise; in such an event, Austria might have enjoyed disproportionate influence over French policy. We know that Metternich gave way before Castlereagh's balance-of-power analysis, but we cannot show that Alexander yielded readily to equilibrist arguments in

[19] The present writer can find no evidence that Hardenberg played any significant role in the restoration of the Bourbons. Two of the most careful students of the problem assign no role at all to him: Webster, *Castlereagh*, 233 ff., and Knapton, "Some Aspects." The same holds true for the works, already cited, of Treitschke and Rain.

[20] Castlereagh believed that the Bourbons would be unaggressive and possess the advantage of not being subject to any complicating obligation to another power: they would be "unconnected equally with any of the Allies, and likely to be too weak for years to molest any of them" (Castlereagh to Liverpool, Jan. 22, 1814, in Webster, *Brit. Dipl.*, 138). To the tsar he declared the Bourbons would "likely . . . be addicted to peace" (Castlereagh to Liverpool, Jan. 29, 1814, *ibid.*, 139).

[21] Castlereagh described it as an "aim at establishing a preponderating Russian influence in France itself" (Castlereagh to Liverpool, Jan. 22, 1814, *ibid.*, 134.

[22] Gentz, *Fragments*, 55. See above, p. 81.

this case. He gave ground slowly. He was faced with a choice between antithetical policies: he could support a balance-of-power policy (exemplified by the Restoration) or a Machiavellian policy of self-interest for Russia (exemplified by the Russian-supported candidacy of Bernadotte). It was no secret that he leaned toward the latter, and it was perfectly clear that Alexander, although active against French preponderance, was in this instance seeking an equally unsettling Russian preponderance. He was fortunately headed off, not only by Metternich and Castlereagh, but by others as well. Pozzo di Borgo, one of Alexander's close advisers in 1814, was ardently pro-Bourbon, and Alexander was literally surrounded by opposition to his own plan. With Bernadotte playing his hand awkwardly and even being out of touch with Russian headquarters, with no indication that his candidacy was strongly supported in France, there was little else for the tsar to do but yield to the all-but-unanimous sentiment of his own allies and advisers. Alexander was, therefore, whether he liked it or not, driven to a decision which was equilibrist in nature.

The case of the equilibrist nature of the decision for the Restoration is, then, markedly evident in Castlereagh's analysis and policy, and it becomes even clearer when Talleyrand's role and ideology are considered. A thoroughgoing balance-of-power statesman, Talleyrand recognized that a restoration of the Bourbons would choke off French dynamism, the first requisite step in re-creating the European balance of power; it would enable France without loss of face to accept her *"anciennes limites,"* the second requisite; and it would give her a legitimate and therefore stable government, a third requisite of the European balance.[23] The greatest advantage of the Restoration, according to Talleyrand, would be the elimination of French dynamism.

---

[23] As to the connection between legitimacy and the balance of power, see below, pp. 228–230. The instructions which Talleyrand took to the Congress of Vienna in September, 1814, describe this connection very explicitly.

Here he went to the heart of the matter. The social, political, and economic changes of the 1790's in France had seemingly invigorated a whole nation, releasing energies that had long been denied expression. "The energies of the French people, released, intensified, and coordinated, gave them an immense advantage over their disorganized and backward neighbors." [24] Here in 1814, however, was an opportunity to stifle, in part, these excrescent energies of France, and a balance-of-power statesman was eager to take it. France under Napoleon was too dynamic, too dangerous to the balance of power; France under the conservative Bourbons could remain in possession of its old territorial extent and still not burst her britches. France would have "once again a government whose principles [would] guarantee . . . the maintenance of peace" [25] and "thus offer to Europe a pledge of security and stability." [26] He reasoned that France was entitled only to a limited power and territory; she had to fit into the larger picture of the European equilibrium. He regarded the reduction of France to her *"anciennes limites"* as no tragedy at all, rather as a formula which should be acceptable to France, beneficial to the European state system, and therefore indirectly beneficial to France herself. [27] One of the great advantages of the Restoration would be the ability of the Bourbons to accept the *anciennes limites* without reservations and without discredit to themselves, since that was their territory, so to speak—the boundaries of 1792 embracing all of the old territory of Bourbon France.

It is clear from these points that the Restoration of the Bourbons was related to the conception of balance of power, Castlereagh as chief architect of the policy and Talleyrand as its

[24] Bruun, *Europe and the French Imperium,* 35.

[25] Martens, *Nouveau recueil,* I, 706.

[26] Talleyrand, *Mémoires,* II, 182.

[27] In Sorel's phrase, Talleyrand "had discerned the aberrations of the conquest" (*L'Europe,* VIII, 313). On Talleyrand's balance-of-power rationale regarding the Restoration, see his *Mémoires,* II, 156 ff.

principal executor both recognizing the intimate connection, not to mention Metternich and others. The tsar, although tempted by other possibilities, was molded to acceptance. In the Restoration we have, therefore, a good example of the conscious majority choice of a balance-of-power policy from among several alternative possibilities.

THE FIRST PEACE OF PARIS, MAY, 1814

With the Restoration launched, the allies were about to embark on the first installment of what would ultimately be an over-all peace settlement for Europe. They planned to write their peace with France first and, with that behind them, turn to the larger and more complicated general European settlement. In April they agreed to negotiate with Talleyrand under the authority of Monsieur, who was now present in Paris as representative of the Bourbons, and they hoped to complete their work on the treaty by the time of the arrival of Louis XVIII, who was not expected for several weeks. The policy of settling first with France was begun with dispatch in the middle of April, only two weeks after the occupation of Paris,[28] and by April 23 a convention was signed between Monsieur and each of the allied powers.[29] This document served as a kind of preliminary peace. It sought "to put an end to the misfortunes of Europe, . . . to found its peace on a just redistribution of power among the states . . . , and . . . to give to France . . . the proofs of their [the allies'] desire to place themselves in amicable relations with her." [30] It provided for a cessation of hostilities, the evacuation from France of the allied armies, the return of administration to Frenchmen, an exchange of prisoners, and arrangements for the more formal peace settlement which would follow. It was a re-

[28] Details of the negotiations are given in Dupuis, *Ministère de Talleyrand,* I, 262 ff.

[29] For the text of the convention, see Martens, *Nouveau recueil,* I, 706 ff.

[30] *Ibid.,* see preamble.

markably moderate beginning by men representing states which had been victimized by French aggression for nearly a generation.

Meanwhile, the statesmen had begun to negotiate the more detailed terms of the peace settlement itself.[31] Here Castlereagh felt that they would be "unanimously disposed to strip the arrangement of anything bearing upon it the character of particular distrust."[32] He himself "inclined to a liberal line upon subordinate questions,"[33] having already secured most of his own program. The allies were willing to allow the Bourbons a moderate extension of French territory beyond its *anciennes limites* and some delay developed over the details connected with this concession. Some further delay arose over the attempt by Prussia and Russia to press for a general statement of the outlines of the larger European settlement. Both Hardenberg and Alexander were eager to settle the matter before their departure from Paris. There were meetings and discussions of a very secret nature, but documentation on them is very incomplete and our knowledge scanty. There is sufficient evidence to show us exactly what Hardenberg wanted, because he drafted and circulated a *"Plan pour l'arrangement futur de l'Europe,"*[34] in which he outlined the main features of the territorial settlement in a form distinctly favorable to Prussia. The tsar's plans and demands were more exorbitant, so that even his ally, Prussia, was alarmed, and the meetings were doomed to a stalemate.[35] It was clearly impossible to secure general agreement on a statement of intentions, and the attempt to include it in the treaty with France was abandoned.

[31] See Dupuis, *Ministère de Talleyrand*, I, 333 ff.

[32] Castlereagh to Liverpool, April 19, 1814, in Webster, *Brit. Dipl.*, 177.

[33] *Ibid.*, 178.

[34] Heinrich von Treitschke, *History of Germany in the Nineteenth Century* (London and New York, 1915–19), I, 661.

[35] See details of the Russian demands in Webster, *Castlereagh*, 281; for the best brief discussion of these meetings, see *ibid.*, 279–285. See also Dupuis, *Ministère de Talleyrand*, II, 42 ff,

Aside from this frustration, the allies had no particular trouble in putting together the articles of the treaty. Flushed with victory, brimming with cordiality, and armed with the products of their earlier discussions of peace terms with France, the statesmen were well prepared with plans and compromises for writing a treaty in May. By the middle of the month, Talleyrand had received the allied project and returned a French counterproject, in which he took exception to the desire of the allies, especially of England, for an immediate abolition of the slave trade; protested against the loss of certain French islands; and sought a further, slight rectification of the northeast frontier.[36] The negotiations appear to have been free from bitterness,[37] and the treaty itself was ready in rough draft by May 23. Finally, by the end of May, the work was complete; disagreement among the allies was ironed out; and on May 30, 1814, the First Peace of Paris was signed.

The treaty was drawn up in four nearly identical settlements between France and each of the four major powers (Great Britain, Prussia, Russia, and Austria).[38] The texts consisted of a preamble and thirty-three regular articles, plus several secret articles and certain "additional" articles which the powers asked for individually. The main body of the treaty provided that French boundaries be returned to the lines of January 1, 1792, with minor accessions going to France; Rhine navigation was to be free; Holland, under the House of Orange, was to be increased in size; German states were to be independent and

[36] Castlereagh to Liverpool, May 19, 1814, in Webster, *Brit. Dipl.,* 183–185.

[37] Prussia balked at the leniency with which France was being treated but did not make a serious issue of this difference of policy (Treitschke, *History of Germany,* I, 657 ff.). For details of the negotiations, see Dupuis, *Ministère de Talleyrand,* I, 333 ff.

[38] Martens, *Nouveau recueil,* II, 1–18; Klüber, *Acten des Wiener Kongresses,* I, 8 ff. A convenient and excellent English source is Edward Hertslet, *The Map of Europe by Treaty . . . since the General Peace of 1814* (London, 1875–91), I, 1–27.

bound by a federal link; Switzerland was to be independent; Italy was to be partly Austrian and partly independent states; Malta was to go to Britain; France was to receive certain of her overseas possessions which had been captured during the war; and plenipotentiaries were to go to Vienna within two months for the completion of this treaty. These provisions were based upon the terms which had been given to Caulaincourt at Châtillon in 1814, as embodied in the draft of a preliminary peace of February 17.[39]

The secret articles appended to the treaty [40] formed an important part of it. The first article contained a significant reference to the balance of power as the principle to govern the settlement "from which there is to result a system of real and durable equilibrium in Europe." The same article provided that disposition of the territory which France had yielded was to be determined at the congress by the "Allied powers." France was to have no voice in it. The five succeeding articles specified some of the disposition, giving to Holland most of the former territory of the Austrian Netherlands to make her "strong enough to maintain her independence by her own means," establishing free navigation of the Scheldt, and providing for use of areas on the left-bank of the Rhine in strengthening Holland, Prussia, and other German states. Again, the third article referred to the balance of power as the principle governing the settlement and held that the strengthening of Holland was essential to it. It is noteworthy once again that the phrase balance of power appeared not only in the Preamble but also in the articles—just one other small evidence of the seriousness with which these statesmen took the balance of power.

This treaty, forming the first major block of the larger peace settlement, is a remarkable document and has been variously

---

[39] Castlereagh to Liverpool, April 19, 1814, in Webster, *Brit. Dipl.,* 177.

[40] Martens, *Recueil des traités . . . conclus par la Russie,* XIV, 257–260. There were also additional articles which varied from treaty to treaty; see Dupuis, *Ministère de Talleyrand,* I, 392, 397 ff.

praised by scholars as "the cornerstone of the new European order," [41] "a masterpiece of constructive thought, the finest model on which statesmen seeking permanent peace after a long war can base their efforts," [42] a peace "honorable and beneficent." [43] By immediately determining what terms France was to get, the treaty gave France a certain freedom of action later on; this freedom came before the allies had been able to agree on the European settlement,[44] and it enabled Talleyrand to influence their later agreements. Moreover, by granting fair terms to France, the Peace of Paris insured the allies against an immediate outbreak of unrest and resentment in France itself and gave them sufficient confidence in French docility to turn their backs and get on with the intricacies of the general settlement. Summed up in a phrase, it was a peace of reconciliation, of moderation. Brinton, the gifted biographer of Talleyrand, has written one of the most incisive comments on the peace:

To our generation, with fresh memories of the Peace of Versailles, the terms granted France in 1814 seem of almost quixotic generosity. Thoroughly beaten, her capital occupied by enemy troops, France was actually permitted to retain some of her revolutionary conquests. . . . Foreign soldiers were to withdraw at once from French soil, and the French garrisons were to be restored. France paid no indemnity.[45]

One of the most interesting aspects of the treaty was its permission to France to retain some of her revolutionary conquests on her eastern perimeter. One would have expected that the generosity of the allies would have been exhausted by their admirable decision to push French territory back no further than 1792. But they added a graceful touch, from the French point

[41] Guglielmo Ferrero, *The Reconstruction of Europe: Talleyrand and the Congress of Vienna, 1814–15* (trans. by T. Jaeckel, New York, 1941), 276.
[42] *Ibid.,* 117.   [43] Dupuis, *Ministère de Talleyrand,* I, 401.
[44] C. K. Webster, *The Congress of Vienna* (London, 1919), 46.
[45] Brinton, *Lives of Talleyrand,* 163.

of view, by giving France several areas which were sufficiently large and populous to be considered somewhat more than token aggrandizement. There were frontier rectifications in seven separate areas, to say nothing of numerous prerevolutionary enclaves which were also promised to France.[46] The largest cessions added plump blocks of territory to France on both sides of the Meuse Valley, directly northeast of Paris, and in the beautiful mountain country of western Savoy, just south of Geneva. The gains were strictly temporary, as it turned out, because they were taken away from France in the following year by the Second Peace of Paris.

The greatest fruit of the policy of moderation was the possibility of survival which it opened before the new French government. A gouty and obese Bourbon had the difficult task of following the dazzling Bonaparte as the head of a nation which yielded more than perhaps any other in Europe to the seductions of *la gloire*. The Bourbons were the choice of the occupation authorities; they represented the type of government which equilibrists wanted; and the allies logically did not make their chosen rulers of France the heirs of their understandable hostility toward Napoleon. The distinction was not an easy one to make, but, once made, it represented distinguished statesmanship. In 1918–1919 the failure to make a similar distinction led to compounded tragedy. With the defeat of the German Empire in 1918, Germany underwent revolution and finally emerged with a republican government which generally represented those elements in the German national life which the west really wanted to see strengthened. Nevertheless, the treaty, a furious document saturated with war hatreds, had to be signed not by the representatives of the German Empire (then dispersed) but by members of the new government, at that time just staggering to its feet. Peacemakers in 1814 made no such fundamental error, although it is only fair to add that the task was more manageable

[46] For a very clear presentation of the French gains, see the maps in Hertslet, *Map of Europe*, I, 28 ff.

in 1814 than in 1919. Talleyrand was well satisfied with the treaty, if not with the secret articles, and felt that his friends "ought to be content" with him for his work.[47]

We see that the First Peace of Paris serves as a stunning and unusual historical example of one of the basic means of the balance-of-power system, which holds that statesmen must see to it that "the different powers which compose the equilibrium . . . [are not] destroyed." [48] The important components of the system must be preserved. In May, 1814, such a dictum meant that France, although the target of much popular hatred for her conquests, disturbances, and cruelties of the last generation, had to be preserved as an effective member of the European balance of power and that the allies could not afford to humiliate her if they expected to re-create a stable peace in their own day.

The . . . [First Peace of Paris] bore the stamp of the moderation of the monarchs and their cabinets—a moderation which did not arise from weakness, but from the resolve to secure a lasting peace to Europe. . . . The peace to be concluded with France could only be looked at either as a revenge on the country, or as establishing the greatest possible political equilibrium between the Powers.[49]

Even Hardenberg was not greatly dissatisfied with the treaty:

The peace with France brings us at last to the end of our efforts. Restored to its ancient frontiers, this kingdom will resume, among the powers of Europe, the place which belongs to it, without compromising the tranquillity of its neighbors and exercising over them a disastrous preponderance.[50]

Within three months of Chaumont the coalition had defeated Napoleon, restored the Bourbons, and written a model peace settlement with France—a record of outstanding achievement, a

---

[47] Talleyrand, *Memoirs,* II, 136. [48] Vergennes. See above, pp. 73–74.
[49] Metternich, *Memoirs,* I, 249. For a discussion of Austrian policy, balance of power, and moderation in this period, see Srbik, *Metternich,* I, 176–182.
[50] Hardenberg to Goltz, Paris, May 31, 1814; quoted by Dupuis, *Ministère de Talleyrand,* I, 403.

solid beginning in the work of pacifying Europe, and a superb initiation of the new experiment in coalition equilibrium.

SUMMER, 1814

Mention has been made of the attempts at Paris in May, 1814, to secure an agreement on the main outlines of the approaching peace settlement.[51] There was no prospect of quick agreements, particularly since Alexander's prestige and popularity were at their zenith—factors which might have enabled the tsar's extravagant demands to carry the field if the statesmen had seriously attempted to settle the main outlines of the peace at that time. For that very reason Castlereagh was disposed to delay any general agreement until the summer visit of sovereigns and statesmen to London, to which they had been invited and where a settlement of the main problems would greatly redound to his own credit and enhance his own prestige.

The change of scene led to many interesting events but did nothing to expedite a general agreement, since the occasion was largely given over to banquets and festivities.[52] The arriving Prussian and Russian monarchs received a warm welcome in England. Metternich, as representative of the absent Austrian emperor, received a courteous but less cordial welcome, the British government having regarded his policy with especial suspicion during the war years because of actual and suspected ties between Austria and France. Alexander made a great splash at first but successfully destroyed his own official popularity by unconventional and headstrong ineptitudes. Instead of cementing the war ties with official Britain, he began to snub the Prince Regent, cultivate the opposition, and capitalize on the Prince Regent's unpopularity with his subjects. Moreover, Alexander's

[51] See above, p. 174.

[52] For the most recent, readable, and detailed account of the London visit of the sovereigns, see Arthur Bryant, *The Age of Elegance, 1812–1822* (London, 1950), 100–164.

sister, the Grand Duchess Catherine, who had preceded him to London, had antagonized the British government by similar tactics. She had also meddled in the unsavory family affairs of the Prince Regent by encouraging his daughter, Princess Charlotte, to balk at the marriage plans which were being made for her. Altogether, Alexander and his sister had soon outworn their welcome in London. Meanwhile, Metternich had scrupulously performed all the correct, diplomatic rituals, cultivating the Prince Regent and avoiding the leaders of the opposition, with the result that Alexander's mistakes and Metternich's tact had soon reversed their positions with regard to the British government.

So much time was spent in hospitality that there was almost no time for negotiation. Documents are virtually silent on what few meetings there were, and we can be rather sure that not much happened. On June 14 the Big Four did agree that the provisional administration of Belgium be handed over to the House of Orange, according to the agreement in May as expressed in the First Peace of Paris.[53] By June 16 the ministers agreed that the Congress of Vienna should be called for August 15 and that the seven powers who had signed the First Peace of Paris should be a preliminary committee. The tsar balked at the date and demanded an opening on the first of October, to be preceded by meetings of the ministers of the big powers. Alexander wanted time for a return to his own capital, from which he had been long absent. Such a journey across the unending flatness of eastern Europe would consume weeks, but the postponement had to be accepted by the others, even though it was a blow to those ministers who had hoped to avoid further delay. They contented themselves with a renewal of the promises

[53] The protocol containing this provision was signed on July 21, 1814. G. J. Renier, *Great Britain and the Establishment of the Kingdom of the Netherlands, 1813–15* (London, 1930), 243 ff., 261, gives the details of the diplomacy leading up to the protocol.

of Chaumont and signed a convention to that effect, each state promising to keep 75,000 troops on foot.[54]

Thus the summer meetings of the Big Four were singularly barren. The British Foreign Office made some progress toward the reconstruction of Europe by working out the details of its agreement with Holland. The boundaries of Holland had been vaguely and indirectly determined by the First Peace of Paris, which had stipulated French boundaries and which had included certain terms concerning Antwerp, the Scheldt, and the Rhine. It was generally understood that Belgium should go to Holland, and the Big Four had implemented this understanding by their agreement of June 14 that the provisional administration of Belgium be turned over to Holland at once.

As to the details, Castlereagh and Hendrik Fagel, the Dutch negotiator, sat down in June to thrash out the various Anglo-Dutch problems. They agreed that Britain should retain the Guiana settlements taken from the Dutch; that Britain would assume an obligation of £1,000,000 to Sweden to permit Holland to retain Guadaloupe, already promised to Sweden; that Britain would assume one-half (£3,000,000) of the Dutch debt to Russia; and that Britain would pay Holland £2,000,000 for the Cape Colony in South Africa, which had been seized by England and which was now to remain in English hands. This sum of two millions was not an unconditional payment to Holland, since the latter had to spend it on barrier fortifications against France. Thus Great Britain assumed £6,000,000 in obligations,

[54] Text of the convention of June 29, 1814, in F. Martens, *Recueil des traités . . . conclus par la Russie,* XI, 207–209. "The Convention . . . seems to have been designed by Castlereagh to secure from the Tsar another pledge that he would not attempt to settle his difficulties by the sword" (Webster, *Castlereagh,* 296). The convention contains an implied, rather than explicit, renewal of Chaumont. In the preamble the general aims of the alliance are restated as "to assure the future repose of Europe and to establish a just equilibrium of the Powers."

only £2,000,000 of which would go to Holland, and that sum was already earmarked.[55]

The point of particular interest in the summer of 1814, as far as British foreign policy was concerned, was the remarkable diplomatic position which Castlereagh now enjoyed, a position that almost any foreign minister in almost any period might envy. Gone were the dismal days of the previous summer when England's voice could scarcely be heard in the councils of central and eastern Europe. Within the space of one year, by the summer of 1814, Castlereagh had already achieved all of the prime points of national interest in his continental policy. In February the big powers had agreed to the enlargement of Holland and the demilitarization of Antwerp, two of the most important aims of British policy. At Chaumont he had secured his long-desired and epochal treaty of general alliance, which had only just been renewed in June. The Bourbon Restoration had been carried off. By the First Peace of Paris France had accepted his points on Holland and Antwerp, and in June the big powers had actually begun to turn Belgium over to Holland. French power had presumably been limited to a size compatible with the general equilibrium, and in the summer the Anglo-Dutch agreement legalized British retentions of the Cape and arranged for Holland's active participation in the barrier system against France. Thus Castlereagh was in an unusually strong diplomatic position. He had what he wanted, in terms of British national interest, even before he began to pack for the trip to Vienna. He was untrammeled by the necessity of fighting for purely British aims, and the question of prime interest had changed to what he intended to do at Vienna with his power and prestige.

[55] Webster, *Castlereagh,* 304–305; Renier, *Great Britain and the . . . Netherlands,* 264–266. Final decisions were not made on the frontiers of the new Kingdom of the Netherlands until 1815 at the Congress of Vienna.

Chapter VII

Congress of Vienna: The Coalition Begins the Settlement

THERE were many conditions, inherent in the times, which almost predetermined the statesmen of 1814 to a relative success with their equilibrist designs. They shared the heritage of a static conception of society, dominantly eighteenth century in its preconceptions. Also, balance-of-power statesmen, once they had created a balanced state system, naturally tended to sit on it, with the expectation that sufficient weight from above would delay and perhaps prevent explosions. The earlier history of the European state system lent plausibility to this attitude, since the membership in the system had not diminished radically between 1648 and the outbreak of the French Revolution, in spite of certain wracking challenges to the system. In addition, the pervasive heritage of cosmopolitanism, which led Europeans to think in continental, as opposed to strictly national, terms, supplied a backlog of common feeling for the peacemakers, a feeling essentially compatible with the necessities of the balance of power. Balance strategy often demanded a shuffling of loyalties, as territory passed from one ruler to another or as former enemy became present ally in the treaty structure, and cosmopolitanism tended to predispose such transference to success. Moreover, the peacemakers had substantial common ground, as their public and private documents bear witness, in their nearly unanimous acceptance of the assumptions, aims, and means of the balance-of-power system. The documents of 1814–1815 show how basically similar were the different plans for the re-establishment of a just equilibrium in Europe. Such a statement might have irritated those statesmen to the point of fury, if it had come to their attention; its truth is, however, undeniable when one looks at their Europe with the detachment of a later century. Their differences of plan were rarely fundamental: the question of yielding in Poland and gaining in north Italy, or the matter of ceding several hundred thousand more souls to Prussia from one quarter and fewer to her from another.

The statesmen all shared a common European legacy and were in rough agreement on an integrated and recognizable framework within which they manipulated their policies. This condition would not again be duplicated in a major peace settlement, because the tidy European framework was destined to become world-wide within the next century. It would include Asiatic and Occidental states alike, as coal, steam, piston, and screw replaced the union of mast, yard-arm, canvas, and trade wind. By 1814 the steam engine had already been known for decades, and men like Fitch, Morey, and Fulton had already had successful trips with it. To be sure, many difficult technical problems remained before the new motive power would be commercially feasible for ocean runs, but inventors and engineers were impatient and the problems would in all likelihood not long remain unsolved.

The statesmen of 1814–1815 were fortunate in that they did not yet have to face and master a whole complex of problems arising from revolutionary forces unleashed in the last quarter of the eighteenth century. The French Revolution had dislocated the equilibrium but had not rendered impossible a return to a balanced Europe; the industrial revolution had not yet fatally smashed the ancient and familiar limits of the European in-group; nationalism and liberalism, both antithetical to the mechanical premises of balance of power, were neither strong enough nor sufficiently articulate in 1814–1815 to confuse the basic design of Vienna. In time, nationalism would give a certain undesirable inflexibility to the units in the balance. It would prevent their being increased or decreased in size without exciting the most violent passions, but that time still lay in the future.

THE GATHERING AT VIENNA

To Vienna in September, 1814, came many of the crowned heads of Europe, most of its statesmen, and countless hundreds of its lesser dignitaries, officials, and hangers-on, to say nothing of the swarm of adventurers, courtesans, spies, and pickpockets.[1] With Talleyrand, head of the French delegation, came the Duc d'Alberg, la Besnardière, and others. Castlereagh was accompanied by Stewart, Cathcart, Clancarty, and a complete embassy staff as insurance against espionage. From Russia came Alexander I, accompanied by Rasumovski and a string of non-Russian advisers—Nesselrode, Stein, Capo d'Istria, Stackelberg, and Pozzo di Borgo. The king of Prussia, present in person, was represented by Hardenberg, Humboldt, Stägemann, Jordan, Hoffmann, and others. Already present in Vienna on behalf of Austria were Francis I, Metternich, von Wessenberg, Gentz, Binder,

---

[1] For an excellent brief description of the personnel of the Congress of Vienna see *Camb. Mod. Hist.*, IX, 580–588. D'Angeberg, *Congrès de Vienne*, I, 255–264, lists the plenipotentiaries and envoys to the Congress. In these two categories there were well over one hundred persons.

and many more. Among the representatives of the smaller powers, there were King Maximilian I Joseph of Bavaria, with Wrede as his chief diplomatist; Count Loewenhielm for Sweden; King Frederick VI, seeking advantage for Denmark; Münster, able diplomatist from Hanover; Cardinal Consalvi, secretary of state of the Pope. Present also were King Frederick I of Württemberg; Grand Duke Charles of Baden; Elector William of Hesse; the Hereditary Grand Duke George of Hesse-Darmstadt; Karl August, Duke of Weimar, well-known to us for his association with Goethe; and many others.

The congress provided the occasion for the greatest social event in the life of Europe since the time before the French Revolution. It became a great, upper-class festival, celebrating the restoration of an earlier magnificence. With so many there for social reasons, the strenuous life of parties, receptions, teas, dinners, and balls absorbed much of the time and energy of the diplomatists. Often social luminaries held open house at dinnertime, tables being regularly set for thirty to fifty guests. The hospitality of Francis I of Austria was extravagant to the point of insanity, his supply of horses, carriages, dinners, balls, and festivities reputedly costing his treasury some 30,000,000 florins.

The effect of all this social activity on the congress was to slow down business. It was impossible for Metternich and Alexander to go the rounds of hospitality, spend hours in the arms of lovely ladies, and still give their best energies to the pressing problems of Saxony and Poland. Contemporaries were properly aroused by the extravagance in Vienna and their disgust did much to color the judgments of historians for a century. Vienna of course did dance, but it somehow produced a peace settlement that possessed merits not attained by the more serious and businesslike conferences of the twentieth century. A contemporary statesman and observer felt that the answer lay in the fact that the unsung experts—Wessenberg, Clancarty, d'Alberg, Humboldt, Gentz, and la Besnardière—did a vast amount of the work at

Vienna.[2] It is true that they did work hard, that they were able, and that they remained aloof from the social whirl. Doubtless much of the success of the final settlement was owing to their dogged labors, although the policy decisions themselves were made at a higher level.

Castlereagh was the first of the principal ministers to arrive in Vienna, on the thirteenth of September. He at once settled with wife and sister-and-law in a large suite in Minoriten Platz in the heart of the formal and ancient part of the city and prepared for the strenous mixture of diplomacy and entertainment which was to be characteristic of the congress. Hardenberg and Nessel-rode followed two days later; Metternich and Gentz on the seventeenth.[3] By the twenty-fourth they had had a series of four preliminary conferences concerning the "form and course of . . . their future proceedings,"[4] to use the innocuous phrase which shielded their intention to keep the initiative in their own hands. In the consideration of organizational problems attendant upon the summoning of the congress into session, there was "but one opinion 'that the conduct of the business must practically rest with the leading Powers.' "[5] The protocol of September 22 made that abundantly clear.[6] They were "agreed that the effective Cabinet should not be carried beyond the six Powers of the first order, with an auxiliary council of the five principal States of Germany for the special concerns of Germany."[7]

It was one thing for the ministers to agree secretly on keeping

---

[2] *Camb. Mod. Hist.,* IX, 580.

[3] Castlereagh to Liverpool, Sept. 24, 1814, in Webster, *Brit. Dipl.,* 193.

[4] *Ibid.*   [5] *Ibid.*

[6] Text in *British and Foreign State Papers,* II, 554. Castlereagh had reservations with regard to this document, since it was "rather repulsive to France" (Castlereagh to Liverpool, Sept. 24, 1814, in Webster, *Brit. Dipl.,* 194).

[7] *Ibid.,* 194. The document which laid down this formula may well have been the first to introduce the concept of "Great Powers" into western diplomacy. See Webster, *Congress of Vienna,* 61 and App.

affairs in their own hands and another to effect it without jeopardizing the congress itself, because representatives of the lesser powers naturally objected. The Big Four were puzzled and embarrassed by the problems connected with a general session of the congress, and much cerebration accompanied their attempts to avoid a full session. The obvious suggestion of summoning such a meeting at once and getting it to nominate a committee which would prepare a project for congressional consideration was quickly discarded as subversive of the authority of the "Powers of the first order." Other suggestions were made, and the outcome was to postpone the general session for a month. At the expiration of that month, the opening was again postponed, with the result that a general session was never convened. Gentz's witticism that the congress never met officially until the signing of the Final Act was technically correct.

THE FIRST PHASE

Poland and the Russian Formula

Among the most significant of the details which bore importantly upon the theory and practice of the balance of power in 1814–1815 were the key statesmen themselves, their attitudes toward the balance of power, and their plans for its reconstruction. Among these men the historian can demonstrate a rather high degree of consistency in the balance-of-power policies of Metternich, Talleyrand, and Castlereagh; he cannot do so for Alexander I of Russia.[8] With Alexander, insofar as the balance of power was concerned, the keynote was inconsistency. We have seen how the Russian decision of the winter of 1812–1813 to pursue Napoleon across Europe was equilibrist in nature, how Alexander's support of the Treaty of Chaumont and his moderation toward France in April–May, 1814, were similarly consis-

[8] The tsar is here treated on the same level with the first plenipotentiaries of the other major powers, because the tsar, unlike other sovereigns, was himself responsible for much of the direction and even execution of policy at Vienna.

tent with the restoration of equilibrium. At the same time his support of Bernadotte's candidacy was distinctly jarring to the European balance of power, and his visit to London was marked by a series of undiplomatic moves which no serious exponent of the balance of power should have made. Moreover, to Vienna Alexander brought one of the crowning inconsistencies of all, a policy toward Poland which was conceived in terms of nationality and moral duty and was defended on equilibrist grounds.

The tsar's interest in Poland went back some years.[9] It was he who had suggested to Napoleon that the latter form a Grand Duchy of Warsaw. In 1810 Alexander and Napoleon had come very close to signing a draft convention to provide against any resurrection of the Kingdom of Poland. Alexander, for his part, feared such a kingdom, because its creation would have stirred Napoleon's desire to add to it the Polish provinces then in Russian hands. Napoleon's subsequent reorientation of policy toward Austria at the expense of Russia prevented their signing the document, however, and led to a profound and mutual

[9] The history of Alexander's attitude toward Poland can be traced in Czartoryski, *Memoirs*, II, 11, 53, 165 ff., *et passim*. Pages 191 ff. record conversations of 1809–1810 between Alexander and Czartoryski in which Alexander reverted to an attitude of cordiality toward the idea of a Polish kingdom linked to Russia, after having both favored and opposed it at various times before. Pages 201 ff. and 213 ff. show Alexander's growth of interest; 222 ff. (Alexander to Czartoryski, Jan. 31, 1811), his specific plans on the subject. Pages 228 ff. (Alexander to Czartoryski, April 1, 1812) declare his expectation of war with Napoleon and his hope to bring the Poles over to the Russian side. On pages 234 ff. (Alexander to Czartoryski, Jan. 13, 1813) the tsar declared that there was no change in his desire for a Kingdom of Poland in personal union with Russia. Volume II of Czartoryski's *Memoirs* gives a very strong impression of Alexander's deep commitment to his Polish plans. On the other hand, his commitment was tempered by the necessity of not estranging Austria and Prussia. If they were to be brought into the Russian camp, the tsar could not afford to frighten them off by an immediate announcement of his aims toward Poland. See Nesselrode, *Lettres et papiers*, IV, 313 ff., for a memoir on this subject to Alexander; also Alexander to Czartoryski, Jan. 13, 1813, in Prince Ladislas Czartoryski (ed.), *Alexandre Iᵉʳ et le Prince Czartoryski, correspondance particulière et conversations, 1801–23* (Paris, 1865), 206 ff.

change of attitude between the two emperors. In 1811 Alexander reversed himself on Poland. Through Prince Czartoryski, he offered the Poles a Kingdom of Poland under personal union with Russia, in order to draw them away from Napoleon. This plan dominated his thinking on Poland during the days of the last campaigns against Napoleon and during the peace conference. It was implied in the negotiations before the Treaty of Kalisch in 1813, when Russian policy insisted on promising to Prussia a restoration of her former proportions but not of her former possessions.[10]

Alexander's new interest in a Kingdom of Poland closely tied to Russia was greatly deplored by Metternich and others as a dangerous expansion of Russian power. It also contradicted earlier treaties. By the Treaty of Reichenbach of June 27, 1813, which marked the accession of Austria to the coalition, the three eastern allies had agreed that the Duchy of Warsaw should be repartitioned among themselves.[11] This agreement had evidenced a retreat by Alexander from his earlier stand at Kalisch, a retreat possibly dictated by his desire to bring Metternich into the coalition. He forgot the agreement, however, and expressed surprise when Castlereagh called it to his attention at Vienna in 1814.[12] At the renewal of coalition bonds at Toeplitz in October, 1813, the allies had promised each other an amicable disposition of the Duchy of Warsaw. Meanwhile, Russian troops sat on the property. By May, 1814, secret meetings of the Big Four at Paris revealed that Alexander's claims to Poland were exorbitant. No progress toward an agreement was possible at that time. There the matter rested, until the Congress of Vienna began to assemble in September, 1814. It was soon clear to all the western statesmen that Russian policy was basically unchanged and would call for most of Poland.

The tsar had been quite secretive about the actual details of his aims until the congress convened. The plan which Nessel-

[10] See above, p. 110. [11] See above, p. 122.
[12] Castlereagh to Liverpool, Oct. 14, 1814, in Webster, *Brit. Dipl.*, 207.

rode finally revealed was dominated by its concern over compensation for Austria, Prussia, and Russia.[13] The design opposed radical changes in the mutual relations of the German states (i.e., no strong Germany) and gave most of the Duchy of Warsaw to Russia. To Prussia it gave Posen, Kulm, and part of Saxony; to Austria, south German accessions, northern Italy, the Illyrian Provinces, and Dalmatia.

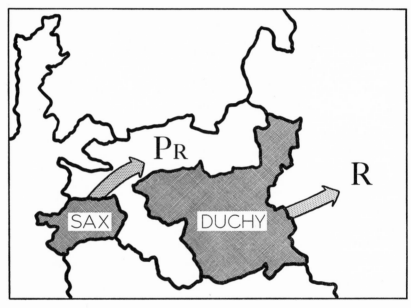

The Russian formula. The heart of Alexander's plan (autumn, 1814) was the cession of Saxony to Prussia and of the Grand Duchy of Warsaw to Russia.

These Russian terms gave rise to the bitterest and most important fight at Vienna: the dispute over the disposal of Poland and Saxony. The two areas were not adjacent, being divided by the width of Silesia; nevertheless, their linkage in the diplomacy of 1814–1815 was so close as to suggest the intimacy of two ele-

---

[13] This important document was drafted in August, 1814. For its contents see Martens, *Recueil des traités . . . conclus par la Russie,* III, 170 ff. It is summarized in Sir E. Satow, "Peacemaking, Old and New," *Camb. Hist. Jour.,* I, no. 1 (1923), 29.

ments in a chemical compound. To separate one from the other would take a powerful catalyst, and the process would predictably generate heat. The real reason for the intimacy may be defined with utter simplicity: the tsar insisted on it, his basic formula for the reconstruction of Europe being

$$POLAND \longrightarrow RUSSIA, \; SAXONY \longrightarrow PRUSSIA.$$

There were the usual fluctuations of attitude within the limits of this formula, as might be expected. The tsar changed his mind from time to time as to how much of Saxony should be given to Prussia and as to what small parts of Poland might remain outside of Russian control, but the formula expresses his general position accurately. Although this formulation of policy made the Polish and Saxon problems inseparable, various other factors (such as Alexander's insistence, the hard fact of Russian occupation of Poland, and Prussian indecision) placed the weight of the early discussions on the Polish half of the compound; and the early history of the congress became largely a story of the struggle over Poland.

The background of Russo-Polish relations had been nasty, brutish, and long. For centuries the two countries had been at each other's throats. One extreme in the struggle had occurred in 1610, during those awesome years known to us as the Time of Troubles, when Polish troops had captured Moscow. The other extreme had only just occurred in 1813, when Russian troops, reversing the process, had occupied most of the former Kingdom of Poland. Poland was an adjacent and vulnerable neighbor; and policy toward her constituted one of the very special concerns of Russian foreign affairs. Alexander's attitudes, like so many other policies of this volatile and idealistic tsar, were subject to as many rapid and unexplained changes as a New England thermometer.

We are accustomed today to thinking of Poland rather as a geographical expression than as a power considerable in her own right and strength. A continuing victim of Russian imperialism early in the twentieth century, she served as a battleground in World War I, enjoyed briefly and chaotically a precarious independence between the great wars, was subjected successively in World War II to invasion and occupation by Germany and invasion and occupation by the Soviet Union, and then was incorporated after 1945 in the Soviet satellite system. Viewed from 1814, rather than from the twentieth century, Poland was much closer to an era when she had commanded international respect. The Poland of the fifteenth century had one of the most advanced constitutions in all Europe; sixteenth-century Poland saw the introduction of Renaissance culture, the creation of organic union within the state, and an era of relative peace; seventeenth-century Poland was able to send troops all the way to Moscow; and in the eighteenth century, although stricken with grave maladies, Poland was large, if not powerful. As recently as 1792, only twenty-two years previous to the opening of the Congress of Vienna and an important year still vividly in the minds of many of the statesmen of 1814, Poland had occupied 200,000 square miles of eastern Europe and was enacting constitutional reforms in a tragically late attempt to put her house in order and to re-establish herself as a sturdy component in the European balance of power. The cynical partitions of '93 and '95 had of course frustrated and nullified that effort. In those partitions, Russia, Austria, and Prussia had added to their respective parts of Poland and then had administered the additions with varying degrees of success for more than a decade. Finally, Napoleon, after defeating Austria and Prussia in 1805–1806, took their shares of the second and third partitions and pasted them together to form the cardboard Duchy of Warsaw, his most easterly satellite. In 1814, therefore, the Polish territories which came on the market at Vienna were not all of Poland, but were the duchy areas which Napoleon had lifted from Austria and Prussia and which had never been under Russian control until the Russian military advance of 1813. The obvious solutions which recommended themselves to statesmen who sought a reconstructed equilibrium were to hand back the areas to their former Austrian and Prussian owners or possibly to re-create the independent Kingdom of Poland. To many of those men it was a new and alarming situation to find the tsar rejecting those alternatives and intent on taking what was for Russia a wholly new slab of territory, that of the Duchy of Warsaw. To be sure, the Russian aim was understandable enough: compensation was in the atmosphere, and this was the obvious area for Russian aggrandizement; Russia was riding the crest of the greatest military exploits in her history and possessed an opportunity to give depth to the nearly featureless vulnerability of her southwestern frontier; Russia was enjoying the triumphant emergence from her frozen distances into the warmth of participation in the west; and she was enjoying the final reversal of the tide of western Christendom which had had successive high marks on the long Russian beach and was only now proven to be steadily ebbing toward the west. From the Russian point of vantage, the duchy lands were much like an exposed sandspit which emerged with the ebb and naturally attracted Russian interest.

The area in question had special significance in the eyes of Poles, too, since it was really the heartland of their historical experience. The Duchy of Warsaw had been shaped like a battered teakettle, with its base running from Cracow east, its sides contained by Silesia and the Bug, its top lying just south of East Prussia, and its spout hooking around the East Prussian frontier toward the northeast. The area within these lines was easily the richest part of what had formerly been Poland, which generally had embraced flat, low country with generous precipitation and slow runoff and was therefore abundantly supplied, like Siberia, with saturated soil and marshes. The duchy area was particularly valuable among such typical Polish land because it was relatively well drained and represented the best of rather poor land. Through its river system its parts were more closely integrated than they were with the destitute areas to the east, where cultural and racial lines became blurred. Two of the four important rivers draining these lands were the Netze in the west, flowing into the Warthe, which itself took a northerly course before angling sharply to the west to join the Oder at Küstrin, only fifty miles east of Berlin. Both of these rivers were important in early Polish history, and their valleys were the first Christianized areas in Poland. Not far to the east, the Vistula, coming from the mountains of the south, traversed the length of Poland before entering the Baltic. Its size, navigability, and valley made it the most important of Poland's rivers. It had on its banks not only Cracow and Warsaw, but more than half the important towns and cities of all Poland. The only other important river was the Bug, a tributary to the Vistula in the southeast and a convenient line in that area indicating approximately where Poles ceased to dominate the population. West of this line and inside the duchy lands, Poles were overwhelmingly in the majority.

The duchy territory, aside from its prominence as the racial heartland of former Poland, also conformed roughly to the three most important nuclei in Polish history—Great Poland, Little Poland, and Masovia. The first of these was the area in the west, traversed by the Warthe and filled with lakes in the vicinity of the ancient cathedral town of Gniezno. It was well-to-do; but in the southwest and on the upper Vistula was the even more fertile area of Little Poland, dotted by one-roomed, white-washed peasant cottages with thatch and simple crosses on the roofs, the roads marked with calvaries and wayside chapels. This area was dominated by old Cracow, whose university had been founded in the fourteenth century; it was the city where Copernicus had studied, where the Polish kings had been crowned, and where the royal apartments had within recent memory been used for quartering Austrian soldiers after the partition of 1795. Masovia, the third portion of particular importance in the heartland of Poland, was in the middle Vistula country, its capital of Warsaw lying two hundred and sixty miles downriver from Cracow. Here was another fertile part of Poland and a fine center for navigation, although Warsaw could hardly claim the distinguished past of Cracow.

These, then, were the areas which Russia sought in 1814 to associate with her already swollen territories to the east. They had indeed an obvious attractiveness for the Russian state, but a Russian retention of them held important implications for the rest of Europe. It meant that compensation had to be found for Prussia's loss in Poland. Alexander's proposal that Saxon areas should become Prussian indicated that he thought of the line of European dominoes as being pushed from the east: as Russia pushed the Polish domino, Prussia should push the Saxon; Austria, the Italian; and so on—all deriving from the original Russian formula. Alexander's policy was a confused mixture of motivation composed of idealism and of Russian self-interest, of a nominal and vigorously rationalized adherence to the balance-of-power system, and of an attempt to reconcile the principle of nationality with that of the balance of power. It was not an easy position to defend in argument with Metternich and Castlereagh, whose equilibrist outlooks did not admit of any recognition of the principle of nationality. To them the over-all balance transcended the national needs of any cultural group like the Poles; mechanical workability was more important to them than cultural affinities and national hopes.

In a letter to Castlereagh, dated October 30, 1814, the tsar expressed the desire to see the allies acquire "dimensions suitable for maintaining the general equilibrium." [14] Such an acceptance of balance-of-power strategy by the tsar seemed only to confuse his intentions as far as Castlereagh was concerned, because Alexander had asserted earlier that his Polish plans were based on a "moral duty" and that the question involved "the happiness of the Poles." [15] The British foreign minister could regard such

[14] D'Angeberg, *Congrès de Vienne,* II, 351. See also Alexander to Castlereagh, Nov. 21, 1814, in Arthur Wellesley, Duke of Wellington, *Supplementary Despatches* (London, 1858–72), IX, 441 (hereafter cited as *Well. Suppl. Des.*).

[15] Castlereagh to Liverpool, Oct. 14, 1814, in Webster, *Brit. Dipl.,* 207.

lofty reasons only with skepticism, and historians have tended to exploit the tsar's arguments as evidence of a meaningless veneer to coat a policy based on nothing more than Russian advantage. The evidence indicates that Alexander, however suspect his designs were at the time, was sincere in his conviction that he brought blessings to the Poles by his plans for their future.[16] His effusion of idealism was probably genuine. Any explanation of his conduct and attitudes must take into account the fact that he was a sensitive individual with profound liberal and moral drives who was nevertheless caught in a harsh system in which his basic emotional make-up could not regularly find satisfaction. An idealist, holding a position of responsibility in an amoral system, he sought to live his idealism and simultaneously manipulate the destinies of his country within that system. The two aims were basically incompatible. He could not deliver Europe from the hated dominion of Napoleon without shedding the blood of countless thousands of soldiers; he could not bring what he felt to be happiness to the Poles without coming very close to plunging Europe into another war in the early winter of 1814; he could not rule his own country happily without reform and could not, in his own mind, reconcile reform with efficient rule. He indicated an awareness of this paradox again and again during his reign by declaring that he wanted to abdicate and lead a life of religious devotion. The paradox became more acute in the years following the settlement at Vienna, and Alexander temporarily sought to solve it by a headlong plunge into reaction. He was the most unusual, the most puzzling, and in many ways the most interesting of the statesmen at the Congress—"a man of high Spirit, and a Prince of very pregnant parts."

The Austrian Axiom and the Strong Center

Among the central figures, Metternich stood as a statesman whose equilibrist record was evident to all. As a young man at the universities of Mainz and Strassburg, he had assimilated the

[16] *Appendix to the Memoirs of the Duke de Ripperda,* 362.

theories of Koch and Vogt, both exponents of the balance of power.[17] The French Revolution, disruptive of continental stability and a fundamental threat to the European equilibrium, was anathema to him. As minister of foreign affairs for Austria after 1809, he was especially sensitive to revolutionary change, because the Hapsburg Empire, a heterogeneous collection of nationalities, had everything to lose by an extension of the revolution and an encouragement of national hopes. For Austria, nationalism meant separatism, weakness, and dissolution.

During the 1812–1815 period, Metternich was rather consistently equilibrist in policy, as already shown.[18] This relative consistency was evidenced in his interest in regaining mobility for Austrian policy, his junction with the coalition, his opposition to undue westward extension of Russian power, his opposition to the candidacy of Bernadotte, his acquiescence in the Bourbon Restoration in France, and his studied moderation toward the new French government of 1814. There is also ample information about Metternich's aims and activities in 1814–1815 to show their consistency. He wanted a state system in balance and had very specific plans for achieving it.[19] At Vienna he was prepared to support Castlereagh's plan for enlarging Holland by the addition of most of what had formerly been the Austrian Netherlands. As a further check against future aggression

[17] On Koch and Vogt, influential teachers of Metternich, see Srbik, *Metternich,* I, 65, 88 ff. For evidence of Metternich's preoccupation with the balance of power in the pre-1812 period, see Metternich, *Memoirs,* II, 29, 30, 38, 272, 289–300, 474–491. For the best comment in English on Metternich and the balance of power see E. L. Woodward, *Three Studies in European Conservatism* (London, 1929), 37–40.

[18] See above, pp. 111 ff. and 128 ff. For a brief review of Metternich's policy in 1813–1814, see Srbik, *Metternich,* I, 163 ff. Srbik has a great deal of material on Metternich and the balance of power; see I, 88 ff., 167, 172, 178–179, 181, 326, 330.

[19] See *ibid.,* I, 182 ff., 317 ff.; and Srbik, "Metternich's Plan der Neuordnung Europas, 1814–15," *Mitteilungen des Instituts für oesterreichischer Geschichtsforschung,* XL, (1925), 109 ff.

by France, he desired Prussia to be strengthened in the west that she might come forward to protect the Rhine frontier, as Austria now reluctantly yielded that responsibility after centuries of guardianship. Germany itself he wanted to confederate in such a way that Prussia might guarantee the security of the northern states and the western frontier, while Austria could guarantee the south and manipulate the destinies of the organization as occasion demanded. He wanted to preserve the sovereignty of the individual German princes and render them dependent upon Austria; he opposed any attempt at organization or centralization which would minimize Austrian influence. He felt that Austrian authority should be reconstituted and enhanced in Italy. Russian westward expansion should be checked and Russia prevented from taking Poland. Ideally, Prussia should regain her Polish domains and be compensated there, such compensation in that area helping to split the close alliance of Russia and Prussia. Prussian compensation in Saxony was to be resisted, except under special circumstances. Austria should regain her earlier territorial losses to Bavaria (at the hands of Napoleon) and regain her former Polish domains. In short, his plans ranged over much of Europe and aimed at the re-creation of a workable equilibrium among the major powers through a systematic use of checks and balances.

As September revealed the shape and strength of Alexander's design for Poland, Metternich's planning tended to shift and reduce itself to a strategic axiom: Austria could tolerate half of the Russian formula but could not permit both Poland to go to Russia and Saxony to go to Prussia.[20] To Metternich, the ces-

[20] This point is made clear by Metternich's conditional consent to the cession of Saxony to Prussia in return for a united front against Russian aggrandizement in Poland (see Metternich to Hardenberg, Oct. 22, 1814, in d'Angeberg, *Congrès de Vienne*, I, 316). Metternich made the same point in a very frank exposition to Hardenberg on Jan. 28, 1815 (see *British and Foreign State Papers*, II, 607). For Castlereagh's testimony regarding Metternich's axiom ("Austria can ill afford to be foiled on *both* these points" [i.e. Saxony and Poland]), see Castlereagh to Liverpool, Nov. 21, 1814, in Webster, *Brit. Dipl.*, 240.

sion of the Duchy of Warsaw to Russia meant an uneasy proximity of Russian soldiery on the immediate north and northeast
frontier of the Hapsburg Empire and a consequent threat to the
Austrian military frontier in that sector. It suggested the un-
wanted necessity of compensating Prussia in Saxony, which
would further weaken Austria's northern frontier, enhance Prussian influence in Germany, tend to consolidate the Russo-
Prussian bond, and stir the potential enmity of Austria and
Prussia. He was especially sensitive on the matter of Cracow,
which was the key to the northern approaches to the Moravian
Gate, that wide and comfortable pass which offered easy approach to Vienna from the northeast. Since the Carpathians
and the mountains around Bohemia generally defied an easy
advance from the north, this bottleneck and its approaches were
of great strategic importance.

The balance of power is, of course, a system of political rela-
tivity. It does not stipulate any absolute maximum or minimum
of power above or below which one state must not go. It would
have been illogical, therefore, for any contemporary statesman
to argue that the addition of new parts of Poland to Russia
would in itself destroy the balance of power. It is noteworthy
that none did so argue. The illogic of the Russian position, in
terms of balance-of-power theory and practice, must be shown
in another manner.

According to the "law" of reciprocal compensation, an unusually large access of territory to Russia had to be balanced by
similarly large compensations for the other principal states in
the equilibrium. Russia could not be permitted to attain the
preponderance of power which the coalition had just successfully denied to France and which would have contained within
it the seeds of a new disruption of the general balance of power.
The new compensations about to be distributed had to be such
that they would not in themselves weaken the general balance
by introducing some new form of insecurity. No west European
wanted to check Napoleon with one hand and unleash Alexander with the other.

According to equilibrist theory and practice, therefore, the "correctness" of the Russian retention of the Duchy of Warsaw was contingent upon Austrian and Prussian compensation which would be adequately large, mutually acceptable, and consistent with equilibrist corollaries. The Russian position must be judged on the basis of whether or not these conditions could be fulfilled. It can be shown that they could not.

The Russian plan, stipulating that Russia retain Poland, that Prussia receive Saxony (as well as compensation in western Germany), and that Austria be compensated principally in Italy, was theoretically feasible from a purely superficial equilibrist standpoint. Nevertheless it was untenable, because it essentially weakened the defensive position of Austria with relation to both Russia and Prussia. Russian power would advance over 200 miles in the direction of Vienna and to a point only 175 miles from that capital, in contrast to her remote position in 1795 after the third partition. The incorporation of all of Saxony in Prussia would give the latter some 200 new miles of common boundary with Austria in addition to the existing 250 miles of common border between Prussian Silesia and Austria. Thus Austria would have new common boundaries with Prussia and Russia which together amounted to almost 500 miles. Both Prussia and Russia were formidable military powers, and, more important, both tended to act in concert from the time of their alliance in the Treaty of Kalisch on.

The Russian proposals were therefore untenable on equilibrist grounds, and the arguments which Metternich used in opposition to them were quite sound from the standpoint of balance of power. He felt that Austria could risk no more than half of the Russian formula. He based his policy toward Saxony upon this premise and was prepared to sacrifice Saxony to Prussia only if he could get the latter to join the opposition against Alexander and block the Russian plan on Poland. One can add further good supporting reasons for Russia's not trying to add new Polish lands to her already bulging empire: Russia

had what we may call her natural frontiers in the west by 1800;
she did not need this area; and she would risk the problems attendant upon trying to solve relations with a higher civilization.
Her best policy would have been a saturation policy with re-

The Russo-Prussian menace to Austria. Fulfillment of the Russian formula
would have radically extended the joint frontiers between Austria and the
Russo-Prussian bloc. Metternich would accept either half of Alexander's
formula, but not both halves.

gard to the western frontiers and a concentration of energies
inside the state. She was never any more successful with Poland
than Britain with Ireland, and she would have done well to stay
out of the Polish heartland.

From the very opening of the congress, Metternich was joined in his opposition to Russia by Castlereagh, whose policies had also been consistently equilibrist in 1813 and 1814. Castlereagh's instructions to his ambassadors in the former year show the balance-of-power content clearly enough, and his own appearance on European soil emphasized it further.[21] Upon his arrival on the Continent in January of 1814, he made it quite obvious to all that his aim was the re-establishment of a balance of power. His use of equilibrist terminology, arguments, and conceptions was demonstrated in his activity against the candidacy of Bernadotte, in his conversion of Metternich to support of the Bourbons, in his attitude toward the consolidation and refinement of the coalition at Chaumont, and in his policy of moderation toward France in April and May.

Then at Vienna in the fall he continued in predictable fashion to make the "establishment of a just equilibrium" the "first object" of his attention and "to consider the assertion of minor points of interest as subordinate to this great end." He intended "to support the Powers, who had contributed to save Europe . . . , in their just pretensions to be liberally re-established." In this aspect of his policy he felt he should "not

---

[21] See above, pp. 134 ff., 141 ff., 166 ff., and 170 ff., for earlier comment on Castlereagh and the balance of power. With regard to his instructions to his ambassadors, see his letter of July 5, 1813, to Cathcart, where he wrote that "in order to lay the foundation of some counterpoise in the centre of Europe to the power of France," it would be "indispensably necessary to require . . . the restoration" of Austria and Prussia "to such extent of power and consequence as may enable them to maintain such a counterpoise" (Webster, *Brit. Dipl.,* 8). Earlier he had declared that "to keep France in order, we require great masses—that Prussia, Austria, and Russia ought to be as great and powerful as they have ever been." (Castlereagh to Cathcart, April 8, 1813, *ibid.,* 1). With regard to Italy, "the main object . . . is to create the most effectual barrier against France in that quarter." In the fall of 1813, Castlereagh pointed out that, before any congress with Napoleon should be allowed, there ought to be an understanding between the allies and Napoleon "upon the basis on which an equilibrium in Europe can be revived" (Castlereagh to Aberdeen, Sept. 28, 1813, *ibid.,* 101). For the best available summaries of Castlereagh and the balance of power, see *ibid.,* xli–xlii, and Webster, *Castlereagh,* 393, 493–498.

be deterred . . . by the necessity of adopting . . . measures which, although not unjust, are nevertheless painful and unpopular in themselves." He would endeavor "to combine this latter duty to . . . friends and Allies, with as much mildness and indulgence even to the offending states, as circumstances would permit." [22] In short, balance of power was his chief aim; reciprocal compensation and moderation were to be his chief means of achievement.

He proposed to secure the "just equilibrium" by creating a system of barriers around France, by strengthening the middle sector of Europe to the point where it could resist aggression from either east or west, and by compensating the major powers for their military activities against Napoleon. For the first aim he desired an enlarged Kingdom of Holland, to give a strong northern anchor to the arc of containment; a strengthening of Prussia in the western part of Germany in order to bring her "more in military contact with France" and to stiffen the arc against the latter; an increase of territory to Bavaria, a strong military state which could offer dogged resistance to France; and a similar strengthening of the northwest Italian states, so they could anchor the southern end of the arc.[23]

He regarded Russian westward extension as a threat to the European balance of power and proposed to check it by weakening the bond of Kalisch between Prussia and Russia and substituting an Austro-Prussian nuclear bond which could serve as the military backbone of central Europe in resisting either Russian or French aggression.[24] Russian designs on Poland he regarded as "not only dangerous but degrading to Austria and Prussia," since they would deny those states "the semblance of a military

[22] Castlereagh to Liverpool, Nov. 11, 1814, in Webster, *Castlereagh*, 350–351; Webster, *Brit. Dipl.*, 232–233. For a good summary of Castlereagh's aims at Vienna and their relation to the balance of power, see A. W. Ward and G. P. Gooch, *Cambridge History of British Foreign Policy, 1783–1919* (Cambridge, Eng., 1922–23), I, 464–466.

[23] Castlereagh to Wellington, Oct. 1, 1814, in Webster, *Brit. Dipl.*, 196.

[24] Webster, *Castlereagh*, 282, 386.

frontier" and create an "undisguised state of military dependence upon Russia;" such a plan "would have the colour of an attempt to revive the system we had all united to destroy, namely one colossal military Power holding two other powerful States in a species of dependence and subjection, and through them making her influence felt in the remotest parts of Europe." [25] On the other hand, he held Saxony to be one of the "minor points of interest . . . subordinate" to the end of checking Russia, and he was willing to see Saxon land used to create a strong Germany. In this connection he wrote to Hardenberg that he considered nothing more important in European politics than "a substantial enlargement of Prussia." [26] He supported the idea of a confederated Germany, the Austrian search for increased power in northern Italy, the re-creation of an unconfederated system of independent states in central and southern Italy, and the claim of Sweden to the control of Norway.

Occasionally the historian is rewarded for his perusal of endless documents of dim importance by stumbling across a letter or memorandum which, transcending paper, throws a beam like a searchlight. Such a document is the remarkable letter which Castlereagh sent to Wellington six weeks after his arrival at Vienna. Here he wrote that a "just equilibrium" in Europe might best be attained by building a strong center and that the only alternative was to pit north against south, an unsatisfactory second choice:

Two alternatives alone presented themselves for consideration—a union of the two great German Powers, supported by Great Britain, and thus combining the minor States of Germany, together with Holland, in an intermediary system between Russia and France— or a union of Austria, France, and the Southern States against the Northern Powers, with Russia and Prussia in close alliance.[27]

[25] Castlereagh to Liverpool, Oct. 2, 1814, in Webster, *Brit. Dipl.*, 200.

[26] Ferrero, *Reconstruction of Europe*, 177.

[27] Castlereagh to Wellington, Oct. 25, 1814, in Webster, *Brit. Dipl.*, 217–218.

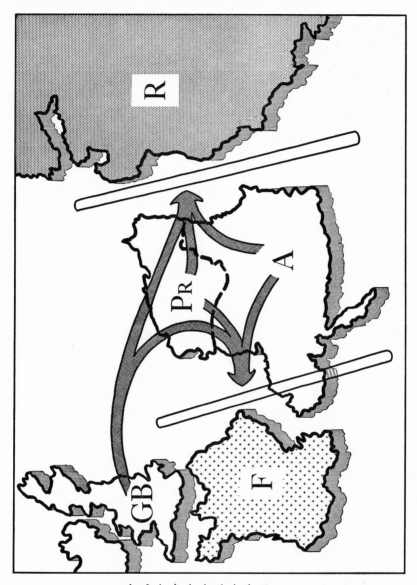

Castlereagh's preferred plan (autumn, 1814): the strong center. Castlereagh expected the other German states to combine with Prussia and Austria in forming the "intermediary system" between Russia and France.

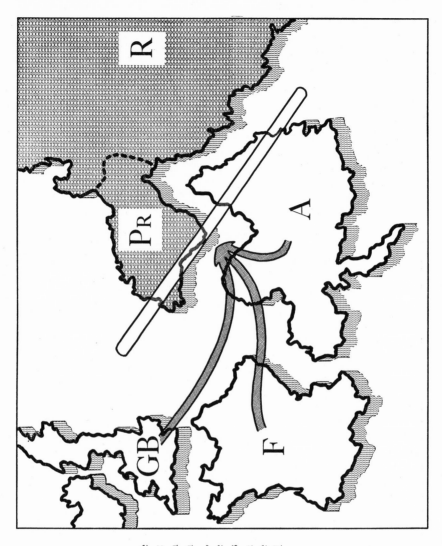

Castlereagh's alternative plan (autumn, 1814): "south" vs. "north." With Prussia against Austria in this strategic arrangement, Castlereagh expected the subordinate German states to take sides—the southern with the Austrian bloc, the northern with Prussia and Russia.

Here was his strategic conception of the territorial equilibrium. He did not want to fall back upon the second choice, because it would be "difficult to cement, on account of the fundamental jealousy existing between Austria and France"; because "it rendered Holland and the Low Countries dependent on France for their support, instead of having Prussia and the Northern States of Germany as their natural protectors"; and because it "presented the further inconvenience, in case of war, of exposing all the recent cessions by France to re-occupation by French armies." [28] He wanted above all a strong bastion in the middle of Europe based on Austro-Prussian co-operation and separating the two poles of aggressive energies in east and west. He was especially eager to reconcile Austria and Prussia with each other, because if they did not agree, they would not be able to present a united front against the Russian plans for Poland; then, when they were unsuccessful on Poland, the settlement would turn on "Saxony, Mayence and other German points, and through the contentions of Austria and Prussia, the supremacy of Russia would be established in all directions, and upon every question." [29]

This Irish lord was, along with all the major statesmen at Vienna, a "great power" equilibrist, believing that the key powers had to operate the balance-of-power system and that the interests of the small powers could justifiably be sacrificed to those of the great if the balancing process demanded it. This principle caused considerable anguish among the representatives of the smaller powers at Vienna, and it later evoked some criticism in Parliament when Castlereagh had to defend his work on the peace settlement. Mackintosh,[30] in April, 1815, pointed out to the House of Commons that the aim of balance-of-power strategy was to preserve the independence of the mem-

[28] *Ibid.*

[29] Castlereagh to Liverpool, Nov. 11, 1814, *ibid.,* 231.

[30] Sir James Mackintosh, a prominent member of the Whig opposition in the House of Commons, who had recently returned from India.

bers of a state system and that it must logically preserve the independence of all the powers, big and small alike.[31] He called attention to the harshness and illogic of strengthening and compensating the major powers by destroying smaller sovereignties, whose kings could often trace their royal descent for hundreds of years. Castlereagh called this concept "a principle of imbecility" and spoke of certain of the ancient states which had been sacrificed as "those rude and shapeless fabrics, which had long been thrown down, and had long ceased to exist in any tangible form." [32] Without bothering to philosophize about his own position, Castlereagh was as sure of its "realistic" workability as Mackintosh was of his own logic.

Castlereagh's balance-of-power policy was given a certain steadiness by virtue of England's geographical position of maritime insulation on the northern flank of Europe. England, although near invasion on several occasions, was never actually invaded and never compelled by occupation to join Napoleon's satellite nations, a fact which goes far toward explaining the striking continuity of British equilibrist strategy, as contrasted with the vacillation of continental statesmen. A Napoleon across the Straits of Dover was less cogent than a Napoleon on one's doorstep or in one's courtyard. While it was true that Britain had Hanover to worry about, England did not have to share her own territorial boundaries with another power in the continental sense; she could lose Hanover and remain untouched herself. Castlereagh's balance-of-power strategy had, therefore, a suggestion of Olympian objectivity about it. Moreover, this objectivity, enhanced by Castlereagh's having earlier used subsidies and colonial cessions to secure British aims, gave him a certain freedom at Vienna. He could act as arbiter, inclining his weight where it would do the most good for the general balance

[31] For the text of the speech see Webster, *Brit. Dipl.,* 405–409. This is a very interesting and revealing speech. According to Mackintosh, the "only useful purpose" of the balance of power was "the protection of independence," i.e. of great and small alike (*ibid.,* 408).

[32] Castlereagh, March 20, 1815, in the House of Commons, *ibid.,* 396.

of power. Talleyrand had a similar advantage, since the territorial extent of France had already been determined to his own satisfaction by the First Peace of Paris, but he could not as readily exploit the advantage. He possessed neither the bargaining power of Castlereagh nor the necessary standing at Vienna in the autumn, because of his representing a defeated power and his consequent exclusion from high councils until rather late in the negotiations. He and Castlereagh did not hold widely dissimilar views on the re-creation of a territorial equilibrium, but there was a tendency for each to embody a different approach to the problem of equilibrium. Talleyrand, the representative of a power against which a coalition remained operative, tended to direct his energies against the coalition and thereby to become the exponent of the alliance balance, whereas Castlereagh, in a very different position, tended to personify the new experiment in coalition equilibrium.

The day after Alexander's arrival at Vienna, Castlereagh had an interview with him in the course of which they discussed Poland frankly, Castlereagh arguing against the tsar's plans. In the first week of October, Castlereagh saw the king of Prussia, and found him "the advocate of the Emperor of Russia, although personally adverse to his measures." [33] On October 12 Castlereagh again debated the matter with Alexander, who defended his plans on equilibrist grounds, saying that Poland would be a check on Russia because the Russian army would be so far away from things.[34] Castlereagh gave him a memorandum and letter stating the case against the tsar's plans on Poland.[35] Under the date of October 30, the Russian reply came in the form of a letter and memorandum arguing the defense of Alexander's plans on practical and ethical grounds.[36] In answer to Castlereagh's citing of the Treaty of Reichenbach,

[33] Castlereagh to Liverpool, Oct. 9, 1814, *ibid.*, 201.

[34] Castlereagh to Liverpool, Oct. 14, 1814, *ibid.*, 207.

[35] *Ibid.*, 206–208; memorandum, 208–210.

[36] Alexander to Castlereagh, Oct. 30, 1814, with memorandum, in d'Angeberg, *Congrès de Vienne*, I, 350–358.

wherein Russia had explicitly agreed to the partition of Poland with Austria and Prussia, the Russian memorandum declared that the treaty referred to was very much a piece of the moment and that, since "its first stipulations were not applicable," [37] the treaty as a whole was no longer binding. The Russians held that the "general equilibrium" did not really stand or fall upon the question of a little territory more or less, nor on the possession of strong positions, but rather on powers having "a common tendency at the moment of the danger" [38]—a reply which attempted to minimize the territorial aspects of a balance settlement and maximize the automatic coalition aspect.

A Balancer and a Winner

Actually there were two powers against one (Great Britain and Austria against Russia), but the numerical superiority of Austria and Great Britain was balanced on the other side by the Russian occupation of Polish soil. With two rather even sides, Hardenberg's position was really one of balancer, and Prussian policy naturally assumed great importance in the eyes of the other statesmen. Hardenberg's activity illustrated vividly the conflict of state interest and equilibrium. His policy conformed to equilibrist demands in the strong and co-operative action of Prussia against the overbalance of Napoleonic France, the interest in restoring the state system re-enforced by a line of barrier states, and the participation in the Treaty of Chaumont. On the other hand, he had played a largely negative role in the Restoration of the Bourbons and then an obstructionist part in the writing of a moderate First Peace of Paris. He had acquiesced, out of necessity, in the implied retention of Poland by Russia and tended to accept it as a fact to which Prussian policy would have to adjust.

Hardenberg appeared at Vienna with quite definite plans for re-creating the European state system and for drafting the constitution of the new German confederation. He had matured the

[37] *Ibid.*, 353.

[38] *Ibid.*, 357; cited by Donnadieu, *Essai sur la théorie de l'équilibre*, 136.

former plan in the spring of 1814, the latter in the summer with the help of Stein. The best summary of his conception of the new Europe lies in his *"Plan pour l'arrangement futur de l'Europe . . . ,"* [39] submitted to the allies in Paris during the negotiation of the settlement with France. In it he called for a barrier system against France to be composed of: an expanded Holland; greatly enlarged holdings for Prussia in western Germany; readjusted frontiers for Bavaria, Baden, and Württemberg; a confederated Switzerland; and increased territory for Austria in Italy. For Germany he specified a confederation which would also include Holland and Switzerland as members. For the new German confederation he envisaged a dual directory of Prussia and Austria, assisted by two councils of the heads of circles and the princes and estates.[40] With regard to reciprocal aggrandizement, he earmarked parts of Poland and Italy for Austria, the lion's share of Poland for Russia, and a whole series of accretions for Prussia, some of them highly controversial (part of western Poland, all of Saxony, the duchies of Berg and Westphalia, and all of the Rhineland from Mainz to Wesel).

His policy was quite naturally one of Prussian aggrandizement, almost to the exclusion of other important matters, because Prussia had suffered great humiliation by Napoleon and had also contributed enormously to the reduction of the French overbalance. Hardenberg had outdone himself in following up Castlereagh's proposal of January, 1814, that Prussian western

[39] See Treitschke, *History of Germany*, I, 661 ff.; H. T. Colenbrander, *Gedenkstukken der algemeene Geschiedenis van Nederland van 1795 tot 1840* ('s Gravenhage, 1905–22), VII, 113–114; and Dupuis, *Ministère de Talleyrand*, II, 62 ff.

[40] There is an unfortunate lack of competent historical work on Hardenberg. Treitschke, "Preussen auf dem Wiener Congresse," *Preuss. Jahr.*, XXXVI (Dec., 1875), 655–714, is helpful for the period of the congress. F. Arndt, *Hardenberg's Leben und Wirken* (Berlin, 1864), 218 ff., is a rather sketchy treatment of Hardenberg at Vienna; Hartmann Freiherr von Richthofen, *Hardenberg, Bilder aus dem bewegten Leben eines grossen Staatsmann* (Berlin, 1933), is for popular consumption and is virtually useless to the professional historian.

holdings be increased. Both men thought of Prussia as the new
guardian of the Rhine frontier against France, as a participant
in the barrier system, and as one of that system's chief supporters. Hardenberg was distrustful of Metternich and Tsar
Alexander.[41] The former heartily opposed the proposed cession
of Mainz to Prussia and Hardenberg's suggested manipulation
of southwest German frontiers.[42] Moreover, Hardenberg could
not count on Metternich's acquiescence in Prussia's absorption
of Saxony. Similarly, he could not be at all sure how much of
Poland Russia would agree to return to Prussia. As will be
shown below, Hardenberg was ultimately to yield to Russian
desires, give up the possibility of regaining for Prussia all her
former holdings in the east, and concentrate his energies on
securing all of Saxony. He thereby became a principal in a plan
which was conceived and defended in equilibrist terms but
which was essentially unsound from a balancing point of view.
His policy was by no means devoid of equilibrist content,[43] but

[41] See Webster, *Castlereagh,* 320, concerning the Hardenberg-Castlereagh
correspondence in the summer of 1814. Hardenberg, *Denkwürdigkeiten,*
is unfortunately useless for this period, since virtually all the papers concern the years up to and including 1807; IV, 423 ff. is Hardenberg's *ex post
facto* account of Prussian aggrandizement and contains some moderately
helpful material. See also Dupuis, *Ministère de Talleyrand,* II, 311 ff. Knesebeck formulated the equilibrist position of Prussia as seeing "that the West
lose its preponderance, that the Center again obtain power, and that the
East not fall into the errors of the West" (Knesebeck memoir, Jan. 7, 1814;
quoted by Treitschke, "Preussen auf dem Wiener Congresse," *Preuss. Jahr.,*
XXXVI (Dec., 1875), 668.

[42] For an alternative suggestion of Hardenberg regarding west-German
frontiers, see his memorandum of late September, 1814, in *Well. Suppl.
Des.,* IX, 301.

[43] See, for example, his letters and excerpts from memoranda in d'Angeberg, *Congrès de Vienne,* 274, 276, 379, 406, 418, 531, 1934, 1941. Humboldt's policy at Vienna was more outspokenly equilibrist in nature than
Hardenberg's. Humboldt was very unenthusiastic over the Russian alliance
and thought that the "natural political system [of Prussia was] an alliance
among Austria, Germany, England, and Holland," i.e., the policy of the
strong middle-Europe. He expounded this thesis very clearly in three

that content was overshadowed by the aggressive and acquisitive character of Prussian aims.

As early as January, 1814, he and Metternich had come to an oral agreement that Austria would support the cession of Saxony to Prussia if Prussia would help Austria block Russian designs on Poland.[44] Then later, on October 9, Hardenberg secretly wrote Metternich, offering support against Alexander in return for an Austrian guarantee of the cession of Saxony.[45] Both Metternich and Castlereagh were at once suspicious of the proposition, thinking that it was a device to get Saxony for Prussia and at the same time offer no real help against Russia. Metternich was disposed to refuse it, but Castlereagh, intent on holding Austria and Prussia together, favored acceptance, thinking that there was still an opportunity of breaking Alexander's stubbornness on Poland. To Castlereagh this was an illustration of how the "establishment of a just equilibrium" should be the "first object" of their attention and that "minor points of interest" should be "subordinate to this great end." Metternich, on October 22, wrote Hardenberg a letter of conditional acceptance, declaring that his action was dictated by the emperor's solicitude for the "establishment of a system of peace based on a just redivision of forces among the powers." [46] Austria would approve the cession of Saxony to Prussia if Prussia and Austria could work

---

memoranda at Vienna: Oct. 23, 1814, in answer to Metternich's proposals of the previous day (Bruno Gebhardt, *Wilhelm von Humboldt als Staatsmann* [Stuttgart, 1896–99], II, 87 ff.); Oct. 25, 1814, in answer to a Castlereagh memoir (*ibid.*, II, 91 ff.); and Nov. 9, 1814, on the Polish question (*ibid.*, II, 104 ff.). See also Treitschke, *History of Germany*, II, 44–45, 51.

[44] Cathcart to Castlereagh, Jan. 16, 1814, in Webster, *Brit. Dipl.*, 132.

[45] Hardenberg to Metternich, Oct. 9, 1814, in d'Angeberg, *Congrès de Vienne*, II, 1934–1936.

[46] D'Angeberg, *Congrès de Vienne*, 316. Gentz later described this letter as having given Metternich "more grief in three months than he has had in all his life" ("The Vienna Congress, a Memoir," Feb. 12, 1815, in Metternich, *Memoirs*, II, 570).

out "an absolute conformity" of policy "in the Polish question," i.e., if Prussia would assist Austria against Russia. Thus a bloc of three was drawn together to check Russian designs on the duchy, but an important condition had been carefully specified by Metternich.

October 24, 1814, was probably the high-water mark of Castlereagh's activity against the creation of a Russian-dominated Kingdom of Poland. On that day Hardenberg, Metternich, and Castlereagh met and put the seal upon their united opposition to Alexander's plan, Castlereagh drawing up a memorandum on their position.[47] Haste was necessary because Alexander was to leave on the following day for Buda, not to return for almost a week. At Buda Alexander was presented with a threat of refusal of Great Britain, Austria, and Prussia to recognize his acquisition of Poland,[48] and he of course blew up, upbraiding both Metternich and Hardenberg before their respective monarchs. His anger carried the day with Frederick William, and the united front of the three foreign ministers was broken. It was probably a "fatal mistake" for Castlereagh to allow Metternich and Hardenberg to handle the affairs when he was not there himself.[49]

The debate between Alexander and Castlereagh through the medium of letters and memoranda continued. On November 4 Castlereagh again attacked the Russian position with the argument that the Treaty of Reichenbach must still be considered as binding.[50] Alexander's second memorandum, dated November 21, held that the linkage of Poland to Russia was justified "as a necessary weight in the balance of the European system." [51]

---

[47] Castlereagh to Liverpool, Oct. 24, 1814, in Webster, *Brit. Dipl.*, 212–215.

[48] Webster, *Castlereagh*, 349.   [49] Webster, *Congress of Vienna*, 103.

[50] Webster, *Brit. Dipl.*, 226.

[51] Alexander to Castlereagh, Nov. 21, 1814, with memorandum, in d'Angeberg, *Congrès de Vienne*, I, 450–456. The quotation may be found on page 453.

The debate was based by both sides on arguments that used balance-of-power terminology and rationale, such usage raising once again the question of whether equilibrist reasoning had any real validity or not, since both sides could use it for divergent purposes.

The opposition to Alexander's Polish designs had been especially strong in October, but, by the decisive interview at Buda in late October, Alexander virtually cut Prussia loose from her joint action with Austria and Great Britain, drawing the former back into the Russian orbit and leaving the latter two in a greatly weakened diplomatic position.[52] Although there was little point in it, Metternich wrote to Hardenberg on November 2, submitting the formal proposals as discussed and agreed upon by the three ministers on October 24.[53] Hardenberg, already considerably compromised by the action of his king, who now followed in the wake of Alexander, was on November 5 given explicit orders to abandon joint action with Britain and Austria on the Polish question.[54] He began to extricate himself from his embarrassing position by giving to Castlereagh a confidential memorandum under the date of November 7, 1814,[55] which confirmed the latter's fears regarding the withdrawal of Prussia from joint opposition against Russia. On the eleventh Castlereagh wrote to the prime minister, preparing him for defeat on the Polish dispute: "as yet, we have no substantial grounds to hope for" Alexander's yielding on Poland.[56] The following day, the twelfth, Metternich wrote Hardenberg a letter recognizing the defeat of the joint opposition against Russia and ascribing that defeat to the failure of Prussia to support the

[52] Gentz: "There was no longer any question about the affairs of Poland; they were tacitly regarded as lost" ("The Vienna Congress, a Memoir," in Metternich, *Memoirs,* II, 566).

[53] D'Angeberg, *Congrès de Vienne,* 379–381.

[54] Webster, *Castlereagh,* 349.

[55] D'Angeberg, *Congrès de Vienne,* 406–408.

[56] Castlereagh to Liverpool, Nov. 11, 1814, in Webster, *Brit. Dipl.,* 230.

others.[57] Neither Castlereagh nor Metternich now hoped for any appreciable concession from Alexander on Poland, since Hardenberg's weight had been withdrawn from their side of the scales. The first phase of the Polish-Saxon dispute was over, and Alexander had clearly won.

[57] Metternich to Hardenberg, Nov. 12, 1814, in d'Angeberg, *Congrès de Vienne,* 418.

Chapter VIII

Congress of Vienna:
The Coalition Breaks Down

WITH the failure of Castlereagh and Metternich to create an effective bloc with Hardenberg against Alexander, the congress entered its second phase, which began a week before the end of November. Hardenberg reported to Castlereagh that he hoped the deadlock "would end in an arrangement," and that Czartoryski had promised to ask Alexander "to make some concessions." [1] Castlereagh expected a "decision, one way or the other, in . . . a few days." [2] On the twenty-fifth he was able to report to London that Alexander had stepped down from the lofty level of his earlier pretentions and had indicated that he was prepared

---

[1] Castlereagh to Liverpool, Nov. 21, 1814, in Webster, *Brit. Dipl.*, 241.
[2] *Ibid.*, 241.

to negotiate on Poland.[3] Hope was reborn in Castlereagh and Metternich.

THE SECOND PHASE

Pivoting on Saxony

Alexander had also asked Hardenberg to conduct the negotiations, and the Prussian minister soon submitted to Russia a project which gave to Prussia Thorn and the line of the Warthe River in western Poland and to Austria the circle of Zamosc in southeastern Poland, Cracow in the southwest, and the line of the Nida River, north and east of Cracow.[4] Hardenberg began well enough, but the Russian counterproject, drafted by Czartoryski and Stein, was a crushing disappointment, indicating that the "intervention of Prussia in the negotiation was little more than nominal."[5] Russia offered merely to neutralize Thorn and Cracow as free cities; she adhered to her former claim to a westward extension to Kalisch and a southern boundary at the upper Vistula and stipulated as a *sine qua non* the cession of all of Saxony to Prussia.[6] It was now demonstrated that Alexander, in spite of his hints to the contrary, was still unprepared to yield on Poland. His "concessions" in this project were negligible. Metternich was greatly upset;[7] the possibility of a Russian advance across Austria's northern frontiers was now all but realized. Castlereagh, similarly discouraged, reported home that "the existing state of affairs . . . may . . . as Europe is more extensively armed than at any former period, suddenly end in war."[8]

While there had been at least a slight hope of reasonable compromise on Poland up to this time, there was now no further reason for Castlereagh and Metternich to hope for a yielding by Russia. Heretofore they had concentrated unsuccessfully on

[3] Castlereagh to Liverpool, Nov. 25, 1814, *ibid.*, 242. The implication was conveyed through Alexander's second memorandum on Poland to Castlereagh, Nov. 21, 1814, in d'Angeberg, *Congrès de Vienne*, I, 450–456.

[4] Castlereagh to Liverpool, Dec. 5, 1814, in Webster, *Brit. Dipl.*, 248.

[5] *Ibid.*, 251.   [6] *Ibid.*, 249.   [7] *Ibid.*, 250.   [8] *Ibid.*, 251–252.

blocking Russian designs on Poland. Other points (among them Saxony) were subordinated to that aim, and the controversy of October–November had pivoted on Poland.

This underscoring of the Polish half of the compound was inevitable. Given the Austrian axiom—according to which Metternich could afford to see either Poland go to Russia or Saxony go to Prussia, but not both—they had had to resist half of the Russian formula. Given Castlereagh's plan for the strong center —according to which they had to knit Austria and Prussia together—they had had to resist a particular half of the Russian formula, namely the Russian extension into the Duchy of Warsaw. Castlereagh and Metternich were therefore logical, according to their assumptions, in throwing their weight first against the cession of Poland to Russia, instead of concentrating their energies in the autumn against the cession of Saxony, as Talleyrand had done. The inevitability of their conclusions was reenforced by the fact that Hardenberg was willing to climb down from his perch on the fence and support Great Britain and Austria in planning for central Europe. Their weight proved insufficient, and they took a thumping defeat. Recognizing the fact that Alexander would get all or most of Poland, they had to direct their weight elsewhere. That elsewhere was also predetermined, because there was only one remaining half to the Russian formula: Metternich, forced to yield on Poland, could not yield on Saxony. To his mind such a conclusion was as easily demonstrable as the second proposition of Euclid. When put into action, it meant that he and Castlereagh had no alternative but to refuse the cession of Saxony to Prussia, even though they had earlier promised it conditionally to Hardenberg. Saxony became the focus of all attention as the negotiations now pivoted on that captive kingdom.[9]

Looked at from the Saxon point of view, this decision was

[9] For evidence on the switch to the Saxon problem, see Castlereagh to Liverpool, Dec. 5, 1814, *ibid.*, 249, 251; see also a letter of Dec. 7, 1814, *ibid.*, 255.

little short of bewildering—and exhilarating. Two of the powers which had been busily selling Saxony down the river in October and November by offering her territories to Prussia now reversed themselves and became adamant and militant champions of continued Saxon independence. There is perhaps no important shift of policy at Vienna which so well illustrates the equilibrist approach of these two statesmen. Neither man was enamored of the Saxons. Neither cared a groat for Saxon independence as such, whether on the grounds of sentiment, legitimacy, or nationalism. Saxony was, in their plans, strictly subordinate to the demands of the European balance of power, specifically of the Austrian axiom and Castlereagh's concepts of over-all balance strategy. Their change was misunderstood for a long time and variously attributed by writers to parliamentary opposition to Castlereagh's policies, to Castlereagh's being muddled, and so on. Only in the present century has Professor Webster made clear the logic of the change according to the Austrian and British points of view.

During an interview with Hardenberg, Castlereagh frankly admitting the failure of the joint opposition to Russia, pointed out that the chief question now was how much of Saxony should go to Prussia, and persuaded Hardenberg to receive a counter-project from Metternich.[10] Reasonable consideration of Prussian claims to Saxony was not, however, easy to achieve at this critical time, and on December 10 a diplomatic explosion resulted from Metternich's formal letter to Hardenberg, in which he refused to yield all of Saxony to Prussia: [11] "All the Prussians and all their partisans cried murder." [12] Hardenberg, thinking to discredit Metternich, sent parts of his correspondence with the latter to the tsar, implying that Metternich refused to give up Saxony because Prussia would not enter a hostile group

[10] Castlereagh to Liverpool, Dec. 7, 1814, *ibid.,* 256.

[11] Metternich to Hardenberg, Dec. 10, 1814, in d'Angeberg, *Congrès de Vienne,* 505–510.

[12] Gentz, "The Vienna Congress, a Memoir," Feb. 12, 1815, in Metternich, *Memoirs,* II, 572.

against Russia. Alexander blew up again and confronted Metternich and Francis I with the evidence. Metternich adroitly put before the tsar his own correspondence with Hardenberg, cleared himself of the worst charges, and put Hardenberg in the somewhat embarrassing position of having to withhold the remainder of his own letters, which were much more incriminating than those of Metternich. This crisis lasted several days and may have cleared the air, because Alexander soon appeared mollified and offered the circle of Tarnopol to Austria as an initial concession toward a solution.[13] The explosion ended the second phase of the Polish-Saxon dispute, which comprised the fortnight of Hardenberg's intervention between Russia on the one hand and Great Britain and Austria on the other. The deadlock continued.

The Possibility of War

One of the by-products of the stoppage over the disposal of Poland and Saxony was the possibility of the dispute eventuating in war among the late allies. Not only had the coalition melted away in the difficulties over the Polish-Saxon disposition, but war talk had become widespread at the congress from early October on. On October 9 Castlereagh reported the "extravagant tone of war" of Austria and the "war language" of Metternich.[14] Wellington, early in November, reported that Blacas, chief minister to Louis XVIII, took a very serious view of Alexander's stubbornness on Poland and contemplated the withdrawal of French plenipotentiaries from Vienna, expecting that "Europe would remain in a feverish state, which sooner or later must end in war." [15]

Liverpool and the British cabinet were disturbed at the prominence which Castlereagh had assumed at Vienna in the Polish question, at his failure to carry his point, and at the

[13] Castlereagh to Liverpool, Dec. 17, 1814, in Webster, *Brit. Dipl.*, 257–259. Tarnopol was in eastern Galicia, off the northeast frontier of the Hapsburg empire.

[14] Castlereagh to Liverpool, Oct. 9, 1814, *ibid.*, 201, 202.

[15] Wellington to Castlereagh, Nov. 5, 1814, *ibid.*, 227.

danger of fresh warfare. On November 25 the prime minister wrote Castlereagh that the worst peace was preferable to the best war at that time.[16] Bathurst, secretary of state for war, followed it with a letter of of his own, declaring the "impossibility of H.R.H. consenting to involve this country in hostilities at this time for any of the objects . . . under discussion at Vienna." [17] Nevertheless, on December 5 Castlereagh wrote Liverpool to prepare the cabinet for possible outbreak of war and the necessary or possible decisions which Great Britain would have to make. The foreign minister himself leaned toward the idea of having Britain and France act as armed mediators and allowing Bavaria and Austria, with their 600,000 troops, to bear the first shock of the attack,[18] a policy reminiscent of Metternich's aim in 1813 that Prussia should shoulder the weight of Napoleonic blows while Austria got ready.

On December 11 the Grand Duke Constantine, younger brother of Alexander and one of the less attractive specimens of the current edition of Romanovs, then in Warsaw to organize a new Polish army, published a proclamation which called on the Poles to gather their strength for a defense of their new independence. Austrian troops were understood to be moving toward the Galician frontier, and France initiated partial mobilization.[19] War remained a possibility until toward the end of the second week of January, 1815, and the crisis appears to have been quite genuine while it lasted, terrible as renewed conflict would have been for Europe and its peoples.

[16] Liverpool to Castlereagh, Nov. 25, 1814, *ibid.*, 245.

[17] Bathurst to Castlereagh, Nov. 27, 1814, *ibid.*, 248.

[18] Castlereagh to Liverpool, Dec. 5, 1814, *ibid.*, 251–254. For further evidence on the war crisis, see *ibid.*, 213, 233, 240, 247, 248, 265, 277, 278, 282, and August Fournier, *Die Geheimpolizei auf dem Wiener Kongress* (Vienna and Leipzig, 1913), 277, 280, 295, 304, 308, 309, 321, 325.

[19] In Gentz's phrase, "troops were concentrated everywhere" ("The Vienna Congress, a Memoir," in Metternich, *Memoirs*, II, 572). See also Treitschke, *History of Germany*, II, 65–66.

THE THIRD PHASE

Castlereagh and Talleyrand

The third phase began with the aftermath of the explosion, when, in the middle of December, both Metternich and Hardenberg sought Castlereagh's intervention in the Saxon question.[20] It was an unpromising offer, since the deadlock seemed so solid and unyielding, but Castlereagh finally accepted the role of arbiter on the assurance that he would be able to make some headway. Within a week Hardenberg sought to maneuver him into acceptance of Prussian claims to all of Saxony. He brought Castlereagh together with Humboldt, Stein, and himself, and the three Germans worked on the Englishman for two hours, marshaling all the arguments which might have moved him. Castlereagh reported that he did not yield and that his opposition apparently produced "more moderate councils on the part of Prussia."[21] He was treading dangerous ground, because he was doing precisely what his cabinet was uneasy about—resuming the role of a principal, against which Liverpool and the others had explicitly warned him.

Prussian claims to Saxony were given a certain cogency by the Prussian fear of traditional French policy toward Germany. France for centuries had been able to play one German prince off against another, and Prussian statesmen were eager to put an end to that diplomatic game. Stein wanted to see Prussia "abide firmly by the principles of the . . . European balance"; he held that she "has saved herself by returning to that principle, as she ruined herself by deserting it, and she has been favoured in her restoration only with the object of supplying her with sufficient power to maintain the European system."[22] To him the cession of

---

[20] Castlereagh to Liverpool, Dec. 18, 1814, in Webster, *Brit. Dipl.*, 260.

[21] Castlereagh to Liverpool, Dec. 24, 1814, *ibid.*, 269–270.

[22] Stein to Hardenberg, Oct. 26, 1814, in J. R. Seeley, *Life and Times of Stein, or Germany and Prussia in the Napoleonic Age* (Cambridge, 1878), III, 260.

Saxony to Prussia could be justified on balance-of-power grounds and was, indeed, essential to a real equilibrium: "If Saxony should be restored to her integrity . . . a Power would be created in the North of Germany which would be hostile to Prussia, would weaken her and furnish a means of influence to France." [23]

The deadlock between Austria-Great Britain on the one hand and Russia-Prussia on the other had resulted both in the breakup of the coalition, so auspiciously successful in the preceding spring, and in the need for a new power alignment. The latter was answered by a return to the more primitive level of alliance balance. Whereas in March, April, and May of 1814 the coalition had been able to act co-operatively and successfully to initiate the work of re-establishing a "real and durable equilibrium" and had thereby briefly approached the ideal of balance-of-power practice, i.e., an effective coalition equilibrium, the Big Four were now deeply fissured with disagreement and hostility and effectually split into two camps.

The situation offered an unusual opportunity for Talleyrand to hold the balance between the two blocs and use his advantage either for purposes of outright self-interest or for the benefit of the general equilibrium of Europe; "he might now have made a great bargain." [24] There is no evidence, however, to indicate that he felt he had a choice in the matter. He was not sufficiently removed from the implications of the decision to enable him to make a free or bargaining decision. He was, in effect, already committed to the Anglo-Austrian position, because it coincided with French interest. Castlereagh and Metternich now opposed the cession of Saxony to Prussia, just as Talleyrand had done for many weeks, and it was inevitable that he should support them rather than the other side.

The rationale of his approach is clearer to us than that of any

[23] Memorandum of Dec. 3, 1814, in Seeley, *Life and Times of Stein*, III, 291.

[24] Webster, *Congress of Vienna*, 110.

of the other statesmen; it was more detailed than any but Castle-reagh's, and even there it had the advantage of being a more articulate, philosophical approach, in addition to being similarly specific.[25] During the preceding summer, when preparations for the peace settlement were afoot, he was charged by Louis XVIII with the task of drawing up the king's instructions for the French representative at the congress. This extraordinary document,[26] conceived by Talleyrand and drafted by la Besnardière, outlined a proposed French and European strategy of peace. It revealed not only the philosophy of Talleyrand's plan but many of the details as well; furthermore, it frankly discussed the balance of power, indicating quite clearly the degree of importance which Talleyrand attached to it.

The congress, he postulated,[27] must be legitimate; that is, it must embrace representatives of all legitimate sovereigns who participated in the war, large and small alike. While the smallest

[25] Talleyrand's papers contain a great deal of material to illustrate his outlook on the balance of power. For example, he repeatedly urged upon Napoleon a policy of moderation toward Austria; see Talleyrand to Bonaparte, Sept. 8, 23, 1797 (G. Pallain [ed.], *Le ministère de Talleyrand sous le Directoire* [Paris, 1891], 139–140, 153–155), and Talleyrand to Bonaparte, Oct. 17, Dec. 5, 1805 (Pierre Bertrand [ed.], *Lettres inédites de Talleyrand à Napoléon, 1800–09*, 156–174, 209–212). Talleyrand wanted to be sure that Austrian power, one of the principal makeweights in the European equilibrium, was not destroyed. Contrary to Napoleon, Talleyrand envisaged the necessity of a *limited* French power, and he urged upon Napoleon the use of moderation and reciprocal compensation in dealing with Austria. Later, in 1808 at Erfurt, Talleyrand helped to sabotage Napoleon's attempt to break Austrian power, by keeping Tsar Alexander informed as to Napoleon's plans (Talleyrand, *Mémoires*, I, 320–321, 393–457). When the Napoleonic overbalance nearly destroyed the European state system Talleyrand would no longer work for Napoleon and did not return to the Foreign Office until the Restoration was in progress.

[26] For the text of the instructions, see Talleyrand, *Mémoires*, II, 214–254, and d'Angeberg, *Congrès de Vienne*, I, 215–238. For a careful discussion of the instructions, see Dupuis, *Ministère de Talleyrand*, II, 333 ff.

[27] The following summary of the contents of the instructions does not observe the order in which they appear in the original. An attempt has been made to categorize the more important points and cut out the less significant passages.

powers should not enter into the great matters which would affect the pattern of Europe as a whole, they had to be allowed to share in those matters which immediately affected them, because their consent must be obtained in order to make the decisions and solutions legitimate and lasting. Here Talleyrand discussed "legitimacy" at length, pointing out that conquest alone did not authorize a change of sovereignty, which must be hallowed by time. He declared that equilibrium "ought to be the principal and final aim of . . . [the congress'] operations" and showed the linkage, as he saw it, between equilibrium and legitimacy. Equilibrium must be the general policy for Europe as a whole, the master plan, the over-all conception; legitimacy, on the other hand, must be used as a device to render stable the units within the equilibrium:

It is not a momentary equilibrium which ought to be established, but a durable equilibrium. It can endure only as long as the proportions on which it is founded endure, and these proportions themselves can endure only so long as the right of possession shall be transmitted in such a way that they are not changed. The order of succession in each state ought to enter as a necessary element in the calculation of the equilibrium, not so as to be changed, if it is certain, but in such a manner as to be rendered certain, if it is uncertain.[28]

Absolute equality of states was unthinkable and might even be dangerous to the equilibrium. France must appear moderate throughout the congress in order to insure the moderation of the allies and the friendship of England, with whom she must attempt to identify herself in certain respects.

The instructions also included such specific aims as a guarantee of the Ottoman Porte for the sake of the general equilibrium; perpetual neutrality of Switzerland; opposition to Prussian gains in Saxony, Mainz, and western Germany (Prussia, he argued, was the greatest threat to the equilibrium in Germany and must be prevented from returning to her pre-Tilsit power); other German states to be strengthened to prevent Prussian expansion;

[28] Talleyrand, *Mémoires*, II, 226–227 (translation mine).

the German confederation to be made strong enough to check
Prussia, but no stronger than this aim would require; opposition
to Austrian possession of parts of Italy; Poland to be independent, but, if this aim proved impossible (as it probably would),
Poland to be restored to the status of the last partition, in order
to prevent Russia from getting all of it; co-operation with England on the abolition of the slave trade to keep her friendship,
but should Spain not be brought into line with British policy,
securing the benefits which were available to Spain.

There is no reasonable doubt about the equilibrist nature of
Talleyrand's thinking on foreign policy.[29] This whole important
document epitomizing his outlook radiates balance-of-power
theory and practice and indicates how balance of power was to
serve as the guiding reason for every one of the major aims of
French policy at the Congress of Vienna. Moreover, it clears up
any doubt about Talleyrand's conception of the relative importance of the principle of legitimacy and the doctrine of the
balance of power.[30] The thesis that the congress was dominated
by Talleyrand's sudden espousal (at a meeting on September 30,
1814) of "that sacred *principle of legitimacy* from which all order and stability spring" [31] is untenable in the light of this docu-

[29] For further commentary on Talleyrand and the balance of power, see
Brinton, *Lives of Talleyrand*, 101, 140, 171, *et passim*. Brinton found that
Talleyrand was thoroughly committed to the balance of power: "Stability
among the European states Talleyrand considered to depend on the working of the old-fashioned balance of power" (*ibid.*, 101). Gentz, outstanding
theorist on the balance of power in this period, declared that Talleyrand's
instructions were "devised entirely on the establishment of a durable peace
and a just equilibrium of power" (Anton von Prokesch-Osten [ed.],
Dépêches inédites du chevalier de Gentz aux hospodars de Valachie, I, 99;
quoted by Donnadieu, *Essai sur la théorie de l'équilibre*, 124–125).

[30] For brief analysis or discussion of Talleyrand and legitimacy, see
Ferrero, *Reconstruction of Europe*, 53; Brinton, *Lives of Talleyrand*, 184;
and Alison Phillips, *Confederation of Europe*, 89.

[31] Brinton, *Lives of Talleyrand*, 169–170. See Webster's comment on the
instructions where he writes: "This brilliant and deservedly famous document based the settlement of Europe on the principle of legitimacy" (*Congress of Vienna*, 51). This remark is misleading, because Talleyrand's first
principle in the reconstruction of Europe was the balance of power. He
conceived of legitimacy as a means to that end, as shown. Donnadieu is one

ment, which discussed both legitimacy and the balance of power in turn and then set them in the perspective which his mind assigned to them. His own testimony indicated a primary concern with balance of power and only a supplementary interest in legitimacy. He showed the interconnection of the two, how one supported the other, how one was an external condition of a state and the other internal, how the lesser principle was an instrument for realizing the greater conception.

His whole role at Vienna is most interesting to follow, because it shows extraordinary virtuosity as well as great insights into the needs of Europe and the diplomacy of its major statesmen. In September the statesmen of the coalition had agreed to limit control of the congress to the Big Four, as noted above.[32] In application this formula meant the exclusion from high councils of France, Saxony, Bavaria, Denmark, Sweden, Hanover, Holland, Spain, Portugal, and the Pope, among many others. It was deeply resented by the small powers, who, in their desire to combat it, managed to achieve a degree of organization and co-operation which would otherwise have been unlikely. Their common opposition pulled them together. Talleyrand, excluded from the central cluster of policy makers, assumed temporary leadership of this protest, adroitly enhancing it to the embarrassment of the allies.

His role as the Socratic gadfly of the congress in the fall was very irritating to the major statesmen during the Polish crisis in October and November. He was especially concerned over blocking substantial Prussian gains in Saxony and less concerned with Russian gains in Poland. Excluded from the secret inner workings of the Big Four, he attempted to check the Saxon cession by strengthening the hand of Saxony and fanning anti-allied sentiment in that kingdom.

---

of the rare writers on the balance of power who has pointed out the relationship between legitimacy and the balance of power as Talleyrand conceived it (*Essai sur la théorie de l'équilibre*, 125).

[32] See above, pp. 188–189.

Castlereagh was deeply critical of Talleyrand's policy. He felt that Talleyrand's actions excited "distrust and alarm" among all the statesmen of the great powers, tended to draw them together in opposition to Talleyrand, and resulted in depriving the latter of "his just and natural influence for the purposes of moderating excessive pretensions, whilst it united all to preserve the general system." [33] Castlereagh held that French policy had put the cart before the horse, that it ought to have opposed Russia first on Poland, and then, if successful, to have worked for a compromise on Saxony. Talleyrand should have acted "upon the broad principles of European equilibrium, instead of fighting smaller points of local influence." [34] Castlereagh wrote Wellington:

The difference in principle between M. Talleyrand and me is chiefly that I wish to direct my main efforts to secure an equilibrium in Europe; to which objects, as far as principle will permit, I wish to make all local points subordinate. M. Talleyrand appears to me, on the contrary, more intent upon particular points of influence than upon the general balance to be established; and his efforts upon the Neapolitan and Saxon questions are frequently made at the expense of the more important question of Poland, without essentially serving either of those interests upon which he is most intent.[35]

Castlereagh attempted to bring pressure upon Talleyrand in order to secure the full weight of his support against Alexander's designs. He wrote to Wellington, who in turn communicated with Blacas, who disliked Talleyrand and readily agreed to help.[36] The king soon sent out orders to Vienna for his minister to co-operate with Castlereagh on Poland, and Castlereagh felt that Talleyrand became much more accommodating as a result,

[33] Castlereagh to Liverpool, Oct. 9, 1814, in Webster, *Brit. Dipl.,* 204–205.
[34] Castlereagh to Liverpool, Oct. 24, 1814, *ibid.,* 213.
[35] Castlereagh to Wellington, Oct. 25, 1814, *ibid.,* 217–218.
[36] *Ibid.,* 217; Wellington to Castlereagh, Nov. 5, 1814, *ibid.,* 227; Wellington to Castlereagh, Nov. 7, 1814, *ibid.,* 228–229; Castlereagh to Wellington, Nov. 21, 1814, *ibid.,* 241.

although it was really too late to make any decisive difference in the outcome.

Talleyrand's action on Saxony during the two-month period from the beginning of the congress offers a good illustration of the polarization of state interest and balance of power, of the tension that exists between them, of the attraction that each pole may exert, and of their effect upon the actions of a statesman. The Saxon-Polish cessions were linked, but the Polish cession was the principal half because Alexander was adamant, whereas Frederick William was willing to see his country compensated in either east or west. Alexander was the key to the situation: if his position were not modified, there would be little or no opportunity of modifying the Prussian stand on Saxony. If Alexander could be forced to yield ground, however, Prussian policy could surely be molded to fit those new circumstances. Castlereagh and Metternich appear to have been correct, therefore, in their initial opposition to Alexander, in their subordination of "minor points of interest" to the over-all picture, whereas Talleyrand, more immediately desirous of preventing an extension of Prussian power which would be of disadvantage to France in her future relations with Germany, permitted himself the mistake of temporarily waging a small diplomatic war for French national interest instead of taking the larger view. Saxony was closer to French interests; Poland, more remote.[37]

[37] There is no question about Talleyrand's tactical adroitness in negotiation. Metternich expressed the universally accepted conclusion when he wrote: "Men like M. de Talleyrand are like sharp-edged instruments, with which it is dangerous to play" (*Memoirs,* II, 285). On the other hand, there is good reason to question his strategy at Vienna, as pointed out in the text above. Estimates of his role at Vienna have varied widely from the disparagement of Gentz, who spoke of "the nullity of the French plenipotentiaries in all the negotiations" ("The Vienna Congress, a Memoir," Feb. 12, 1815, *ibid.,* II, 560) to the lavish praise of Ward and Ferrero. Ward described Talleyrand's role as "brilliant" (*Camb. Mod. Hist.,* IX, 584); Ferrero held that "Talleyrand seems to have the right of precedence over all the statesmen who have appeared in the Western world since the Revolution" (*Reconstruction of Europe,* 344–345).

It has often been said in favor of Talleyrand that he correctly foresaw the defeat of Castlereagh and Metternich on Poland. This prevision is taken as evidence of the correctness of his attitude. It is possible, however, that Talleyrand might have prevented the failure of the concept of the strong center by an earlier support of Castlereagh and Metternich. Had he joined them before October 24, the three-power bloc against Russia would have been a four-power group, an increase which might have kept Prussia in line instead of defecting to Alexander. The question is complex, and conclusions must remain speculative; we may, however, be sure that both Metternich and Castlereagh believed that support by Talleyrand would have forced Alexander to back down on the duchy.[38]

Whether one regards Talleyrand as correct or mistaken in his Saxon policy during October, his stock had risen a good deal by December. On December 5 Castlereagh, fully aware of this enhanced importance of France in the current deadlock, wrote to Liverpool, preparing him for the possibility of war among the allies [39] and suggesting that Britain might best act with France in joint intervention or armed mediation. The precept of mobility of action, well illustrated by the Saxon pivot, is even more dramatically pointed up for balance-of-power purposes when England and France, mortal enemies for more than a century, began this quick equilibrist approach to each other.

On December 12 Talleyrand made a written overture to Metternich and followed it with another letter on December 19, indicating the same desire for *rapprochement*. In arguing against the cession of all of Saxony, he reiterated his stand on balance of power and legitimacy and the integral relation between the two, declaring:

When the treaty of May 30 proposed that the ultimate result of the . . . Congress should be a real and durable equilibrium, it did not

[38] See Metternich to Hardenberg, Nov. 12, 1814, in d'Angeberg, *Congrès de Vienne,* I, 418; Webster, *Brit. Dipl.,* 239.

[39] See above, p. 224.

mean to sacrifice to the establishment of that equilibrium the rights which it should guarantee. . . . it wished that every legitimate dynasty should be either preserved or re-established, . . . and that the vacant territories . . . should be distributed conformably to the principles of political equilibrium.[40]

In the second letter he argued very closely the equilibrist rationale of his position:

The disposition which they wished to make of . . . Saxony, pernicious as an example, will be still more so by its influence on the general equilibrium of Europe, an equilibrium which consists in a reciprocal agreement between the forces of aggression and resistance in the different political bodies; and these it will injure in two ways, both very serious.

1st. By creating a very strong aggressive force against Bohemia, and thus threatening the safety of the whole of Austria. For the special force of resistance of Bohemia must be proportionately increased, and this can only be at the expense of the general force of resistance of the Austrian Monarchy.

2nd. By creating in the midst of the Germanic body . . . an aggressive force out of proportion to the others, putting the latter in danger, and forcing them to seek support from without and thus render void the strength of resistance which, in the system of a general equilibrium in Europe, the whole body must offer, and which it can only have by the intimate union of its members.[41]

Metternich replied to Talleyrand on December 16, making the first regular overture of Austria to France and enclosing his earlier note to Hardenberg in which he refused to yield all Saxony to Prussia.[42] This was the beginning of the formation of the Triple Alliance of January 3, 1815. In interviews with

[40] Talleyrand to Metternich, Dec. 12, 1814, in Metternich, *Memoirs*, II, 594–595.

[41] Talleyrand to Metternich, Dec. 19, 1814, *ibid.*, 597–598.

[42] Metternich to Talleyrand, Dec. 16, 1814, in d'Angeberg, *Congrès de Vienne*, 540.

Castlereagh, Talleyrand was "urgent in his language" to get an engagement among Austria, France, and Great Britain.[43]

At the same time, Liverpool, unaware of the degree of involvement of his foreign minister, was writing to Castlereagh of the *rapprochement* with France as "most desirable at the present moment" as a move to prevent France from lining up with any other powers, to exert a measure of control over French policy, and to prepare the ground for possible joint action.[44] He also urged him to treat the idea of armed mediation with caution.

Talleyrand and Metternich drew closer to agreement on the nature of their joint plans, but Castlereagh was still uncommitted to them, although very near the point of a definite decision. As principal promoter of the conception of a coalition equilibrium, Castlereagh was naturally reluctant to see his structure come tumbling about his head without first exploring every possible remedy to its ills before stepping down to the more primitive level of the alliance balance. The mid-December decision of Alexander to yield Tarnopol to Austria, although meager in the extreme, at least encouraged the British minister to attempt one more device which might bring agreement.

One of the persistent sources of difficulty during the fall of 1814 had been the disagreement of the allies on population figures and other statistical facts.[45] Accordingly, Castlereagh urged the creation of a statistical committee to draw up accurate information on the territories involved. The allies approved the proposal and selected delegates to the committee at once, enabling them to begin work on December 24. The committee held six sessions between then and January 19, and, although fertile

[43] Castlereagh to Liverpool, Dec. 25, 1814, in Webster, *Brit. Dipl.*, 273.

[44] Liverpool to Castlereagh, Dec. 23, 1814, *ibid.*, 265–267.

[45] See for example the disparity in Austrian, French, and Prussian statistics concerning Prussian losses and proposed compensations (d'Angeberg, *Congrès de Vienne*, 509–510 [Austrian], 582–585 [French], and 602–604 [Prussian]). See also conflicting British and Russian statistics in Webster, *Brit. Dipl.*, 227, 244.

in disagreement, was very helpful to the work of settlement.[46] It is significant in this context because it illuminates the equilibrist conceptions of the statesmen and because it served as the threshold for Talleyrand's entry into the central group of statesmen and the expansion of the Big Four into the Big Five.

The committee, with the aid of Hoffmann, the distinguished Prussian statistician, grappled with the problem of how many "souls" had been taken from Napoleon and might therefore be considered to be at the disposal of the congress. The work of the committee was typical of the contemporary conception of the balance of power, which was necessarily based on the assumption of measurable, or "estimable," power. In this instance the committee simplified "power" to one of its basic ingredients— population. Talleyrand had earlier protested against this narrow basis, writing that it would be "a very great error to consider, as the sole elements of equilibrium, those qualities which political arithmeticians enumerate." [47] Once again he protested to Castlereagh on December 23, when he urged that qualitative differences in areas be taken into account. The suggestion was not taken, so far as the committee work went, but it was a sound, if complicating, argument and was never wholly unheeded by the statesmen.[48]

[46] The work of this important committee is treated briefly in Dupuis, *Le principe d'équilibre,* 60 ff.; Webster, *Congress of Vienna,* 90–91; and Webster, *Castlereagh,* 368–369. The minutes and documents relating to the work of the committee may be found in d'Angeberg, *Congrès de Vienne,* I, 561–568, 573–579, 594–597, 638–660; and Klüber, *Akten des Wiener Kongresses,* V, 9 ff., 17 ff., 23 ff., 54 ff., 82 ff., 88 ff., 94 ff., 96 ff. The final report of the committee, Jan. 19, 1815, may be found in d'Angeberg, *Congrès de Vienne,* I, 644–660. The committee reported that almost 32 millions of Europe's population were at the disposal of the congress, i.e., that number had been taken from Napoleon and lay outside the new boundaries of France (*ibid.,* I, 647).

[47] Talleyrand to Metternich, Dec. 12, 1814, in Metternich, *Memoirs,* II, 595.

[48] Metternich also urged that the committee's work on population should not be confined to a simple report of quantity, but that it should report quality (d'Angeberg, *Congrès de Vienne,* I, 562).

A more important development was Talleyrand's bold inclusion of himself in the membership of the statistical committee. When the committee held its first meeting on December 24, he appeared uninvited and pretended that there could be no question of his right to membership. The tempest which this stirred behind the scenes resulted in Lord Stewart's being sent by the allies to inform the French minister that he was not to participate in the committee's work. Talleyrand's immediate threat to withdraw from the congress was enough to guarantee his place, and his membership became an accepted fact. Having crossed the threshold, it remained for him to complete his entry into the secret councils of the big powers by being included at the ministerial level, his next objective.

The Treaty of January 3, 1815

With the Polish-Saxon crisis still unresolved after Christmas, Castlereagh finally wrote to Talleyrand on December 27, welcoming his support in an arrangement "both with respect to Saxony and Naples, as may tend to establish a just equilibrium among the Powers of Europe and procure a general and solid peace." [49] This vague statement was significant in implication: England was ready to join some agreement with France. Earlier, on the day before Christmas, Alexander had requested that the Big Four confer formally on the Polish question, something which had yet to be done for the first time, since the angry autumn had been confined, in a technical sense, to informal consideration of the problem only.

When the ministers of the four had convened on December 29 to consider the problem, Metternich and Castlereagh took up the cudgels for Talleyrand and insisted that France be included in the discussions.[50] Such action would have meant the realization of Talleyrand's greatest aim at the congress. The demand produced an immediate and agitated protest from both Hardenberg and Nesselrode, who recognized that this eventu-

[49] Webster, *Castlereagh*, 369–370.
[50] Castlereagh to Liverpool, Jan. 1, 1815, in Webster, *Brit. Dipl.*, 276.

ally would create a majority of three against their two and force them to compromise on Saxony.[51] Forty-eight hours later the question was still unresolved, Talleyrand was still excluded from the ministerial conferences, and feeling was bitter to the point of anger and hostility. Hardenberg, usually the most discreet of diplomatists and capable of exploiting his deafness by not hearing proposals which he disliked, this time had not only heard the motion concerning Talleyrand but had declared that a refusal to recognize the cession of Saxony to Prussia would be tantamount to war. Castlereagh, capable himself of assuming the formal stiffness of an icicle, objected to Hardenberg's statement and stated with cold British fury that the congress had better be adjourned.[52] The meeting once again broke up in deadlock and anger. The congress, with nothing yet done on the peace treaty, tottered toward dissolution and war.

The next day, New Year's 1815, Castlereagh submitted his draft alliance to both Metternich and Talleyrand and secured agreement to its terms.[53] He felt that although Prussia might accept a liberal settlement and compromise on Saxony, the "utmost vigilance" must be observed regarding her.[54] Prussia was reported to be organizing her army for the field and fortifying Dresden, and he feared a sudden move by both Prussia and Russia against Austria.

The situation continued precarious, while Castlereagh, Metternich, and Talleyrand gave their attention to their new *rapprochement*. Their work was soon done, and on the third of January, 1815, they signed the Triple Alliance of Great Britain,

[51] The official records of the meetings of Dec. 29, 30, 1814, and Jan. 3, 1815, do not reveal the controversial and explosive nature of these meetings but briefly and soberly record the positions of Prussia, Russia, and Austria on Poland and Saxony (d'Angeberg, *Congrès de Vienne*, II, 1858–1877). For information on the real nature of the meetings, see Webster, *Brit. Dipl.*, 276 ff., and Botzenhart (ed.), *Freiherr vom Stein*, V, 202 ff.

[52] Webster, *Brit. Dipl.*, 277–278.   [53] *Ibid.*, 279.

[54] *Ibid.*, 277.

Austria, and France.[55] It specified mutual support if any one of the three were attacked; 150,000 troops from France and Austria, and the equivalent in subsidies or mercenaries from Great Britain; Bavaria, Hanover, and the Netherlands to be asked to join; and a military commission to draw up a plan of operations. Also, on January 3 the Russian and Prussian ministers tried once again to secure the approval of Metternich and Castlereagh for their plans for Saxony.[56] They were anxious to come to a decision on the matter before France could be brought into the inner council. Their attempt was blocked. At the end of the session, Hardenberg told Castlereagh that on the morrow he would recommend the immediate introduction of the French plenipotentiary.[57] This meant, in effect, that the crisis had been passed without resort to hostilities.

These moves occurred on January 3, 1815. Although Talleyrand had not yet made a formal appearance at the ministerial councils of the big powers, he was now sure of doing so very soon. He was ecstatic over this consummation of his policy to divide the allies and insert France among them on equal terms. "All my efforts," he wrote, "were directed to the prevention of so great a misfortune" [58] as the continued isolation of France. He had been very persistent in voicing and following this aim. It was asserted in his instructions, was repeatedly implied or mentioned in his letters to Louis XVIII, and was made evident throughout his actions at Vienna in the autumn.

Now, in a triumphant letter to the king, he announced with confidence and delight that the coalition had been dissolved and an alliance formed among France, Great Britain, and Austria. It

[55] For the text see d'Angeberg, *Congrès de Vienne*, I, 589–592, and *British and Foreign State Papers*, II, 1001–1005.

[56] Castlereagh to Liverpool, Jan. 3, 1815, in Webster, *Brit. Dipl.*, 280–281.

[57] *Ibid.*, 281.

[58] Talleyrand to Louis XVIII, Jan. 4, 1815, in G. Pallain (ed.), *The Correspondence of Prince Talleyrand and King Louis XVIII during the Congress of Vienna* (New York, 1881), 242.

was a great moment for him, and his account to the king made the most of it (indeed, too much, as events were to prove):

The spirit of the coalition and the coalition itself had survived the Peace of Paris. . . . If the plans which, on arriving here, I found had been formed, had been carried into execution, France might have stood alone in Europe without being in good relations with any one single Power for half a century to come. . . .

Now, Sire, the coalition is dissolved, and for ever. Not only does France no longer stand alone in Europe, but your Majesty already has a federate system such as it seemed that fifty years of negotiation could not have procured for her. France is in concert with two of the greatest Powers, and three States of the second order, and will soon be in concert with all the States which are guided by other than revolutionary principles and maxims.[59]

Castlereagh was himself pleased with Talleyrand's conduct. He had quite reasonably feared that Talleyrand would bargain for a rectification of the French frontier, but Talleyrand was too adroit for that, too aware of the genuine merit of the First Peace of Paris, and too much delighted over his own diplomatic success to bother with what he regarded as lesser details. One of the key clauses in the recent Triple Alliance was an affirmation of the French frontiers as defined in the First Peace of Paris, and Talleyrand endeared himself to Castlereagh by expressing "great satisfaction" with those frontiers.[60] An important equilibrist hurdle was thus taken without a break in stride.

On the following day, Hardenberg, still desirous of an agreement on Saxony before France should formally enter the new Big Five, proposed to Castlereagh in a long interview that the king of Saxony be given a kingdom in the west.[61] The suggestion

[59] *Ibid.*

[60] Castlereagh to Liverpool, Jan. 1, 1815, in Webster, *Brit. Dipl.*, 279.

[61] This proposal had been in the air for several weeks. It had been seriously considered by Prussian and Russian statesmen since Dec. 13, 1814; it had been formally promoted by letter (Hardenberg to Alexander, Dec. 16, 1814, in d'Angeberg, *Congrès de Vienne*, I, 531–535), and it had been included in the Russian project which was submitted to the second

comes as a shock to the nationalist reader of a later day. To a prenationalist and balance-of-power statesman like Castlereagh, the proposal was something to be argued down, but it was not one to shock him. The reason lies in the essential difference in

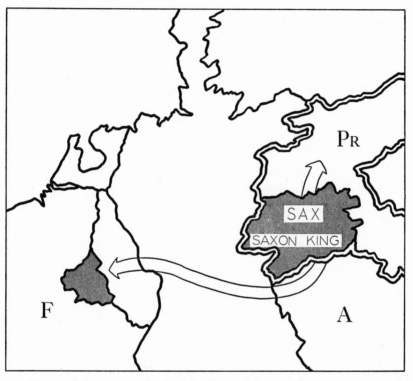

Proposed "transportation" of the king of Saxony (January, 1815).

point of view which a century of nationalism has built between Castlereagh and ourselves. Where we may think of Alsace-Lorraine, the statesman of 1815 was still unused to passionate, mass support of the "nation." Moreover, there were even some points to recommend the transportation of the Saxon king.

---

formal meeting of the Big Four on Dec. 30, 1814 (*ibid.*, 1873). The details relative to the creation of a new state of 700,000 souls out of Luxembourg, Trèves, and other Rhineland areas may also be found in *British and Foreign State Papers*, II, 592.

Saxony had been a migrant entity among German states for centuries, slowly making its way toward central Germany, where it rested at the time of the Congress of Vienna, and one other move would not have been unthinkable. The suggested move would also have unlocked Prussian intransigence at the congress.

Nevertheless, Castlereagh was not to be taken in. He objected on the grounds that this new kingdom would be both weak and adjacent to France; it would come under French domination, and, in effect, weaken the barrier system against France in that general area. Talleyrand, again, could have used his enhanced bargaining position to secure a special advantage for France. He did not—and for equilibrist reasons. He pointed out that "for purposes of ambition and conquest he must favour the plan; but as his sincere desire . . . was to put a restraint upon any extension of the existing boundaries of France, he was against the project." [62] Castlereagh was again satisfied with Talleyrand's support against the Prussian proposal.

Hardenberg having made his attempt to soften up the strong-minded Britisher, Alexander took up the proposal and urged it on Castlereagh on January 7 in a "very long interview." The British minister again argued against it, declaring the impossibility of his consenting "to place a Prince in circumstances so dependent upon France, in a very centre of our line of defense. . . . the obvious policy in military prudence, was either to place there a great military Power such as Prussia, or if that could not be, to bring forward some secondary Power such as the Prince of Orange." [63] In the same interview, the tsar, suspicious of the recent British familiarity with Talleyrand, asked Castlereagh outright about the rumored treaty among the western powers. Castlereagh was surprised, but he was equal to the question. He neither denied nor admitted the existence of a treaty but contented himself with saying that Alexander had nothing

[62] Castlereagh to Liverpool, Jan. 5, 1815, in Webster, *Brit. Dipl.*, 283.
[63] Castlereagh to Liverpool, Jan. 8, 1815, *ibid.*, 283.

to fear if he acted on the principles just avowed in their conversations.[64]

On the ninth, Hardenberg, true to the spirit of his word, recommended the inclusion of the French plenipotentiary in the inner councils of the congress. Talleyrand appeared at the next meeting—on the twelfth, and joint action among the Austrian, British, and French delegates was apparent at once. It was evident that together they would oppose the outright cession of Saxony to Prussia and more than likely that Prussia and Russia would not risk war against three formidable powers acting in concert. The powers, having skirted disaster for so long, all began to recede from it. The crisis was over. The deadlock had been broken by a reversion from coalition equilibrium to alliance balance, in which Great Britain, France, and Austria were aligned against Prussia and Russia, in the fashion foreseen and feared by Castlereagh. Whatever the loss in unity, the great powers had avoided the return of war and arrived at a point where the general settlement could really commence.

[64] *Ibid.*, 284.

Chapter IX

Congress of Vienna: Creation of

a New Territorial Equilibrium

THE war crisis was solved, but the problem of Saxony had yet to be ironed out.[1] Hardenberg had indicated only that a deal could now be made; he had agreed to nothing more; and for bargaining purposes, he continued to press the Prussian claim to all of Saxony. On the surface the Prussian position was unchanged; in the same fashion, Metternich persisted in asking that only a small part of Saxony go to Prussia. Nevertheless, if a good medi-

[1] Only the major territorial problems are treated here. The facts are too well-known for needless repetition. Good summaries of the details leading up to and including the territorial settlement at the Congress of Vienna are available in the *Camb. Mod. Hist.*, IX, 598 ff., 647 ff., and in Webster, *Castlereagh*, 380 ff. For general questions and the abolition of the slave trade, see the latter, 413 ff.

ator could now find the magic point between the two extremes, there was every chance of compromise. Searching for that point, Castlereagh spent an incredibly busy month. One element which contributed to his ultimate success was the winding up of the Polish dispute. During the struggle over Saxony, such progress had been made toward agreement on Poland that by January 3 the new west Polish frontier was virtually settled.

On the third, Metternich had placed before the plenipotentiaries of the four courts an Austrian reply to the Russian draft agreement of December 30.[2] Although the two documents were worlds apart on Saxony, they registered complete agreement on the details of the western boundary of Poland between the obscure villages of Neuhoff in the north and Gola on the Silesian frontier. This carefully specified line proved to be the final congress boundary in that area.[3] Hardenberg's position on Saxony was weakened by this success of his Russian allies in securing their specific aims on Poland, because the Russians, having won their own point, became less disposed to support Prussia unto death over Saxony. Utilizing this advantage, Castlereagh was able to secure the tsar's support for compromise on Saxony as early as January 8 and could then spend the remaining weeks of January in putting pressure on Austria and Prussia to modify their pretensions.[4] By the end of the month, both Hardenberg and Metternich were reconciled to the principle of compromise, and the bargaining over the carcass of Saxony had begun in earnest.

The Kingdom of Saxony itself was a victim of Napoleon, its own geographic position, and the balance of power. The switch of its king's loyalty from Napoleon to the allies had come rather

[2] The minutes of the formal meetings of the Big Powers in the winter months of 1814–1815 may be found in *British and Foreign State Papers*, II, 577 ff. For the Russian draft agreement of Dec. 30, 1814, see 590–593; the Austrian counterproject of Jan. 3, 1815, follows on 594–596.

[3] See Hertslet, *The Map of Europe*, I, map facing p. 218.

[4] Castlereagh to Liverpool, Jan. 22 and 29, 1815, in Webster, *Brit. Dipl.*, 292, 293, 296–297.

later than the changes of Russia, Prussia, and Austria, and that fact was held against its representatives at Vienna, although so many states had changed sides on so many occasions that—to quote Talleyrand's famous phrase—it was little more than "a matter of dates." Although the king had had some control over his own destiny in the summer of 1813, the balance-of-power dicta and the political geography which victimized Saxony at the congress were matters over which he had no control. The Austrian axiom and Castlereagh's strong center, those geometric propositions which had determined Austrian and British strategy at Vienna, were related to matters and conceptions of international politics quite beyond the reach of Saxon influence.

Saxon geography became a matter for hasty study at Vienna. The kingdom lay in east-central Germany, and was bisected by the Elbe. It was immediately south of Brandenburg, its frontier being only about thirty miles from Berlin, and virtually its entire north and east lay next to Prussian lands. To the south stood Bohemia, cut off by tumbled mountain country which the Elbe pierced as it rushed north, but since the river cut through a rough valley, it had little communicative effect. The kingdom was roughly rectangular (if such an outrageous generalization can be made about any frontiers in the political chaos of eighteenth-century Germany), with a ragged tail flying west toward the Rhine. Saxon territory had fluctuated a good deal, from the original large holdings of the medieval Duchy of Saxony in northwest Germany to the early nineteenth-century compactness of the kingdom around Leipzig and Dresden. The most interesting speculative point in that progression was the seventeenth-century prominence of Saxony in German life and the possibility that Saxony might have gone on to give Germany the leadership which later, and unfortunately, came from Prussia. The acceptance by the Saxon kings of the Polish throne in 1697 and their concomitant adoption of Catholicism were the critical steps which cost them their following in the Protestant north. By the end of the eighteenth century, the Saxon kings had lost not only the Polish throne but had passed their opportunity in Germany to that harsh northern neighbor which now was in a position to digest parts of Saxony itself.

The Saxony at the disposal of the statesmen of 1815 was largely mountainous, parts of it very picturesque. In limited areas around Leipzig and in the north it lay in the northern European plain, which belts the continent for immense distances from west to east. As a whole, the kingdom was one of the most fertile parts of Germany, its productivity diminishing toward the south. To the rich wheat areas of the north and the lush pasturage of the river valleys were added valuable mining country as well. With numerous long-established towns and the two prominent cities of Leipzig (population 30,000) and Dresden (population 55,000), the kingdom was an obvious attraction for covetous eyes. The covetous eyes were Prussian, and the areas which were sought extended in from the northern and eastern frontiers toward the heart of the kingdom.

Compromise on Saxony would obviously cut Prussian gains short of Dresden, which was safely distant in the south, but Leipzig was more exposed in its central position in the west, and Metternich was determined to prevent its falling to Prussia. When on January 28 he communicated to the Big Five the formal, on-the-record, Austrian offer of Saxon land to Prussia, Leipzig was not included.[5] The Prussians were persistent, and agreement seemed hopelessly remote.

Early in February Castlereagh persuaded Russia and Hanover to lubricate the negotiations by additional concessions to Prussia: from Russia, Thorn on the Vistula, which would give Prussia a nip of her former duchy territory; from Hanover, an area embracing 50,000 "souls" (to be compensated by a cession from the Netherlands). Prussia accepted and settled for somewhat more than half of the Saxon lands, without Leipzig, and for somewhat fewer than half of Saxony's "souls." This agreement on February 8, 1815, enabled the matter to be sent into subcom-

[5] *British and Foreign State Papers*, II, 604 ff.

mittee for drafting. Prussia received her portion of Saxony, some areas in Poland, and large areas in western Germany. Russia retained most of Poland, while Austria had yet to receive her compensation in Italy. Prussian statesmen had done well by their monarch. They gained title to valuable land, the king of Saxony renouncing (according to the text of the final treaty) "in perpetuity for himself, and all his descendants and successors, in favour of His Majesty the King of Prussia, all his right and title to the provinces, districts, and territories." [6] The Prussian monarch also picked up a small handful of titles: "those of Duke of Saxony, Landgrave of Thuringia, Margrave of the two Lusatias, and Count of Henneberg." [7] The grant of large areas in western Germany designated Prussia as heir to the historic Austrian role of defender of the Rhine. Prussia was quite consciously brought forward to hold the line against a possible resurgence of French power. It was a calculated risk of great importance, and one which Englishmen of a later century wished had never been taken, but it conformed nicely to the equilibrist strategy of Castlereagh, as inherited from Pitt. The Polish areas which Russia agreed to pass over to Prussia were small when compared with the massive Russian gains in the duchy, but they were not negligible. They amounted to about one-sixth of the duchy and were larger than the parts of Saxony which Prussia received. They included a useful section of the Vistula; the entire Netze Valley, an ancient and hallowed part of Poland; and over half of the Warta Valley to a point above the city of Posen.

Relative to the balance of power, one of the particularly noticeable characteristics of the negotiations was the extraordinary mathematical approach to the problem of reciprocal compensation. On January 12, for example, Hardenberg had submitted to the Big Five a "Plan for the Reconstruction of Prussia" (see following page).

[6] Article XV of the Final Act, in Hertslet, *The Map of Europe*, I, 221.
[7] Article XVI, *ibid.*, 223.

Plan for the Reconstruction of Prussia *

	Prussia		
	Has lost since 1805	Has regained possession of	Has not recovered
	Subjects	Subjects	Subjects
1. The circle of Bialystok, ceded to Russia	183,300	—	183,300
2. The districts in the Duchy of Warsaw	2,357,626	—	2,357,626
3. City and territory of Danzig	79,015	79,015	
4. Circle of Cottbus	34,671	34,671	
5. The Old Mark of Brandenburg	110,000	110,000	
6. Magdeburg, on the left bank of the Elbe	208,000	208,000	
7. Halberstadt and Quedlinburg	113,000	113,000	
8. Mannsfeld, Prussian part	27,000	27,000	
9. Hohenstein, Prussian part	26,662	26,662	
10. Eichsfeld, with Treffurt, Mühlhausen and Nordhausen	108,000	108,000	
11. Erfurt, Untergleichen, Kranichfeld	51,000	51,000	
12. Wernigerode	11,280	11,280	
13. Hildesheim	119,500	—	119,500
14. Goslar	5,500	5,500	
15. Paderborn	96,920	96,920	
16. Ravensberg	90,000	90,000	
17. Minden	69,000	69,000	
18. Mark, Lippstadt, Hohenlimburg	137,890	137,890	
19. Cleves, on the right bank of the Rhine with Elten, Essen, and Werden	80,456	80,456	
20. Münster and Kappenberg	126,291	126,291	
21. Tecklenburg	20,059	20,059	
22. Lingen	25,021	25,021	
23. East Friesland	119,500	119,500	
24. Ansbach	276,788	—	276,788
25. Bayreuth	243,001	—	243,001
	4,719,480	1,539,265	3,180,215
Total of what Prussia has not recovered	—	—	3,180,215

* *British and Foreign State Papers,* II, 602–603 (translation mine).

Plan for the Reconstruction of Prussia (*continued*)

	Subjects	Subjects	Subjects
Prussia, being bound to cede:			
1. To Hanover .... 250 to 300,000			
of which	119,500		
are already in its possession, in return for the district of Hildesheim, and there remain to be ceded		180,500	
2. To Weimar, the district of Erfurt; while reserving the fortifications of this place, with the right to put garrisons there		51,000	
It is necessary to add	—	—	231,500
Total of the compensations which Prussia can claim in order to attain the State of 1805	—	—	3,411,715

	Subjects	Subjects
Prussia appears to be able to find them suitably only by the following acquisitions:		
1. The Kingdom of Saxony, without the circle of Cottbus, of which Prussia has already regained possession	2,051,240	
2. Part of the Duchy of Warsaw, according to the arrangement agreed upon with Russia	810,268	
3. The Duchy of Berg	299,877	
4. Koenigswinter, etc.	3,000	
5. The Duchy of Westphalia, for which it is necessary to indemnify Darmstadt on the left bank of the Rhine	131,888	
6. Dortmund and Corbeye	19,500	
7. The portion of Fulda, to assist in arrangements with Hesse	48,628	
The other portion of Fulda would fall in partition to the Duke of Weimar		

		Subjects	Subjects
8. On the left bank of the Rhine			
—the *département* of the Ruhr	625,228		
—from the *département* of the Ourthe	50,000		
—from the *département* of the Lower Meuse ...	24,000		
—from the *département* of the Rhine and Moselle	30,000	729,228	
TOTAL		4,093,629	4,093,629
SURPLUS			681,914

Hardenberg at this date was obviously still looking to Saxony for the bulk of Prussian gains. When Metternich replied to these mathematics with the Austrian counterproject of January 28,[8] he turned open the spigots of arithmetical compensation and trebled the Prussian effort. He might have known that the Hapsburgs could not compete with the north Germans in a game of this nature, because Hardenberg's rejoinder of February 8 topped everything with nine pages of material, as printed for us in the *British and Foreign State Papers*.[9] The figures, so charged with meaning for the congress statesmen, are of no great value to us today, but their usage is superbly illustrative of the tidy mechanics of the balance-of-power approach: *quid pro quo* with a measuring cup.

The Saxon question had been so intimately connected with concessions on numerous frontiers that its solution began a chain reaction. Bavaria had been reluctant to cede to Austria areas which the latter had lost in the wars of 1805 and 1809 and which had been earmarked for return to Austria. Nevertheless, the return was effected, Bavaria being compensated in

[8] *British and Foreign State Papers*, II, 609–612.
[9] *Ibid.*, 620–629.

Würzburg, Frankfurt, and the Palatinate. Mainz, long coveted by Bavaria, was made a confederation fortress under the sovereignty of Hesse.

The old Hanoverian electorate, Britain's sprawling north German satellite on the Continent, emerged as the enlarged Kingdom of Hanover, in contact with the new Prussia in the east and south and possessing a contiguous frontier with the Netherlands. At the height of the Napoleonic empire, Hanover had disappeared for several years, split between France and the artificial Kingdom of Westphalia, and then later bobbed to the surface with Napoleon's downfall. The congress tinkered with the old Hanoverian frontiers, adding and subtracting in several areas, the only large change coming in the west where very noticeable additions were made between the Dutch border and the Duchy of Oldenburg. To Hanover's already strong position on the lower Weser and Elbe, this new bloc of territory added the control of the lower Ems, which meant that Great Britain, through her client states of Holland and Hanover, had something to say about every river, large or small, which flowed into the North Sea from Dunkirk to Denmark.[10] For a country committed to sea power, these arrangements were little short of heaven. Critics of the settlement were quick to point out that the new land brought to Hanover a sandy area of marshes, poverty, storms, and fog. Moreover, Hanover had not been given Oldenburg, a part of the ancient Saxon lands, which in 1815 thrust from the shores of the North Sea into the heart of the new Hanover. A critic who rebelled at the addition of East Frisia to Hanover, however, could not logically contest the exclusion of Oldenburg, itself one of those poor, foggy, Protestant lands of moors, peat, dykes, marshes, and ague. Hanover's frontier was the product of much bargaining which shows how interlocked the whole central European settlement was. East Frisia, which had belonged to Prussia, was traded to Hanover in return for Lauenberg on the Elbe; Prussia then "used it [Lauenberg] to barter from Den-

---

[10] Castlereagh to Liverpool, Feb. 13, 1815, in Webster, *Brit. Dipl.*, 303.

Compensations at the Congress. The principal net advances of 1815 over 1789.

mark Pomerania and the Isle of Rügen, which Sweden had ceded in return for Norway." [11]

Details were filled in on the Netherlands' frontiers. The main outlines had been laid down in the previous year at the Treaty of Paris and the summer negotiations between Holland and Britain. The southern Netherlands were now added to Holland, plus Liège and the Duchy of Limburg. The king of Holland received the Duchy of Luxembourg, although not as a part of Holland—rather as a member of the German confederation, with the city of Luxembourg being garrisoned by Prussia. Castlereagh served to mediate the overlapping demands of Hanover and the Netherlands.

Thus the settlement progressed. Once the Saxon war crisis had passed, the frustrations of months were resolved in several active weeks. Castlereagh left Vienna in mid-February to assist his government in Parliament, Wellington succeeding him as first British plenipotentiary at Vienna. Early in March the news of Napoleon's return to France struck Vienna, touching off the fury of the Hundred Days. [12] After a series of swift and efficient readjustments to this new situation, the plenipotentiaries in Vienna again settled down to work.

The Italian settlement, largely determined by Metternich, now followed relatively quickly. Several months' stalemate had prevented appreciable progress on Italian frontiers, the incorporation of Genoa in Piedmont having been the only Italian decision which the congress made in the fall of 1814. A unique, complicating factor had been the alliance between the Hapsburgs of Austria and Murat of Naples. Joachim Murat, son of an innkeeper, had risen as a soldier under Bonaparte, married the latter's youngest sister, commanded the French armies in Spain, and been made king of Naples. In January, 1814, after much service under Napoleon, he had secured Austrian support for his throne and switched to the allied side. Thus Austria was bound to support him, while Talleyrand held out for the

[11] Webster, *Castlereagh*, 390–391.   [12] See below, pp. 262 ff.

return of the legitimate Spanish Bourbon dynasty of Ferdinand I. The disposition of this Neapolitan crown split Austria and France on a rather important matter of policy in the autumn of 1814, but the Polish-Saxon difficulties at Vienna made French support necessary to Austria and Britain, with the result that both Metternich and Castlereagh sought means for cutting Austria loose from Murat.[13] Although they were still unsuccessful in realizing that aim, by the time Talleyrand had joined them in the alliance of January 3, they continued to seek it. In the end, Murat himself solved the dilemma by offering Napoleon his support in the Hundred Days and attempting without success to unite Italy against Austria. The Kingdom of the Two Sicilies was awarded to Ferdinand I, and Murat was followed, captured, and shot.

The remainder of the Italian settlement went rather quickly. The allies recognized Italy as an Austrian preserve, according to the law of reciprocal compensation, and French opposition to Austria was dispersed when the flight of the king of France during the Hundred Days robbed Talleyrand of any importance in the final settlement. The upshot was a miniature system of ten states in Italy, five under the Hapsburgs. The enlarged Kingdom of Sardinia (Piedmont) embraced Sardinia, Savoy, Nice, Piedmont, and Liguria. Its new size and stature were owing to its function as a barrier state against France. Austria united much of northern Italy in the new Lombardo-Venetian kingdom under the emperor of Austria. To the emperor's brother went the Grand Duchy of Modena; to his daughter, the Parma duchies. Papal authority was reaffirmed in central Italy, and Bourbon authority was established in the south.

Switzerland proved to be a difficult problem, but it, too, yielded to solution. The problem was complicated by acute dif-

13 For an unraveling of the fantastic complexities of the diplomacy surrounding Murat in 1814–1815, see Webster's short and lucid accounts in Ward and Gooch, *Camb. Hist. of Brit. For. Policy,* I, 483–490, and Webster, *Castlereagh,* 397–407. Murat was the rashest, bravest, and most successful cavalry leader of his generation.

ferences among the Swiss. The congress had established a special committee on Switzerland, which finally emerged with a settlement providing for a loose union among twenty-two cantons and for frontiers which were finally accepted by the Swiss. Once in 1814 and twice in 1815 the Big Five guaranteed Swiss neutrality, a sound act of statemanship and a compromise acceptable to both France and the other big powers. One of the less important decisions of the period, it proved one of the most lasting; the neutrality was, to be sure, violated in 1815, but its reaffirmation in November of that year proved to be durable, and Switzerland emerged from its bloody past into long vistas of peace.

The constitution of the new Germanic confederation was particularly slow in taking shape. By the time the congress assembled in September, 1814, certain basic conditions had become evident. For one thing, the creation of a German empire had been eliminated as a real possibility by the reaffirmation of the power of German princes, who were naturally opposed to an empire. Both French and Russian policy sought an inert Germany with sovereignty scattered among the princes,[14] an outcome which was predictable at the opening of the congress.

Allied policy, moreover, agreed in principle on the creation of a confederation. At Vienna the big powers quickly decided to leave the drafting of the new constitution to the German states themselves. They established a German committee which met in October and November, 1814, discussed the various constitutional drafts, and finally stalemated itself in good congress fashion. Disagreements suspended work for five months until spring, 1815. When negotiations began again, an Austrian draft precipitated compromise and the eventual creation of the essential structure of the new constitution, based on a federal diet and a voting differential for various states. The result was a Germanic Confederation of thirty-four princes and four free cities; a diet under Austrian presidency, with representatives from each state;

[14] See Treitschke, *History of Germany*, II, 92 ff., and Sorel, *L'Europe*, VIII, 437 ff.

stipulations against separate negotiations of the princes in time of war and against their contracting alliances contrary to the good of all. The confederation had no strong machinery, but it did give some organization to German politics, and it brought Prussia and Austria into the same structure, creating some semblance of Castlereagh's dream of a strong center for Europe, able to throw its weight against either east or west.

After some dispute, the powers agreed to consummate their work with a general treaty. Delay in preparing it as a whole led to the signing of numerous "Treaties, Conventions, Declarations, Regulations, and other Instruments," each representing a completed part and each later annexed to the final treaty, which came to resemble a recipe book for a fifteen-course Chinese feast.[15] On June 9, 1815, the plenipotentiaries signed the great treaty—the Final Act,[16] whose 121 articles served as a general roundup of all the odds and ends of completed negotiation. It lay down regulations on myriad matters, from the great central decisions on Poland, Saxony, West Germany, and Italy to the hierarchy of "diplomatic characters," the privileges of shepherds and drovers in areas which had changed hands, and the maintenance of towpaths for the rivermen. International lawyers now had a fascinating new toy, and the fourth and final phase of the Congress of Vienna was over.

Examination of the over-all picture of compensations shows that the pattern conformed closely to the Pitt-Castlereagh strategic conception of the balance of power with regard to the containment of France. The arc bordering the east of France was theoretically complete, north to south, with the enlarged Kingdom of the Netherlands; the linkage of Luxembourg to that kingdom; Prussia, immensely increased on the Rhine and even

[15] For a listing of the "Annexes," see Hertslet, *The Map of Europe*, I, 275–276; for the texts, see *ibid.*, 60 ff. or Klüber, *Akten des Wiener Kongresses*, IV, 447 ff.; V, 121 ff.

[16] For the text, see d'Angeberg, *Congrès de Vienne*, 1386 ff.; Martens, *Recueil des traités . . . conclus par la Russie*, III, 231 ff.; Martens, *Nouveau recueil*, II, 379 ff.; and Hertslet, *The Map of Europe*, I, 208 ff.

brought to the French frontier; Bavaria also with land on the French frontier; both Baden and Württemberg strengthened; Switzerland neutralized; and Sardinia increased to anchor the

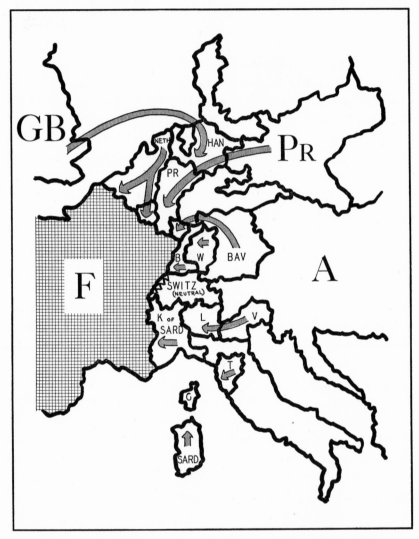

The Pitt-Castlereagh arc of containment against France, 1815.

line on the south. Thus France's small neighbors were strengthened. Three major powers, moreover, were placed in excellent positions to back up this relatively light line: Great Britain, closely associated with both Hanover and the Netherlands, could give weight to the line on the north; Prussia, owing to the curious shape of her new western holdings, was both in contact with France and in a position to back up the Netherlands against her; and Austria, compensated in Italy, could support Sardinia from Lombardy and threaten the French island of Corsica from Tuscany if need be. The balance-of-power strategists had shown a clever appreciation of military affairs in their new allocations and had incidentally disclosed the affinity of equilibrist strategy and military planning. This affinity in turn reveals to us the essentially tough character of balance-of-power theory and practice. These men were not hopeful of perpetual peace, they were not prepared to forget the bloodletting of recent experience, and indeed they were not even optimistic about the piece of work which they had just completed. Gentz, who was intelligent and of course very well informed on the inner workings of the congress, expressed his dismay as early as mid-February, by which time the main decisions had been made. He then wrote: "This congress . . . has only been . . . a source of embarrassment and trouble to everybody, and particularly to Austria, and the results . . . will do little towards the foundation of a lasting peace in Europe." [17] The settlement was never popular, and the work of the congress was widely abused by contemporaries and later generations. While much of the criticism was the product of nationalist writers who passionately rejected the cold calculations of the balancers, there was abuse from observers who accepted the assumptions and aims of the balance-of-power system. Such a critic was G. F. Leckie, who argued in his postwar book on the balance of power that "the peace of Europe will be durable only in proportion to the perfection of its political balance," [18] and that the salvation of that balance lay in simplification and consolidation on the map of

[17] "The Vienna Congress, a Memoir," Feb. 12, 1815, in Metternich, *Memoirs,* II, 584–585.

[18] Gould Francis Leckie, *Historical Research into the Nature of the Balance of Power,* 242.

Europe: "the more complicated the system of nations be, and the more numerous the independent states become, the more will be the points of collision and consequently the causes of disputes." [19] He was particularly hostile to the clustered states of Italy and the Rhineland:

Like a collection of rooks' nests, which a gust of wind dislocates, these little principalities are liable to be over-run and plundered in every political squall. Were there no such clusters of small independencies in Germany and Italy, there would be no commodious theatre for war: powerful princes would be obliged to attack the territories of powerful princes, and the simple construction of the European system would not only be better understood, but fewer clashing interests would exist, to produce the motley arrangements which are exhibited in every treaty. The solid and compact states of Europe would be less liable to be shaken on every sudden emergency; fewer causes of disorder would arise; and whatever differences might occur, it would be so difficult to gain any decisive advantage by hostilities, that negotiation would come more quickly, as well as more seriously, to the relief of nations.[20]

He was a "fluid" equilibrist who found the Final Act of Vienna timid and unimaginative. Specifically, he wanted a greatly increased Kingdom of the Netherlands, embracing not only the Belgian areas which the congress had given to Holland, but much of west Germany as well; [21] Austrian compensation in south Germany, instead of Italy; [22] Prussia confined to areas east of the Elbe and given all of the former Duchy of Warsaw; Italy united in the south; [23] and Denmark, Norway, and Sweden compacted in the north.[24] It all sounds rather radical and fantastic after perusal of what really happened at Vienna, particularly as a result of Russian demands, but the author makes an interesting case for his proposed territorial balance of power. By eliminating the small, weak powers one would remove tempta-

[19] *Ibid.,* 111.   [20] *Ibid.,* 348–349.   [21] *Ibid.,* 353.
[22] *Ibid.*   [23] *Ibid.,* 354–355.
[24] *Ibid.,* 355–356; also 232.

tion from powerful neighbors; and powerful states, when faced with each other, "would find more difficulties in executing their ambitious projects; and consequently be less disposed to entertain any." [25] He deeply feared the influence of Russia on Europe, since the congress boundaries for Poland enabled Russia to penetrate between Prussia and Austria and weaken their frontiers against herself. He paraphrased with relish a remark of the Abbé de Pradt to the effect that: "A barbarous people . . . commanded by civilized chiefs, and inhabiting cold and inhospitable regions, have a tendency to migrate to milder and more fertile parts of the earth." [26] The consolidated Scandinavia and the grant of Polish land to Prussia (to "make Prussia the palatine of Europe against the Scythians") [27] would help to check the Russians. But the congress statesmen, by their failure to adopt a program along these lines, left the door open upon a gloomy future: "The Congress of Vienna has now re-established the old system of division, with all its defects, (one might say) to prepare things for the next conqueror who may appear; and who will profit by this mistaken policy, to establish an empire perhaps more solid than that of Buonaparte." [28] Castlereagh had stood for a much milder program than Leckie's, but he was not sanguine about the future of the edifice which he had been so prominent in building.

[25] *Ibid.*, 243–244.   [26] *Ibid.*, 369–370.   [27] *Ibid.*, 354.   [28] *Ibid.*, 313–314.

Chapter X

France's Frontier Redefined

ON THE night of March 6–7, 1815, in the midst of the Congress of Vienna and when most of the important problems were either solved or well on the way to solution, the news of Napoleon's escape from Elba burst upon Vienna. Bonaparte had left Elba on February 25. Landing at Cannes, he was soon on his way toward Paris, his way blocked by troops which had been sent by Louis XVIII to intercept him. In one of the most romantic of all episodes in his career, Napoleon, without much initial support, simply began his journey toward the capital. The march soon turned into a Napoleonic snowball, with accretions of troops rallying to his banner every few miles. Within two weeks of his landing in the south, he was holding a reception at the Tuileries and forming a new government, a process virtually completed within forty-eight hours. Louis XVIII fled France and proceeded to Ghent.

COALITION EQUILIBRIUM REVIVED

No sooner had Metternich received word of the escape of Napoleon from exile than the congress bristled with plans to meet this emergency. There was very little division of opinion in Vienna on the matter of action against Napoleon; it was generally believed that his return was "incompatible with the peace and security of Europe." ¹ On March 13, 1815, the eight signatories of the First Treaty of Paris signed a declaration to the effect that "Napoleon Bonaparte has placed himself outside of civil and social relations, and . . . , as an enemy and disturber of the peace of the world, he has delivered himself to public hatred." ² He was designated an outlaw.

On March 12 Wellington was able to write Castlereagh of the general disposition of armies against Napoleon. Military plans, which had been settled quickly, provided for 150,000 Austrian troops in Italy; a build-up on the upper Rhine to 200,-000 from Austria, Bavaria, Baden, and Württemberg; the middle Rhine to be covered chiefly by the Prussian corps under General Kleist and the Austrian garrison of Mainz; British and Hanoverian troops under Wellington to defend the lower Rhine; a Russian army of 200,000 in reserve in Württemberg; and the remainder of the Prussian army, also in reserve, on the lower Rhine.³ Thus the territorial strategy of the congress was put to work before it was even finally written into international law in the omnibus peace treaty.

The minds of the statesmen immediately reverted to the idea of renewing and reaffirming the coalition against Napoleon; the alliance balance structure of January–February, in which the allies had overindulged in disagreement, vanished almost overnight. Castlereagh, then in London, quickly dispatched word to Wellington, urging the latter to

¹ Castlereagh to Wellington, March 12, 1815, in Webster, *Brit. Dipl.*, 309.
² Martens, *Nouveau recueil*, II, 110–111.
³ Wellington to Castlereagh, March 12, 1815, in Webster, *Brit. Dipl.*, 312.

lose no occasion of calling their [the other ministers'] attention to the Treaty of Chaumont, as the only safe basis upon which their conduct can now be founded. . . . there is no safety for Europe but in a close and indissoluble union of the Four Great Powers, supported by all the other states, who will rally round their standard.[4]

In anticipation of just such instructions, Wellington had already discussed the idea with Alexander on March 12, and the two had agreed in principle to sign a new treaty something like that of Chaumont.[5] Agreement in principle was merely the prelude to disagreement over details; it proved to be no easy matter to secure general approval of the treaty because of the insistence of Alexander and others on a British grant of subsidies at the same time and because of the disagreement among the German states over the command of troops in north Germany.[6]

Nevertheless, agreement was reached after a difficult period for Wellington, and the coalition was re-created on March 25, 1815. On that day the Big Four signed a treaty [7] specifying their intention "to apply to that important circumstance, the principles consecrated by the Treaty of Chaumont . . . to preserve against every attack, the order of things so happily re-established in Europe." [8] The document contained nine articles, virtually all of which were important: reaffirmation of the First Peace of Paris; each of the Big Four to supply 150,000 troops; no separate peace; this treaty valid only for the war emergency, the Treaty of Chaumont to go back into effect afterwards; all Europe to be invited to join; and Louis XVIII to be asked to sign. By an additional convention, Great Britain agreed to set aside £5,000,000 for subsidies up to April 1, 1816, if war should continue that long.[9] The lesser powers lost little time in joining the new coali-

---

[4] Castlereagh to Wellington, March 16, 1815, *ibid.*, 314.

[5] Wellington to Castlereagh, March 12, 1815, *ibid.*, 312.

[6] Wellington to Castlereagh, March 25, 1815, *ibid.*, 316.

[7] For the text, see *British and Foreign State Papers*, II, 443–450.

[8] *Ibid.*, 444.   [9] *Ibid.*, 452–455.

tion. By the end of April, 1815, Hanover, Portugal, Sardinia, Bavaria, Holland, and numerous German princes and cities had acceded to it. The month of May swept in Baden, Switzerland, Hesse-Darmstadt, Saxony, and Württemberg.[10] Denmark brought up the rear in September. Great Britain concluded parallel subsidy treaties with the new signatories.[11]

Thus the coalition was launched with model efficiency and speed: within five days of the first indication of a need for it, two of the major participants had already agreed on the general outlines of its creation and a general disposition of armies had been planned and begun; and within two weeks of that time, the coalition had been signed and subsidies promised. Inside another fortnight, three secondary powers had joined, and another seven weeks gave the coalition eight more signatories; meanwhile, the allied armies were on the march and military preparations were proceeding with speed.

This swift re-creation of the coalition against a potential enemy serves as a nearly unique and perfect illustration of the operation of a coalition equilibrium as well as of the principle of mobility of action. Within a few hurried weeks every necessary diplomatic move had been made; the danger had been recognized, agreement secured, and joint action taken. Speed and success here were the products of unusual and fortunate circumstances. For one thing, most of the major statesmen of the great powers were together in Vienna; capable generals were also there. A rather obvious common danger, about which there was little dispute, had arisen and had come to their ears with a dramatic and unifying suddenness. Moreover, the armies of the great powers were partially available at once; subsidies were forthcoming, and military prospects were good. In addition there were also the factors of both a common and recent experience with coalitions and the existence of a general instrument in the Treaty of Chaumont, designed for just such an emergency. In other

[10] *Ibid.,* 456 ff.   [11] *Ibid.,* 484 ff.

words, the diplomatic deck was thoroughly stacked in favor of a new coalition, an extraordinary phenomenon which coalition-minded statesmen might never again witness.

The new coalition should be viewed as the application of the Treaty of Chaumont to a specific situation. In effect, it put into operation the substance of the scheme in Articles VI–XVI of Chaumont.[12] The coalition of March 25, 1815, virtually repeated the provisions of the first four articles of Chaumont. Moreover, it specified that the more universal provisions of the Treaty of Chaumont would go back into force at the end of the emergency. Thus the new coalition equilibrium began its trial run.

While the men at Vienna were so busy with these events, Napoleon tried to detach Great Britain and Austria from the coalition and failed. He discovered the French copy of the Triple Alliance of January 3, 1815, and attempted to sow dissension among the allies by disclosing it to Russia, but this maneuver failed too; it merely emphasized his own diplomatic isolation and made even clearer to him the urgency of war preparations.

He had inherited an army of 200,000 from Louis XVIII.[13] Louis, in one of his few popular acts during his year on the throne, had abolished conscription, and his successor now hesitated from March until June before reviving it. Bonaparte had to fight time. By June, after nearly three months of military preparations, he had raised his regular army to 284,000, an unsatisfactory figure for one in his isolated posture. He called upon the National Guard for service in fortresses, but he had difficulties in getting substantial numbers of them and by June 15 had only 135,000. Together with naval personnel, which he used in this emergency to swell his land forces, all his auxiliary troops totaled about 250,000 and could not be considered strong. In June his total armed forces amounted to something over 500,000, a figure which he felt could be raised to perhaps 800,000 by October, if only he were given that long.

[12] See above, pp. 153–155.
[13] The military figures are taken from the *Camb. Mod. Hist.*, IX, 618–619.

He was fortunate in the return of most of his former officers, who willingly left their inactive status on half pay. The temper of France, however, was markedly different from that of an earlier day. To appease it, he issued his *Acte additionnel,* with its guarantee of a liberal constitution, and then found, much to his disgust, that the new lower house, which was brought into the world by the *Acte,* was genuinely liberal in character. The temper of this aging "son of the Revolution" was understandably short under the circumstances. In the diplomatic field, moreover, he now had but one supporter, Murat, his brother-in-law at Naples, who was soon to discredit himself and precipitate his own defeat and death. To cap the arch of insecurity, Napoleon was faced with the most formidable coalition of his career and was soon to meet in battle two generals who had no fear of him.

The coalition had agreed to put 600,000 men in the field. In June, Belgium held two main concentrations of allied arms— 105,000 British, Dutch, and German troops under Wellington and 117,000 troops under Blücher, located some fifty miles to the east of Wellington's position in the Scheldt Valley.[14] Napoleon decided that his best move would be a swift advance on the junction point of these two allied armies. Against their united 220,000 he could use only 125,000, and he had to deal with them separately if he were to deal with them at all. He hoped by his swift advance to gain three days' march on them, meet and defeat them separately, then deal with Austria and Russia in much the same way, catching the former before the latter could come to her aid.

On June 15 he began his thrust into Belgium toward the gap between the allied armies.[15] By the morning of the sixteenth his position was excellent, although on that day troops under Ney were checked at Quatre Bras and Napoleon himself was victorious only after a difficult, costly, and bloody engagement

[14] *Ibid.,* 623.
[15] See *ibid.,* 624 ff., for a good brief account of the military campaign which culminated at Waterloo.

with Blücher at Ligny. Nevertheless, his plans were working. Then, on the following day, Napoleon allowed himself the costly luxury of wasting some of the precious time which his rapid advance had gained him, and Wellington reformed his army on Mont St. Jean, hoping to give battle to the Emperor on the morrow, if Blücher could get to him with support. The help was promised, and the battle was joined as planned on Sunday, June 18. Wellington's victory is a familiar tale; it was compounded of British fortitude, cool generalship, the late but important arrival of the Prussians on the French right wing, Napoleon's mistakes, and numerous other known and unknown factors. By 8 P.M. the main battle was over and Napoleon in headlong retreat.

On June 21 the legislative chambers in Paris declared themselves in permanent session. Napoleon considered a purge of his enemies and the establishment of a dictatorship, rejected the idea, and resigned in favor of his son on June 22. Wellington urged on Louis XVIII a speedy return to Paris. The king entered France on the twenty-fifth, and the first Prussian troops arrived on the hills north of Paris on June 29. Napoleon, having remained at Malmaison from the twenty-fifth to the twenty-ninth, was almost caught by the Prussians. Blücher was prepared to shoot him, but Bonaparte disappeared and was not accounted for until he sent a message to Captain Maitland of the British navy on July 10. Meanwhile, the allies had surrounded Paris, Blücher intent upon the alternatives of unconditional surrender or assault. Wellington's unbending insistence upon mildness resolved the disagreement. Blücher gave way, and a capitulation of the provisional government was affected on July 3, particularly through the efforts of Fouché and Davout, the one the able and ruthless head of the Paris police under Napoleon, and the other perhaps his most important marshal. Both were key figures inside the city but had some difficulty in persuading the chambers of the wisdom of the policy of surrender. On the seventh of July the allies staged a second triumphal entry into

Paris, and Louis XVIII was back in the Tuileries on the following day. The flurry was over and the Bourbons safely back on their throne, this time for a somewhat longer tenure.

MODERATION ON TRIAL

French frontiers had been settled once in the First Peace of Paris in May, 1814; French statesmen had participated in the Congress of Vienna in the fall; and France had become a member of the Big Five in January. But the diplomatic fortunes of France, so low in April, 1814, so high in early 1815, had again changed with a swiftness which must have chilled the heart of Talleyrand, who now actually signed the new coalition in the name of France, aligning the French government in exile against the Napoleonic government in residence and creating a situation which left him shorn of influence at Vienna and in the awkward position of fighting his own countrymen. After Waterloo and the occupation of Paris, moreover, many statesmen took the Hundred Days as evidence that their earlier moderation in dealing with France had been wrong. There was strong sentiment for partitioning France to weaken her. The problem of moderation had to be faced once again, and all the old arguments against France were brought up, this time re-enforced by the recent unhappy experience with Napoleon.

While Wellington was seeing that Louis XVIII returned to Paris as soon as possible, Fouché, inside the city, was preparing the ground for the second Restoration. He repeatedly urged the importance of satisfying the allies on as many counts as possible, since it would dilute their wrath in dealing with France. Meanwhile, Prussian and Bavarian soldiery were looting and pillaging the French countryside, much to the discredit of allied arms and the discomfiture of allied statesmen, who feared disintegration of the coalition before its work was properly done.

On July 12 at Paris the allies set up a ministerial committee, sometimes known as the Committee of Four, which continued to meet rather regularly until well into September and thereafter somewhat less often until the signing of the Second Peace of Paris, November 21, 1815.[16] The committee, representing the final *de facto* authority in France, fell into disagreement at once over the problems of how to reduce French power, what to do about war criminals, how to stop the looting by the Prussians and Bavarians, and how to preserve the coalition.

Everyone agreed on the basic proposition of reducing French power, but disagreement arose over the means to effect it.[17] Most controversial of all was the question of whether or not to dismember France in order to reduce her power. Sentiment in favor of a harsh peace was naturally strongest among those powers which were most exposed to French aggression: the Netherlands, Prussia, Bavaria, and Württemberg, whose representatives were very vocal in their demands against France. The statesmen of the smaller powers flew around Paris like ill-fed horseflies, buzzing the urgency of a partition.[18] Prussia was the most formidable because of her membership in the Big Four, her participation in the defeat of the French, and her position as one of the chief occupying powers, with 280,000 troops on French soil. Moreover, her generals wanted a harsh peace for France. Among the military figures, Knesebeck and Gneisenau were perhaps the most important in their opposition to moderation. Blücher had shown where he stood in his demand for unconditional surrender and his plans for Napoleon. Both

[16] The official records of these meetings are not especially revealing, but, for what they are, they may be followed in d'Angeberg, *Congrès de Vienne,* 1465–1510, 1514–1516, 1522–1523, 1526–1527, 1529–1530, 1565–1580, 1588– 1589, 1590–1591, 1592–1594. The diplomacy of the summer and fall of 1815 is best summarized in Webster, *Castlereagh,* 462–478. See also Treitschke, *History of Germany,* II, 208 ff.

[17] Webster, *Castlereagh,* 463 ff.

[18] *Ibid.,* 459–460, 462, 470–471. Castlereagh reported plans for the "partial dismemberment" of France as coming from "the King of the Netherlands; . . . the Prussians . . . Bavarians . . . Wurtembergers" (Castlereagh to Liverpool, July 24, 1815, in Webster, *Brit. Dipl.,* 350). See Treitschke, *History of Germany,* II, 212–213; and Gebhardt, *Humboldt,* II, 177 ff.

Gneisenau and Knesebeck worked hard during the summer to secure the partial dismemberment of France and new accessions of territory to Prussia.[19]

The upshot of this pressure was an increase in the difficulties for Hardenberg, who was caught between the opinions of the Prussian military and an equally stubborn sentiment among his British and Russian allies, who had quite different opinions. His policy conformed rather closely to the demands of the militarists, and he sought to show that Europe's "generous confidence" in France had failed and that a repetition of "such generosity would be unpardonable." [20] In much the same vein, Humboldt argued that moderation to France was now impossible, that France must be punished, and that Prussia must be rewarded for her decisive role in the recent campaigns.[21] Hardenberg presented the Committee of Four with a series of detailed proposals for diminishing French power.[22] The plan called for the cession of three historic chains of fortresses, which had been constructed by Vauban, to the Netherlands, the German states, and Switzerland and the cession of all of Savoy and Alsace-Lorraine. These demands represented one extreme. Within two weeks the opposite extreme was defined.

Castlereagh's policy from the beginning of the Hundred Days had been to defeat Napoleon, restore Louis XVIII, and prevent a revengeful peace. By July 8 the first two points had been gained. The third offered difficulties. He encountered opposition from Liverpool and the British cabinet, as well as from Prussia and the other "barrier" states to the east of France. Liver-

[19] For a brief discussion of Prussian demands see Treitschke, *History of Germany,* II, 208–212; Gebhardt, *Humboldt,* II, 177 ff. See also Knesebeck's "Supplement to the memoir of the undersigned," Aug. 13, 1815, in *Well. Suppl. Des.,* XI, 117–121. The Prussian demands emphasized a large occupation force, indemnity, and many territorial cessions, among them Alsace-Lorraine.

[20] Hardenberg, Memorandum of Aug. 4, 1815, in d'Angeberg, *Congrès de Vienne,* 1479–1480. See also Treitschke, *History of Germany,* II, 206 ff.

[21] Gebhardt, *Humboldt,* II, 181 ff.

[22] *Ibid.,* II, 177; Treitschke, *History of Germany,* II, 208.

pool was a rather mild exponent of a harsh peace. Although not vindictive himself, he recognized the sentiment of the country and cabinet as being opposed to moderation. In the middle of July, within a week of the second Restoration, he wrote Castlereagh that it "might have been not unwise last year to try the effect of a more magnanimous policy; but in the result of that we have been completely disappointed; and we owe it to ourselves now to provide . . . for our own security." [23] He felt that the "prevailing idea" in Great Britain was to take back the conquests of Louis XIV and occupy France until the barrier should be completed. With the support of the cabinet, he urged upon Castlereagh the necessity of making an example of the war criminals. "The forbearance manifested at the present moment can be considered in no other light than weakness, and not mercy . . . . A severe example made of the conspirators who brought back Bonaparte could alone have any effect." [24]

Castlereagh was not insensitive to the temper of opinion in England, but he was unwilling to jeopardize the peace structure by yielding to what he considered transient and foolish desires. With regard to making examples of war criminals, he merely went through the motions of carrying out his instructions. On July 17 he suggested to the allied ministers that they urge Louis XVIII to "adopt some measure of vigour" against the worst war criminals.[25] Nevertheless, he expected laxness because Fouché was the head of the police and would let them slip through his fingers. More important, the matter could not be pressed too far, because the authority of Louis was in question and the loyalty of the army was uncertain.[26]

To humiliate France by partition would only undermine the authority which the British wanted to strengthen. It would weaken the government of Louis, render France unstable, and possibly light the fuse which would set off future disturbances.

[23] Liverpool to Castlereagh, July 15, 1815, in Webster, *Brit. Dipl.*, 346.
[24] Liverpool to Castlereagh, July 15, 1815, *ibid.*, 345–346.
[25] Castlereagh to Liverpool, July 17, 1815, *ibid.*, 347.
[26] Castlereagh to Liverpool, July 14, 1815, *ibid.*, 344.

The cabinet remained unconvinced, and Liverpool was writing as late as August 18 that the British public would be "grievously disappointed" by the proposed moderation toward France.[27] Castlereagh was convinced that his own policy conformed to sound equilibrist strategy. He wanted to check French power by temporary devices, negative in character, and render it harmless by a positive reliance upon the coalition of great powers which would act upon the principles of the Treaty of Chaumont. He was satisfied that the frontiers of France were not incompatible with the essentials of a territorial balance of power in Europe. He realized that French power must be diminished with discretion and that allied power must be readily available to check it on the field of battle. His formula, therefore, provided for discreet and temporary checks on French power, plus a genuine reliance upon a coalition equilibrium directed against France.[28] Throughout the summer, Wellington was a great source of strength to those who favored moderation. He had opposed Blücher's immoderate demand for the unconditional surrender of France and had seen that a capitulation was accepted. It was he who was perhaps chiefly responsible for the second Restoration of Louis XVIII. It was he also who drew the initial outlines of the policy of occupation before the statesmen arrived at Paris. Wellington felt that France had been left too powerful relative to the rest of Europe, and he agreed that French power must be reduced, but he argued that it must not be done by "any very material inroad upon the state of possession of the Treaty of Paris." [29] Such a move would defeat the purpose of the allies, alienate France, and necessitate a continuation of the expensive war footing of the allied powers. The best course, therefore, was

[27] Liverpool to Castlereagh, Aug. 18, 1815, *ibid.*, 368.

[28] "Principles upon which the proposed Negotiation with France ought to be considered," enclosed with Castlereagh to Liverpool, Aug. 24, 1815, in *Well. Suppl. Des.*, XI, 138–142. This document and the accompanying letter lay bare the inner structure of Castlereagh's policy during the period of the summer negotiations of 1815.

[29] Wellington to Castlereagh, Aug. 11, 1815, in Webster, *Brit. Dipl.*, 357.

"temporary occupation of some of the strong places" and temporary maintenance of an armed force in France to strengthen the French government.[30] For someone of his background and bluntness, his policy of moderation was singular in its wisdom.

> If the policy of the united Powers of Europe is to weaken France, let them do so in reality. Let them take . . . its population and resources as well as a few fortresses. If they are not prepared for that decisive measure, if peace and tranquillity for a few years is their object, they must make an arrangement which will suit the interests of all the parties to it, and of which the justice and expediency will be so evident that they will tend to carry it into execution.[31]

The Austrian reaction was also moderate, although Metternich did not at once disclose his policy. On August 6, 1815, he finally presented it to the Committee of Four and showed that he did not belong outright to either one side or the other, although he wished to follow a policy somewhat nearer to Castlereagh's moderation than to the German spirit of annexation.[32] The Austrian memorandum of early August, 1815, in which Metternich laid down the rationale of his policy was a good equilibrist document.[33] In it Metternich argued that the war of 1815 had not been fought as a war of conquest and must not be allowed to degenerate into such. The allies had every right to insist upon occupation, indemnity, and limited territorial cessions, provided that these measures conformed to the aims of converting France from an offensive power to a secure defensive one and of stabilizing France and Europe. He attempted to show that France's elaborate system of fortifications "is out of

[30] *Ibid.,* 358.

[31] Memorandum, Wellington to Castlereagh, Aug. 31, 1815, *ibid.,* 374–375.

[32] Srbik is satisfied that in Metternich's summer policy "European interest played the first role" and German interest a secondary one (*Metternich,* I, 220).

[33] For the text, see d'Angeberg, *Congrès de Vienne,* 1482–1487.

proportion to the means of defense of the neighbor states." [34] From that, he reasoned that France should lose her "offensive points," i.e., her first line of fortresses, and that they be destroyed or given to the barrier states. Thus it became increasingly clearer that Prussia, if unmoved, was at least diplomatically isolated. With Prussia and the barrier states actively urging the partition of France, with Metternich not decisively committed one way or the other, Castlereagh and Wellington could never have prevented a revengeful peace without support from the tsar.

Fortunately, Russian national interest was not immediately involved, Alexander was in one of his most amiable and benevolent phases when he came to Paris,[35] and Russian policy consistently followed a line of limiting France's power moderately while opposing "any permanent reduction" of her territory.[36] Castlereagh pointed out the fact that "Russia, being remote, rather inclines to protect France."

At the end of July, 1815, a long memorandum, inspired by Castlereagh, drafted by Capo d'Istria, and submitted by Alexander, stated the case against dismembering France, since the objects of the war had already been achieved.[37] The memorandum carefully went over the aims of the recent war and canvassed the possible ways of dealing with France. It argued that a revision of French frontiers would involve the creation of an entirely "new system of equilibrium." [38] It placed emphasis on the unity of the coalition and called for a renewal of the Treaty of Chaumont.

[34] D'Angeberg, *Congrès de Vienne*, 1484.

[35] Phillips has pointed out that one of the most crucial moments for the success of the balance of power was when Castlereagh and others were waiting for Alexander's entry into Paris in early July, not knowing whether he would listen to his Prussian allies or to the British counsels of moderation (*Confederation of Europe*, 124). See also Castlereagh to Liverpool, July 12, 1815, in Webster, *Brit. Dipl.*, 341.

[36] Castlereagh to Liverpool, July 24, 1815, *ibid.*, 350.

[37] Memorandum of Capo d'Istria, July 28, 1815, in d'Angeberg, *Congrès de Vienne*, 1470–1476.

[38] *Ibid.*, 1471–1472.

Alexander's religious experience of the spring of 1815 had deeply moved him and left a strong mark on Russian diplomacy throughout the year. The tsar's generosity toward France is doubtless explained to a large degree in terms of that experience. One may note in passing, nevertheless, that Russian policy also conformed to the demands of one type of balance-of-power conception. Russian generosity toward France would enable France to maintain a strong position in the west, a position which would minimize any central European tendency to direct its energies solely against Russia. The vulnerability of Prussia in the west, moreover, would render Prussia continuously dependent upon Russia. There was the further possibility of regarding France and England as offsetting the power of each other, Prussia and Austria similarly balancing one another, while Russia enjoyed a relatively free hand in the east.[39]

There were two important and immediate reactions to the Russian memorandum: the outcry of the Prussians and the clarification of Austrian policy. Humboldt, by no means the most aggressive of the Prussian figures, declared the Russian plan to be "the most disastrous for Prussia that could possibly have been imagined."[40] It is noteworthy that he took the occasion to urge upon Hardenberg once again the desirability of a wholly new system of alliance for Prussia, based on his conception of a strong middle-European barrier against both east and west.[41]

[39] See Donnadieu, *Essai sur la théorie de l'équilibre,* 168; and Treitschke, *History of Germany,* II, 204–205.

[40] Humboldt to Hardenberg, Aug. 4, 1815, in Gebhardt, *Humboldt,* II, 180. See also Treitschke, *History of Germany,* II, 210–211.

[41] In a very confidential memorandum of Aug. 4, 1815, in Gebhardt, *Humboldt,* II, 181 ff. The divergence of Russian and Prussian policies tended to breach the Russo-Prussian alliance which had been so much in evidence since its inception at Kalisch in February, 1813. The weakening of this bond, which Humboldt disliked anyway, gave him his opportunity to urge the system he wanted, i.e., the alliance system among England, Austria, and Germany. See above, p. 214, n. 43.

THE BALANCE REAFFIRMED:
SECOND PEACE OF PARIS

The lines of battle were very clearly drawn by the end of the first week of August. Preponderance lay with the policy of moderation, since Castlereagh, Wellington, and Alexander all supported that policy, and Metternich's plan was not substantially different. Nevertheless, Prussia would not give way. Hardenberg summoned Stein from Germany to appeal to the tsar—to no avail.[42] Gneisenau likewise attempted to convert the tsar to the Prussian demands—but without success.[43]

Castlereagh had found himself seriously embarrassed by lack of British support for his own policy. The London press was opposed to moderation toward France, and the cabinet expressed a similar disagreement with Castlereagh. To solve this dilemma, Castlereagh dispatched his brother, Lord Stewart, to London to convince the cabinet of the validity of a policy of moderation. With him he sent to Liverpool a letter and supporting documents.[44] He restated the arguments for moderation, pointing out how the

Prussian object is to augment their possessions; put Hanover and the Pays Bas between them and France, for their own security; and involve Hanover and the King of Pays Bas so irreconcileably with France as to render them dependent on Prussia for support, and then to demand her own terms for her support.[45]

[42] Treitschke, *History of Germany*, II, 212. See also Lehmann, *Freiherr vom Stein*, III, 460 ff., and, for Stein's memoir of Aug. 18, 1815, Botzenhart (ed.), *Freiherr vom Stein*, V, 259–261.

[43] Hans Delbrück, *Das Leben des Feldmarschalls Grafen Neithardt von Gneisenau* (Berlin, 1882), I, 269 ff. Treitschke described the Russian reply of Sept. 5, 1815, to Gneisenau as a "masterpiece of oriental pulpit oratory" (Treitschke, *History of Germany*, II, 217).

[44] Castlereagh to Liverpool, Aug. 24, 1815, in *Well. Suppl. Des.*, XI, 137–142.

[45] *Ibid.*, 138.

Suddenly, at the end of August and during the first week of September, precipitation of an agreement began. On August 28 Hardenberg indicated that he would no longer demand the cession of upper Alsace and would modify Prussian demands.[46] Lord Stewart returned from London with the cabinet's backing for Castlereagh's policy,[47] and Castlereagh drew up for circulation a statement of the Anglo-Russian diplomatic position.[48] Meanwhile, Gneisenau had launched the last big Prussian appeal to the tsar, soon answered by the unsympathetic restatement of Russian policy noted above. The diplomatic pot simmered. Hardenberg continued to balk at moderation toward France, but the tsar, unwilling to have his Prussian ally suffer a humiliating diplomatic setback, finally indicated that he would support a policy of moderate territorial cessions from France. The allies were in substantial agreement by September 8, and their worst troubles were over. In their ultimatum of September 20, 1815, the conditions were given to France: occupation, indemnity, and the frontiers of 1790.[49]

Talleyrand rejected the allied ultimatum, much to the surprise and anger of the coalition,[50] but his successor, Richelieu, accepted for France early in October, after the allies had made slight alterations in their terms. The drafting of the various documents which were to comprise the Second Peace of Paris absorbed several weeks, their signing taking place on November 20, 1815. On that day the major powers signed the Treaty of Paris,[51] supplementary conventions [52] regulating the execution

[46] Treitschke, *History of Germany*, II, 215.

[47] Liverpool to Castlereagh, Aug. 28, 1815, in *Well. Suppl. Des.*, XI, 145–146.   [48] *Ibid.*, 147.

[49] D'Angeberg, *Congrès de Vienne*, 1523–1527.   [50] *Ibid.*, 1531–1535.

[51] *Ibid.*, 1595–1601; Martens, *Nouveau recueil*, II, 682–691.

[52] "Convention . . . relative to the payment of the indemnity," d'Angeberg, *Congrès de Vienne*, 1604–1606; Martens, *Nouveau recueil*, 692–695. "Convention . . . relative to the occupation," d'Angeberg, *Congrès de Vienne*, 1607–1616; Martens, *Nouveau recueil*, II, 695–701. "Convention . . . relative to the liquidation of . . . claims," d'Angeberg, *Congrès de Vienne*, 1616–1636.

of the treaty, a new guarantee of Swiss neutrality,[53] and a new treaty of alliance among the Big Four.[54]

The Treaty of Paris gave France the frontiers of 1790 with slight modifications; provided for the destruction of the fortress of Huningen; subjected France to a three-to-five-year occupation by not more than 150,000 allied troops, whose location and conduct were carefully circumscribed; and provided for the payment by France of an indemnity of 700,000,000 francs.

These details of diplomacy during the summer and fall of 1815 show the process by which the four courts arrived at a new settlement with France and successfully resisted the demands of one of their members for a harsh rewriting of the peace. As at Vienna, each power related its plans to the mother conception of the balance of power, however different the plans might have been. Tsar Alexander and Castlereagh both justified moderation on equilibrist grounds. Metternich desired moderate cessions from France, also on equilibrist grounds. Humboldt argued for larger cessions on similar grounds. To us it seems valid that the statesmen should have accepted the Metternichian thesis of a slight blunting of French offensive power and Castlereagh's formula of not humiliating a new government which they really wanted to render secure. Both of these policies were quite sound balancing methods.

[53] "Guarantee of the perpetual neutrality of Switzerland," *ibid.,* 1640–1641.

[54] *Ibid.,* 1636–1638; to be discussed below, pp. 287 ff.

Chapter XI

Territorial Equilibrium Re-enforced

THE negotiations which led up to the Second Peace of Paris also included a search for a formula of enforcement in order to give some structural strength to the new territorial equilibrium. The enforcing of a territorial balance of power is by no means automatic: it has usually been done by individual powers or by the crisscrossing of alliances which is typical of alliance balance. It could also be performed by the action of a coalition. Although the conception of a coalition equilibrium suffered several setbacks in 1815, notably at Vienna in January and at Paris in July, there was still a strong tendency to strengthen and implement it.

GUARANTEES

One of the ideas which presented itself as a means of such implementation was that of guaranteeing the peace settlement of

Vienna. The history of the European state system offered numerous examples of the guarantee of different parts of Europe.[1] For example, Britain's long-standing defensive alliance with Portugal amounted to a kind of British guarantee of the Portuguese Empire.[2] In the seventeenth century a very precise type of guarantee was often employed, with carefully stipulated obligations. Guarantees were often used in the eighteenth century. The Treaty of Tilsit contained a guarantee clause, and in 1815 the integrity and neutrality of Switzerland were guaranteed. In general, we may say that a guarantee was wedded to the *status quo* and implied a freezing of the boundary or agreement to which it was applied. Enforcement of guarantee lay in the hands of the participants, the implication being that they would support their guarantees by diplomacy and, ultimately, by force of arms.

While there had often been these guarantees of individual states, there had never been a general guarantee of a peace settlement by several powers. In 1804–1805 such a guarantee was contemplated by Pitt and Alexander, and in the autumn of 1804, when a renewal of war with Napoleon seemed likely, Alexander had sent Novossiltsov to London with the proposal of a new coalition, as noted above.[3] His instructions included a stipulation that Pitt be asked to join in the creation of a new kind of international law. We have seen how Pitt was greatly interested in the suggestion and how, in his reply of January 19,1805, he specified "a general agreement and Guarantee." [4] He called for its formation "at the restoration of peace." Any peace settlement which omitted these measures would be "imperfect." He wanted

---

[1] For articles on guarantees, see E. Satow, *"Pacta sunt servanda,"* *Camb. Hist. Jour.,* I, no.3 (1925), 295–318, and J. W. Headlam-Morley, "Treaties of Guarantee," *ibid.,* II, no. 2 (1927), 151–170.

[2] Great Britain and Portugal have had defensive alliances since 1373. Headlam-Morley, *op. cit.,* 151, distinguishes guarantees from defensive alliances, and makes a point that there was never any British guarantee of Portugal in the strict sense of the word.

[3] See above, pp. 105–106, 143.   [4] See above, p. 144.

the big powers to "bind themselves mutually to protect and support each other" and especially to restrain "any projects of aggrandizement and ambition." He asked that the treaty be put under the "special Guarantee of Great Britain and Russia." Thus he wanted a general guarantee by all the powers and a special, bilateral guarantee by two of the most powerful of the states. The idea of a guarantee was written, in vague form, into the Anglo-Russian Treaty of Alliance of April 11, 1805,[5] but the war ended with Napoleonic victories, and the allies had no opportunity to put their conception into practice.

Pitt's plan slept for the better part of a decade, and then in 1813 Castlereagh once again began to consider it as capable of practical use in European affairs. Although he was active with plans for a consolidating alliance in 1813, he did not press the idea of a general guarantee. Nor did Alexander. Too much groundwork remained to be done in the preliminary consolidation of the coalition and the reconcilation of animosities within its ranks. Nevertheless, with the appearance of the Treaty of Chaumont in March of 1814, the necessary first step had been taken in laying the base by creating a situation in which a general guarantee could be effected.

At Vienna the reversion to alliance balance corrupted the atmosphere for a general guarantee; in December and early January, 1814–1815, it would have been out of the question. Then the admission of France to the inner councils of the great powers broke the deadlock over Saxony, precipitated constructive action on the general settlement, and produced a relative congeniality among the major statesmen. The diplomatic configuration of the great powers, however, remained somewhat confused. The Treaty of Chaumont, although at that time almost a dead letter, was still on the books and available. It united

---

[5] Rose, *Select Despatches*, 274. For a very specific enunciation of Anglo-Russian equilibrist aims in the 1805 negotiations, see Gower to Mulgrove, April 7, 1805, *ibid.*, 129. Gower was British ambassador to Russia; Mulgrove, British foreign minister.

four against one. The more recent Triple Alliance, uniting three against two, made France, which had been the victim of Chaumont, a ranking, majority member of the new alignment and split the old foursome in two. Moreover, the common actions and responsibilities of the major powers as members of the five courts created a bond which was antithetical to either of these sundering alliances. It was not surprising that Alexander wanted a clarification of the alignment.

There were several ways of clearing up the confusion. Three separate and conflicting relationships lay in a tangle, but the powers, by renewing or strengthening one of the three, could cut a path through the tangle. Alexander let it be known in interviews with both Wellington and Francis of Austria that he favored a renewal of the Treaty of Chaumont. Metternich and Talleyrand indicated that they wanted to continue along the lines of the Triple Alliance. On the other hand, Castlereagh, in company with Wellington, saw the tsar on February 12 and proposed "that the Powers who had made the peace should . . . announce to Europe . . . their determination to uphold and support the arrangement agreed upon; and, further, their determination to unite their influence, and if necessary, their arms, against the Power that should attempt to disturb it." [6] Castlereagh argued that they should include France in order to strengthen Louis XVIII at home. In essence, he was suggesting the broadening of the Treaty of Chaumont to remove its anti-French character and make it unequivocally a general instrument for use against any aggressive state which might threaten the balance of power.

Alexander agreed, and by the following day, the 13th, Talleyrand, Metternich, and Hardenberg had all given their approval.

[6] Castlereagh to Liverpool, Feb. 13, 1815, in Webster, *Brit. Dipl.*, 305. See also Webster, "Some Aspects of Castlereagh's Foreign Policy," *Transactions of the Royal Historical Society*, 3d ser., VI, 70. See Webster, *Castlereagh*, 427 ff., for a brief summary of the attempt to promote a general guarantee.

Gentz immediately drafted a declaration [7] which embodied the conception of this general guarantee. The declaration was so certain of going into effect that Castlereagh issued a circular letter to British ambassadors on February 13, declaring that there was

every prospect of the Congress terminating with *a general accord and Guarantee* between the great Powers of Europe, with a determination to support the arrangement agreed upon, and to turn the general influence and if necessary the general arms against the Power that shall first attempt to disturb the Continental peace.[8]

The draft itself called upon the sovereigns "to subordinate all other considerations to the inviolable maintenance of the peace" and to stifle at once "by common and well concerted measures," or, if that should fail, "by the . . . union of all the means which Providence has entrusted to them," any "project which would tend to upset the established order and provoke anew the disorders and calamities of the war."

At this promising turn of events, Metternich and Castlereagh decided to request the inclusion of the Ottoman Porte in the agreement. In another interview with Alexander, Castlereagh received from the tsar "the most distinct and satisfactory assurances of his disposition to concur with the other Powers, including the Ottoman Porte, in the general Guarantee." [9] Alexander stipulated one condition—that Russo-Turk difficulties be reviewed by the joint mediation of Austria, France, and Great Britain. In spite of the success with which statesmen had surmounted the early obstacles and arrived at agreement on this general guarantee, the declaration was never issued. It was first halted by the unwillingness of the Porte to sign and then abandoned when the Hundred Days threw their shadow over Europe. Although the collapse of the idea of a general guarantee is not

[7] For the text, see d'Angeberg, *Congrès de Vienne,* 864–866.

[8] Webster, *Brit. Dipl.,* 307.

[9] Castlereagh to Robert Liston, Feb. 14, 1815, in Webster, *Brit. Dipl.,* 305–306. Liston was British ambassador in Constantinople.

minutely explained by the documents of the period, it was virtually inevitable. Its success was dependent upon the active and reliable participation of all the five courts, but the position of France as a major guarantor of the peace settlement was completely undermined in the eyes of the other statesmen as a result of the return of Napoleon. It was natural that they should have lost interest in the general multilateral guarantee and have fallen back on the earlier suggestion of the tsar that they renew the Treaty of Chaumont. Thus the general guarantee died an obscure death in its infancy, having been quickly conceived, born, and killed within the space of a few weeks. Alexander, surprisingly enough, did not lose sight of the idea, and a Russian circular of May, 1815, showed that it was still a part of Russian policy.[10] It was nevertheless too vague a conception to hold its place in Castlereagh's policy after the events of the Hundred Days, and Castlereagh never reverted to it in its original form. When Russia brought it forward again in 1818, at the Congress of Aix-la-Chapelle, the British foreign minister rejected it.

Its acceptance in February, 1815, would have reconstituted the coalition equilibrium, but reconstituted it by implication rather than by specific formula. The general guarantee would have implied the necessity of a coalition whenever the *status quo* was attacked or upset, but the guarantee would not have specified the composition of such a coalition nor made its detailed operation clear. Its vagueness, moreover, would have raised the perennial problem of deciding when it should be invoked.

CHRISTIAN FORBEARANCE

Throughout the remainder of the spring, the statesmen were busy either with the last details of the peace settlement or with decisions regarding the campaign against Napoleon. In July and August they were laboring in Paris over decisions regarding their treatment of France after her resounding defeat at Waterloo, but by September, when they were once again facing the

10 Webster, *Castlereagh*, 431–433.

problem of enforcement of the territorial balance of power in Europe, the idea of a general guarantee, which had so taken the fancy of Alexander in February, suddenly reappeared in an important Russian project—Alexander's Treaty of the Holy Alliance.[11] By it the signatory monarchs would declare their "immovable determination" to base their international relations on the "precepts of . . . holy religion, precepts of justice, charity and peace, which, far from being solely applicable to private life, must on the contrary directly influence the decisions of princes." The monarchs would make of themselves "a true and indissoluble brotherhood."

The document was, and is, astonishing. It represents the purest flight of idealism in any serious state paper of the period, possibly of any period. While Alexander ascribed the origin of the Holy Alliance to a conversation with Castlereagh early in 1815,[12] in which the idea of a general guarantee was doubtless the subject under discussion, his embellishment of the idea owed much to his study of the New Testament and the influence of Frau von Krüdener.[13] In September the concept of a guarantee emerged fully clad in the terminology of Christian charity and love. To be sure, the language of idealism was not unknown in diplomatic discourse; it was one of the clichés of diplomacy and as such was never to be literally interpreted or actually employed as the real basis for diplomatic conduct. The text of the Holy Alliance was astonishing just for the reason that it did envisage the precepts of Christ as the real basis for the conduct

[11] For the text, see d'Angeberg, *Congrès de Vienne*, 1547–1549. The Holy Alliance may best be studied in William P. Cresson, *The Holy Alliance* (New York, 1922); Hildegard Schaeder, *Die dritte Koalition und die heilige Allianz* (Königsberg and Berlin, 1934); and Ernest J. Knapton, *The Lady of the Holy Alliance* (New York, 1939). For an excellent bibliographical roundup of works on the Holy Alliance see E. J. Knapton, "An unpublished letter of Mme. de Krudener," *JMH*, IX (1937), 483–492.

[12] Castlereagh to Liverpool, Sept. 28, 1815, in Webster, *Brit. Dipl.*, 382–383.

[13] For a highly skilled discussion of the relation of Frau von Krüdener to the Holy Alliance, see Knapton, *Lady of the Holy Alliance*, 147 ff.

of princes—something of a nightmare to the other statesmen of the period. Its appearance was greeted with surprise and sarcasm. Within twenty-four hours of their first knowledge of it, Metternich and Castlereagh were exchanging mutual cynicisms.[14] Metternich was sure that Alexander was out of his mind, and Castlereagh wrote the same conclusion to Liverpool, adding his own characterization of the Holy Alliance as "this piece of sublime mysticism and nonsense." [15]

The Holy Alliance is relevant to an analysis of the balance of power in 1815 only insofar as it was conceived to be a way of enforcing the territorial balance of power. It was one of several plans for administering and preserving a European equilibrium. It was, of course, directly connected with the earlier project for a general guarantee, which was itself conceived as a means of enforcement of the *status quo*. As an effective instrument for preserving the European equilibrium, its importance was negligible in 1815. It was signed on September 26, 1815, by the fellow sovereigns of Alexander, more as a concession to avoid an incident with the tsar than as an act of serious statesmanship. Several years later the Holy Alliance did assume an important role in the balance of power, but its original purpose had been perverted by then and its Christian idealism watered down to the dilution appropriate for European statecraft.

QUADRUPLE ALLIANCE

The problem of enforcement of the territorial balance of power was not solved by either the idea of guarantees or the Holy Alliance, since the original project of the former was dropped in March, and its later disguised appearance in the Holy Alliance was without immediate significance to the preservation of the European equilibrium. For enforcement, statesmen turned to a renewal of the principles of the Treaty of Chaumont.

The treaty of March 25, 1815, had represented a return to

[14] Webster, *Brit. Dipl.*, 383.   [15] *Ibid.*

coalition equilibrium after the momentary reversion to alliance balance in the preceding winter at Vienna. While it brought the coalition to life and concentrated its energies against France, it was merely a war measure, destined to die with the end of the military emergency. Article IV, which limited the duration of the treaty to the war, stated that the Treaty of Chaumont would go back into effect at the war's end.[16] Thus Chaumont had continued alive, and the intention to preserve its principles remained relatively constant throughout 1815. Statesmen planned to renew it as soon as the appropriate time presented itself. There can be no doubt of constancy on the part of Castlereagh. The principles crystallized in the Treaty of Chaumont represented the product of his heritage from Pitt and the culmination of specific plans of his own since 1813. He had played a leading role in the creation of the treaty and had remained the last and most reluctant of the major statesmen to shed its ties in the winter of 1814–1815. He was eager to secure its renewal as soon as Napoleon returned from Elba and maintained its principles as cardinal tenets of his foreign policy through the rest of 1815. In July he sought to prevent its disruption in Paris, when interallied disagreements threatened the unity of the coalition, and, in his presentation of measures to be taken in dealing with France, he stated the necessity of preserving the alliance in the strongest possible terms:

In deciding upon any arrangement, the first object to attend to is that it shall preserve unimpaired the Alliance to which Europe already owes its deliverance, and on the permanence of which union it ought in wisdom to rely above every other measure of security for its future peace and preservation.[17]

Similarly, Alexander signified his desire to preserve the new form of the coalition equilibrium. His interest in it had virtually a parallel history to that of Castlereagh: initially interested in it

[16] D'Angeberg, *Congrès de Vienne*, 973.

[17] Castlereagh, "Principles upon which the proposed negotiations with France ought to be considered," in *Well Suppl. Des.,* XI, 139.

in 1804–1805 and receptive to its principles during 1813, he had supported them at Chaumont, acted upon them in Paris in 1814, been partly guilty of their temporary setback at Vienna in the winter of 1814–1815, and then returned to them as a defense against the Triple Alliance of January 3, 1815. At the outset of the Hundred Days he had come to a quick agreement with Wellington on the renewal of the Treaty of Chaumont, and he continued to support its principles at Paris in the summer of 1815. The Russian memorandum of July 28, 1815, one of the important documents of the summer negotiations, urged another renewal of the Treaty of Chaumont as necessary to prevent any "harm which France might in the future bring to the security of the European states." [18]

The first definite move toward the renewal came as the outcome of a conversation between Castlereagh and the tsar. Capo d'Istria drafted the text of a proposed treaty embodying the principles of the Treaty of Chaumont, and this was submitted to Castlereagh by Alexander in early October on the eve of the tsar's departure from Paris.[19] It was too vague for Castlereagh, whose mind operated along more specific and practical lines. He objected to the fact that it possessed "too strong and undisguised a complexion of interference." [20] He submitted his own version, which was slightly modified by Capo d'Istria and Rasumovski and soon accepted by the other statesmen.[21]

The treaty of alliance was finally signed on November 20, 1815.[22] It was composed of identical bilateral agreements, each of seven articles, between the members of the various pairs of

[18] D'Angeberg, *Congrès de Vienne,* 1473.

[19] See Liverpool to Bathurst, Oct. 17, 1815, in *Well. Suppl. Des.,* XI, 201–202; and Castlereagh to Liverpool, Oct. 15, 1815, in Webster, *Brit. Dipl.,* 386–387.

[20] Castlereagh to Liverpool, *ibid.,* 386. Castlereagh regarded the "conservation of the alliance as the great measure of European security" ("Principles," in *Well. Suppl. Des.,* XI, 139).

[21] See Martens, *Recueil des traités . . . conclus par la Russie,* IV, 27–28.

[22] For the text, see Martens, *Nouveau recueil,* II (1814–15), 734–737; d'Angeberg, *Congrès de Vienne,* 1636–1638.

the four powers. The allies, "wishing to employ all their means in order that the general tranquillity . . . be not troubled anew," resolved to give to the principles consecrated in the Treaty of Chaumont and the treaty of March 25, 1815, an application best adapted to the actual state of affairs and to fix in advance the principles which "they propose to follow to guarantee Europe from the dangers which can still menace it."

By Articles I and II, the allies agreed to maintain in force the Second Treaty of Paris and to prevent by arms the return of Napoleon. The third and fourth articles provided that if France should attack the army of occupation, the allies would each support that army with 60,000 troops, and more if necessary. Article V provided for the continuance in force of the first two articles after the occupation of France should end.

The only novelty in the brief text of the treaty came with Article VI, which provided for periodic conferences of sovereigns or ministers "to assure and facilitate the execution of the present treaty and consolidate the intimate relations which today unite the four sovereigns for the good of the world." These conferences, whether convened "under the immediate auspices of the sovereigns or by their respective ministers," would devote their energies "to the great common interests and to the examination of measures which would be judged the most salutary for the repose and prosperity of the peoples and for the peace of Europe."

The implications of Article VI were of the utmost importance. Webster has noted that the Quadruple Alliance "marked definitely the ascendance of the Great Powers and the principle of the European Concert" [23] and that Article VI established the legal basis for the "diplomacy by conference" which characterized the next decade of international relations in Europe. It inaugurated "the period of a great international experiment." [24] For our purposes, however, the Quadruple Alliance represented the serious attempt of European statesmen to carry over into

[23] Webster, *Congress of Vienna*, 143.
[24] C. K. Webster, *The European Alliance, 1815–25* (Calcutta, 1929), 1.

peacetime the appartus of the coalition equilibrium which had been built during the wars against Napoleon. Article VI was a specific and very significant implementation of that conception. It promised neither success nor failure; it offered no slick panaceas; but it did assure Europe of a new departure in equilibrist statecraft, a tardy experiment with a new institution. Its principle was neither new nor antithetical to the theory of the balance of power, but directly derived from it—a refinement of balance practice long envisaged by equilibrist writers and occasionally practiced in the great continental war emergencies of Europe.

With the crystallization of the Quadruple Alliance and the signing of the various documents of the Second Peace of Paris on November 20, 1815, the great peace settlement of 1814–1815 was rounded out, incomplete in many details, unfortunate in many aspects, destined to endless revision in the coming decades, and yet markedly consistent, in major outlines, with the conception of a Europe in balance. It represented the last great European peace settlement which could be consciously, and with relative consistency, based on the principles of the balance of power. Equipped with a refined system for preserving the European equilibrium, statesmen could turn their faces hopefully toward the future.

Chapter XII

Epilogue to Peacemaking

THE years 1816 and 1817 were years of dislocation and reconstruction, more notable for concern on the part of statesmen with domestic difficulties than with foreign policy. The chief fact of those years in European foreign affairs was the military occupation of northern France in accordance with the provisions of the Second Peace of Paris. This occupation was skillfully administered by the Duke of Wellington with a minimum of friction between the veterans who had fought French soldiery so fiercely and for so long and the French populace. Since occupations involve trying problems and typically have bad reputations, the duke's achievements were impressive, although French public opinion did turn against him.

Although there had been small reason for an international conference in the immediate postwar years, by early 1818 there were suffcient problems to raise the question of activating Article VI of the Quadruple Alliance and taking a hand at the application of the coalition equilibrium to the peacetime decisions of the new Europe. Castlereagh took the initiative, Alexander seconded him, and other statesmen and monarchs joined in supporting the first of what were to be four big postwar conferences. They agreed to meet at Aix-la-Chapelle, a popular spa with ample accommodations for royalty and aristocrats and the former capital of the Holy Roman Empire. To this conference, "the first ever held by the Great Powers of Europe to regulate international affairs in time of peace," [1] came most of the familiar figures of the Congress of Vienna. Castlereagh, appearing for the last time at a European conference, was joined by Wellington, whose occupation headquarters were conveniently nearby. Richelieu, representing France, was a new figure, but from Russia came Alexander, Nesselrode, and Capo d'Istria, while Prussia was represented by her monarch, as well as by Hardenberg, Humboldt, and the usual group of generals. The Austrian emperor came with Metternich and Gentz, the latter resuming his familiar role of protocolist for the conference.

Business chiefly concerned France. When the latter offered to pay off the remainder of her indemnity quickly, the conference accepted and made the appropriate arrangements. Acting under the urgings of the Duke of Wellington, the sovereigns and ministers also agreed to terminate the occupation, which was done forthwith. But when Richelieu sought entry for his country into the Quadruple Alliance, he posed a more difficult problem. It was ultimately handled ambiguously by an agreement

[1] Webster, *The Foreign Policy of Castlereagh, 1815–1822* (London, 1925), 121. This second volume of Sir Charles Webster's great study of Castlereagh is one of two brilliant works of research by English scholars on the diplomacy of the postwar era. The other is *The Foreign Policy of Canning, 1822–27* (London, 1925) by Harold Temperley.

In the postwar decade, the congress became a new means for preserving the equilibrium of Europe in time of peace. This means was not put to work until after 1815 and therefore is not examined in the theoretical section of the present study.

to include France and then a contradictory and secret renewal of the Quadruple Alliance itself. The only major discord of the conference arose over the Russian attempt to put through a guarantee of both the territory and governments of the states of Europe, a guarantee which could be used to repress revolution anywhere on the Continent. Castlereagh, already under attack in England for his policy of involvement in continental affairs, rejected the suggestion outright. In spite of this disagreement, the conference enjoyed remarkable successes in the statesman-like handling of relations with France, although the disappearance of the French threat to Europe increasingly meant the concomitant disappearance of harmony among the opponents of France. The high-water mark of postwar work of the coalition equilibrium was achieved in this first conference, and co-operation tended to recede in subsequent years.

Later conferences were held at Troppau, Laibach, and Verona in 1820, 1821, and 1822. The meetings were concerned primarily with the recurrent problem of revolution in Italy, Spain, and Portugal, and the degree to which the coalition equilibrium should be concerned in the internal problems of states in those areas. Castlereagh took the position that internal change had to be permitted unless there was a demonstrable danger to the state system.[2] He saw no such danger in the areas under question. The tsar took the initiative in pressing the opposite policy at Troppau in the Russian circular of December 8, 1820, in which he sought agreement to the propositions that any state which suffered change of regime ceased to be a part of the European alliance and could be resisted by coercive force of the other members. The eastern monarchies adopted this approach at Laibach, in spite of British opposition, and went on to apply it systemmatically to specific revolutionary situations in southern Europe in the early twenties.

[2] See his great analysis of the problem of intervention in the State Paper of May 5, 1820; Temperley and Penson, *Foundations of British Foreign Policy*, 48–63.

This intervention was regarded by the British cabinet as an abuse of the powers of the coalition and has been widely excoriated. One should notice that for all its repressive conservatism, it represented a mild type of international government. It even possessed an apparatus of co-operation which went somewhat beyond the joint use of armed forces, since these same years saw the repeated use of ambassadorial conferences in various European capitals. The degree of co-operation, while not breathtaking, is quite impressive when seen against the long background of earlier centuries, and it is well worth examination by modern students of international government.

This edifice of the coalition, so difficult to build and so hard to maintain, was soon torn down by the rush of new circumstances. Contributing importantly to the destruction were the alienation of Great Britain by the reactionary use of intervention and the removal from the scene of two of the most important figures associated with the coalition. Castlereagh, its architect, broke down under the strain of immense cabinet responsibilities in 1822 and took his own life during the summer of that year just before he was to leave for the Congress of Verona. He was succeeded by a brilliant and persistent critic of his policies, George Canning, who at once made it clear that Britain would no longer participate in the European coalition. Three years later, when the system was tottering toward dissolution, Alexander disappeared from the European stage, either through death or through a pretended death which veiled his abdication and secret withdrawal to Siberia to live the life of a religious devotee. The facts are not yet wholly clear, although some very skillful research has been done on the subject.[3] Whatever the actual truth, a certain romantic haze now surrounds the figure of Alexander and softens the incompetence and

[3] It is possible to follow the outlines and some of the details of this fascinating research in Leonid Ivan Strakhovsky, *Alexander I of Russia* (New York, 1947). The case for believing in the abdication is circumstantial, but very persuasive.

cruelty of his last years as emperor. His death or abdication in 1825, whichever it was, removed a second major figure who had been committed to the experiment in mild internationalism. The stage was left to Metternich and to a type of statecraft which was built more upon the virtuosity of one man than upon a cluster of able men, as in the case of the years of the coalition equilibrium.

Chapter XIII

Summary and Conclusions

HAVING trekked through the arid uplands of the theory and practice of Europe's classical balance of power, one can now outspan, rest, and contemplate the landscape. Glancing back, it is possible to say that the theory of equilibrium made particular assumptions, had special aims, and used certain means.

The theory assumed the existence of a state system, an understood territorial extent for it, a certain homogeneity of the member states, and a rational system of estimating power. The theory aimed at the survival of the individual states, at the creation of group-consciousness and group action as the best way of preserving the individual state, and at the prevention of preponderance by any one member state. The theory envisaged the use of vigilance, appropriate alliances, intervention, holding the balance, reciprocal compensation, preservation of components, coalitions, and warfare.

This theory was adjusted to work best through absolutism and under the warm sun of cosmopolitanism, since it demanded both flexibility and moderation. It had an affinity to conservatism and a close, although not crippling, tie to the *status quo*. Possessing an idealistic side, it was nevertheless secular and amoral, and it was more the property of the big powers than the small, although both benefited by it. It possessed its own geographical base and was to a degree inbred and parochial. Intimately related to international law, it was an improvement over international anarchy, in spite of its harshness and cold mechanics. Its dream of the good life was modest, attainable, and mundane —more like that of Islam than the wild and remote Christian dream of the Kingdom of Heaven. It promised liveability and workability for Europe's brilliant, competitive, and barbarous states, rather than peace on earth. The doctrine of counterpoise accepted these states as they were, without demanding either the perfection of their constitutions or a reform of human nature.

One sees that this theory was not simply a casual, haphazard matter of self-interest, but that it was a moderately well defined and relatively systematic approach to the problems of statecraft in the European state system. It lent itself to theoretical exposition and was capable of logical explanation. One should recognize its separateness and uniqueness and set the theory apart from other systematic outlooks; it was not Machiavellian, for example, in any literal meaning of that word, but represented somewhat more self-restraint and considerably more group interest than the latter. It should not be confused with "power politics," which is a much more general term characterizing the totality of the struggle among states which are compelled to rely upon their own strength for security and survival. "Power politics" implies no set aim or policy; it embraces all methods, equilibrist or expansionist alike, whereas the balance of power means a particular condition or policy and is thus a more specialized phrase. Although this theory of counterpoise was not as systematic as twentieth-century astronomy nor as fully and brilliantly rationalized as Thomistic theology, it was quite as comprehensive and carefully worked out as the mercantilism of the 1600's and 1700's, Benthamism, nineteenth-century capitalism, or pre-1900 socialism, and it was quite as important in its separate way as any of these. Observers who risk a denial of its systematic properties should logically venture the assertion that none of the other above-mentioned systems represents a systematic approach to the facts of economic and political life.

While it would be absurd to overemphasize the systematic character of the balance of power—it was after all not as tightly logical as geometry—it is just as incorrect to underestimate its cohesion, as has been done with regularity in our historical literature. It was perhaps too precise and overcategorized, making arbitrary assumptions and possessing its own bigotry. At the same time it was an important, logical, and widespread response of European statesmen to the problem of running a state system under circumstances where no ordinary statesman could control more than his own state, if that much. As such, the theory of balance occupied a position of unusual importance in history after the emergence of modern Europe in the sixteenth century, an importance which we begin to appreciate now that we have witnessed in the twentieth century the disregard of the theory and the political collapse of historic Europe.

The assumptions of this theory were really the foundation of a broader outlook than one at first suspects. By making them, a statesman was committing himself to some form of philosophical optimism. Although he may not have agreed with Voltaire's Dr. Pangloss that this was the best of all possible worlds, he did hold that a state system could be perpetuated by analysis, measurement, and certain adjustments of policy; and, more fundamentally, he implied that man was not a cork bobbing along on a terrible ground swell, but that he had an appreciable influence over his environment and could exert effective control over his destiny through his own intelligence. Although some writers, notably Rousseau and Kant, did not find that man had much control over the system, even they believed in an inevitable improvement of the system and were optimists after their own fashion.

The theory had as well a quality of patness which enabled it to be reduced to a series of precepts: check preponderance; be watchful; intervene where necessary, but only when necessary; hold the balance when possible; be mobile; divide the cake evenly; do not pull the pillars down; normally, use alliances—ideally, use an automatic coalition; and so on. The degree of patness represented the margin of error, since few subjects offer more complexities than the history of international relations. Part of the patness was the inevitable and appropriate comparison of the balance of power with chess. With men and squares one had a state system of a given territorial extent; there was a certain homogeneity of pieces; a chessman had calculable properties; and a given move had a limited number of accepted responses. There was thus an approach to simplification and still a recognized complexity. One never rose in patriotic wrath to smash the board; the players, winning, losing, or drawing, treated each other with courtesy and moderation, shook hands, and left the table discreetly.

This analogy suggests the position of the individual in the balance-of-power system. Here was a remote and artificial stratosphere, high above the world of the French peasant tending his vineyard with loving hands; distant also from the honest German burgher, content with his church, his music, and his beer; or from the lacerated soldiers screaming with pain on the battlefield of Leipzig as the statesmen made their tour of inspection. The theory said nothing of trench feet, rats, lice, syphilis, amputations, and gangrene. The peasant, the burgher, and the soldier all belonged to a more real world for the individual than the chess squares and mathematical arabesques of the equilibrist. Of the latter's classical theory, Herman Melville might have written, as he did of something else: "Thou belongest to that hopeless, sallow tribe which no wine of this world will ever warm."

Turning from the cold formality of theory to the world of application, a glance back over the years 1812–1815 shows us that the period was rich in the materials of the balance of power. Before the formation of the last coalition, there was manifested a clear concern for the re-establishment of a state system, the basic condition for an equilibrium. When Austria joined the coalition, the restoration of a European balance of power became the official aim of the coalition, enunciated first at Reichenbach, confirmed at Toeplitz, repeated in the Declaration of Frankfurt, and reaffirmed at Châtillon, Chaumont, and Paris.

It was usual for statesmen at that time to use balance-of-power terminology very freely. And their usage suggests a striking difference between our twentieth-century attitude and that of the eighteenth and early nineteenth centuries toward the theory of equilibrium. To us, conditioned in a different climate of opinion, the balance of power too often possesses the distasteful overtones which liberal criticism has attached to it. To eighteenth- and nineteenth-century diplomats, equilibrist strategy was an obvious necessity, honored by theorists and employed by statesmen. For most of them, it had connotations as pleasant as those which the word "democracy" enjoys in the occident today. Flattering things were said, and in abundance, about the balance of power. One could wax lyrical about it without eliciting from the gallery a shower of curses.

Nevertheless, widespread use of a certain type of phraseology does not in itself prove that the theory back of it was taken seriously in practice. Usage could have been nothing more than lip service. That its value was more than a pleasant meaninglessness is at least implied by the fact that it was incorporated in the articles of treaties as well as in their preambles, i.e., it was used in text which was legally binding. This implication becomes stronger and more persuasive when one examines the great policy decisions of the period. Corroborating evidence declares that the balance of power governed the Russian decision to carry the war into Europe in the winter of 1812–1813; it lay at the bottom of the Treaty of Kalisch, which dominated Russo-Prussian relations for many years and cast its shadow over Europe at large; it permeated Metternich's thought and action as he separated Austria from the French alliance in 1813; it inspired the formation, and became the official aim, of the last coalition; it lay behind the spectacular "refinement" of balance strategy at Chaumont; it served as the soundest argument against the candidacy of Bernadotte and for the restoration of the Bourbons; it governed the peace of reconciliation with France in May, 1814, a high point in European statecraft; and it played a tremendous role at Vienna and Paris, 1814–1815, in molding the strategic conceptions of the most prominent statesmen. We may conclude that the balance of power was not only the intellectual matrix to which virtually all lines of argument were related in the period, but that it was the dominant political and military strategy of those years.

The congress itself is one of the most fruitful historical areas to examine for insights into the classical balance of power. Congressional attention was chiefly concerned with the creation of a territorial balance and was principally focused on the redivision of territory, since a dominantly agricultural society thought of power largely in terms of square miles and "souls." The congress began when the conception of a coalition equilibrium was still strong. The coalition solidified at Chaumont in March, 1814, had won the war, restored the Bourbons in France, and written an excellent, moderate peace with France—in short, it had passed through a crucial period of reconstruction without appreciably wavering in its loyalty to the balance-of-power ideal for which it had fought the war. The congress itself was controlled by the great powers which had been the chief instruments in the defeat of Napoleon. Their intention was to exclude France and the lesser powers from the inner negotiations, and the coalition equilibrium still possessed an anti-French character. The peace settlement was delayed by the disagreement of the members of the coalition over the disposal of Poland and Saxony. Disagreement was heightened by the fact that the decision on those two areas would determine to a large extent the nature of the new territorial equilibrium in Europe, since it would affect the strength and internal tension of the center. Each approach to the problem, whether British, Austrian, or Russian, could be recommended on some kind of equilibrist grounds, although the last-named plan was unsound, in that it involved a severe weakening of the defensive position of Austria. Deadlock on these problems split the coalition into rival camps, temporarily blighted the new coalition equilibrium, nearly produced a new war, and demonstrated the necessity of a new power alignment. In effect, this turmoil momentarily dissolved the coalition equilibrium in favor of a return to an alliance balance. The Triple Alliance of January 3, 1815, aligned France, Austria, and Great Britain against Russia and Prussia, and the crisis was solved by compromise. Although interrupted by the frenzy of the Hundred Days, statesmen swiftly renewed the coalition equilibrium, and the congress went on to complete its work. The Final Act was signed on June 9, 1815, re-creating a territorial balance of power.

To say that the theory of equilibrium was more than a gloss to an existing situation and that it had an important influence on events is not to say that it dominated the conference negotiations to the exclusion of other conceptions. Legitimacy, nationality, and state interest all played their parts. It can be shown, however, that legitimacy was less important in the grand strategy of the congress than the balance of power, and that they were closely related—the one a matter of internal policy and the other a strategic conception of organizing a continent. Also, the idea of nationality was generally suppressed in favor of the balance of power. Antithetical to the latter, it was still too inarticulate and powerless to thrust aside the older conception. It played its part in Poland and in the outlook of Alexander,

Stein, and lesser figures, but it gained no victories beyond those.

State interest as a motivation at the Congress of Vienna was also subordinate to the re-establishment of a balance of power. The history of the congress must be written largely in terms of state interest *vs.* equilibrium, but with the greater emphasis on equilibrium. While state interest repeatedly diverted individual statesmen from equilibrist policies, there were always other statesmen present to check these excursions and redirect them along balance lines. Exorbitant demands of Austria, Prussia, and Russia were all eventually whittled down to sizes compatible with the shape of a new equilibrium. This subordination of state interest to balance of power may be largely explained by two circumstances. The settlement was the work of five states of nearly equal power. This was the overwhelming fact of the era. As a result, no one state could dominate the new outlines of Europe as France had been able to do in earlier years. Moreover, the four great powers which dominated the settlement were being amply rewarded for their earlier efforts against Napoleon. Thus balance of power and state interest, antithetical in many matters, were in this case virtually synonymous as far as the great powers were concerned.

The redivision of territory at the congress followed two principal lines of policy: containment and reciprocal compensation. A barrier was built against France comprising an arc of states to her east—the Netherlands, Luxembourg, the western holdings of Prussia, Bavaria, Baden, Württemberg, a neutral Switzerland, and Sardinia. The barrier ranged in depth from 200 miles in the north and central areas to 100 miles in the south. It was further strengthened by the backing of interested great powers—Great Britain, Prussia, and Austria. It was constructed with much attention to detail; witness, for example, Castlereagh's January opposition to the Russo-Prussian plan of transporting the king of Saxony to the left bank of the Rhine. Such a new, weak state would inevitably have fallen under French influence and weakened the barrier system. Castlereagh successfully opposed it. From Castlereagh's point of view, the decisive point was a strong center. He had pinned his first hopes on an Austro-Prussian bloc. Failing that, there was still a strong check against French aggression in the barrier system, stiffened by Bavarian soldiers, Prussian involvement by virtue of its westward extension, and the contiguous, Dutch-Hanoverian area in the north. Against possible Prusso-Russian aggression, there remained the defensive strength of the German princes, supported by Austria, Great Britain, and France. Thus the territorial settlement offered rather good strategic possibilities for preserving the balance. With regard to the policy of reciprocal compensation, Russia received most of Poland; Prussia, areas in Saxony, Poland, and western Germany; Austria, extensive holdings in Italy; and Great Britain, important overseas areas. By the Second Peace of Paris, slight modifications were made in the French frontier with an eye to diminishing French aggressive power. Occupation of France by coalition soldiery was provided to weaken France's offensive power further without forcing upon her a permanent, humiliating, and unwise partition.

The eighteenth century may have conceived the balancing system to have a certain beauty of design, a delicacy of poise, with the formal beauty of the cattleya orchid, but harsh realities were very evident in the new Europe. Policy on Poland could be questioned. Many small princedoms had been swallowed. Little awareness of the problems of nationality had been evinced. And the treaty, whose very authors were unhappy about it, had been possible only after the sacrifice of several million men, dead through battle wounds and disease. Nevertheless, looking at it with equilibrist precepts in mind, there had been more successes than failures, and the statesmen had not as strong a case for profound gloom as they thought.

The years 1812–1815 are especially meaningful to the student of the balance of power for the further reason that they witnessed the temporary evolution of a coalition equilibrium from the antecedent, eighteenth-century system of alliance balance. The wars of the French Revolution and Napoleonic dominion had provided the terrible anvil upon which coalitions were forged; and the statesmen of the great powers attempted to consummate their experience of wartime coalitions by the creation of an automatic coalition which would solve the problem of enforcement for the state system in the postwar period. As a result, the particular, the distinguishing, and the most fruitful subject to study in these years is the conception of the coalition equilibrium which emerged at Chaumont, suffered various vicissitudes at Vienna, and remained, after the dust had begun to settle, as the chief means of enforcing Europe's new territorial balance. The choice between the alliance and the coalition is a very fundamental decision, since the consequences are so different. Both may start near the same point, but they diverge quickly and widely as one advances along their paths, and they end at separate places. For example, if enforcement by coalition sticks, certain means of the alliance balance should wither away, such as the magpies' nest of bilateral alliances and holding the balance. The major allied powers of 1815 chose the coalition and wrote this conception into the Quadruple Alliance of November 20, 1815, where they provided for periodic conferences of sovereigns or ministers to deal with the major postwar problems, this decision laying the legal basis for the international conferences of the next decade by which European statesmen hoped to give a peacetime reality to their new coalition equilibrium.

The principle behind this instrument illustrates the linkage between the eighteenth-century balance of power and its nineteenth-century development; it demonstrates how the latter was merely a refinement of the former, a logical evolution of earlier equilibrist theory and practice. One of the great difficulties of the alliance balance had been its haphazard character. As the product of numerous statesmen acting for the most part independently, it was a kind of disorganized counterpoint, a clutter of independent pieces only loosely co-ordinated. The new instrument of 1815 was a step toward order, simplification, and organization.

When seen in the total context of Europe's international relations, this step illuminates the rather obscure tendency of a balance-of-power system to supplant itself ultimately with a federation. The tendency is not strong, but it exists. It is a movement from freedom toward organization, from anarchy toward federation. It may be stated as the progress from anarchy to alliance balance to coalition equilibrium to confederation to federation. This tendency was never very vigorous in modern Europe before the world wars of the twentieth century, and its orderly realization was rendered impossible by the luxuriant growth of hostile tendencies which became powerful and articulate shortly after the balance-of-power system had reached the zenith of its achievement in 1812–1815, when equilibrist theory was so consistently applied. The classical balance-of-power system, based on mechanical premises, cosmopolitanism, and the existence of a limited framework, was dated as soon as the great new forces of the nineteenth century gained their feet. Nationalism rooted out the principle of moderation fundamental to equilibrist theory and practice. Liberals attacked the amorality of the theory of balance of power and pointed to the bloody history of its practice. The industrial revolution created a world market, solved transportation problems, and multiplied the overseas connections of European states, thereby effectually smashing the limited framework of the European state system. Romanticism was inimical to the mechanical premises of counterpoise. Together, all these forces corrupted the environment for the balance of power and created tendencies beyond its scope.

One can see from the larger context that "collective security," far from being alien to the "age-old tradition of the balance of power," not only derives out of the latter, but also must be regarded as the logical end point of the balance-of-power system, the ideal toward which it has been moving, slowly and halt-ingly, for several hundred years. This contention leads to the hypothesis that the League of Nations and the United Nations, when considered as instruments for maintaining the "continued co-existence of independent governments in contact with one another," were merely further refinements in balance practice— namely, organizations representing a world-wide state system of sovereign, independent, and armed states, intent on preserving their security and independence and prepared to use an auto-matic coalition to prevent the dangerous expansion of any mem-ber state. Added to this were certain other embellishments of balance practice: the location of the organization in one city and the invention of a system of permanent representation there for the member states, an innovation which was to the new type of equilibrist organization what the system of permanent embassies was to the older types of balance practice. At bottom, however, the collective security of 1919 or 1945 was merely an elaboration and refinement of the coalition equilibrium of 1815, just as the latter was an elaboration and refinement of the alliance balance. This relationship was never understood by the chief proponent of collective security. Woodrow Wilson, who did much to discredit the balance of power and popularize the idea of the League of Nations, conceived the two to be antipodal, the one to rest on an unstable balance between opposing factions and the other to lodge on the secure founda-tion of a preponderance of power. An examination of the his-tory of equilibrist theory, however, indicates that his conception was seriously wrong in this respect.

The emergence of the coalition equilibrium in 1814–1815 marked off that period from the earlier history of Europe's system of counterpoise, and the era of the Treaty of Chaumont became the New England Indian summer of Europe's classical balance of power. Appearing some time after the disappearance of the regular summer, it was similar and yet different, with a special quality and brilliance of its own. Its similarity lay in the application of the standard precepts of the classical theory to the territorial arrangement of the peace settlement. Here was classicism with its clearest lines. The dissimilarity lay in its reliance on the continued sharp focus of the coalition.

One of the many services performed by this period of Indian summer is to illustrate for us more clearly the differences of our nation-state diplomacy from the classical diplomacy. The foreign minister, in the era of the latter, did not have to court the press, the voters, and parliament; his analysis was the restricted analysis of foreign monarchs, their moods, their advisers, and their courts, without the harrowing imponderable of the sovereign will of the people. Wars were limited, fought for provinces, and followed by negotiated, and not dictated, peace treaties. There was a certain universalism in the concept of Europe, in the recognition of the historical state, as opposed to the more modern and unhistorical nation-state; the passionate middle-class patriot had little place in this cold-hearted and aristocratic world of mathematical observers and analysts.

If one can look at this different world for a moment, it is possible for one to appreciate the insight of a contemporary German historian who has suggested that the "classical diplomacy . . . must be considered as one of the great accomplishments of old Europe." [1] At the very least, the age of the classical balance of power is astonishing for the accumulated efforts which went into maintaining the state system in equilibrium, just as the more recent era of science and big business is amazing for the man-hours of nervous energy which have been devoted to the pursuit of its aims. The practitioners of the classical balance did not pretend a devotion to the search for truth that the research scientist may have, but they were just as busy and often as rigorous in their mental processes. Their contribu-

[1] Franz Schnabel, "Bismarck and the End of Classical Diplomacy," *Measure*, II (Fall, 1951), 378.

tion to European life helped maintain the separate cultural identities of Europe's states by preventing the predominance of a single member. By the perpetuation of a modified competition in international relations, they contributed much for good and for ill, the former outweighing the latter as long as the practice of the balance was confined to an era of limited warfare.

Bibliographical Essay

IT IS an extraordinary experience, much of it pleasurable, to work in a discipline like European history, where so many gifted scholars have left evidences of their labors and enthusiasms. If one takes time to look up from the task at hand, the sight of the landmarks of scholarship is exciting and, indeed, awesome. The sensation of awe is particularly evident in the field of Napoleonic studies, where one's attempted contribution appears miserably small. The feeling is less oppressive when one works among the writers on the theory of the balance of power, since the scholarship there has so far been slighter and less formidable.

1. *Theory of the Balance of Power*
   A. *Bibliographies*
   There is as yet no really good bibliography of theoretical works on the balance of power. For that reason it has been necessary to use incomplete and inadequate lists. The most suggestive and helpful have been Max Immich, *Geschichte des europäischen Staatensystems*

von 1660 bis 1789 (Munich, 1905); Comte d'Hauterive, "Conseils à un élève du ministère des relations extérieures," *Revue d'histoire diplomatique,* XV (1901), 161–224, a list of suggested readings for young members of the French diplomatic service written early in the nineteenth century; E. Kaeber, *Die Idee des europäischen Gleichgewichts in der publizistischen Literatur vom 16. bis zur Mitte des 18. Jahrhunderts* (Berlin, 1906), a rather good bibliographical commentary; Hanns Frederich, *Die Idee des politischen Gleichgewichts* (Wurzberg, 1914,) which contains a small and reasonably good bibliography; and Ernest Nys, "La théorie de l'équilibre européen," *Revue de droit international et de legislation comparée,* XXV (1893), 34–57, one of the most useful studies of the balance of power, containing limited comments on many of the seventeenth- and eighteenth-century treatises. This article by Nys was to have been followed by another, but the present writer has been unable to find a trace of it among the extensive writings of its author. An article by J. L. Kunz, "Europäisches Konzert" in Karl Strupp (ed.), *Wörterbuch des Völkerrechts* (Berlin, 1924), I, 697 ff., is useful. See also G. F. von Martens, *Summary of the Law of Nations, Founded on the Treaties and Customs of the Modern Nations of Europe* (Philadelphia, 1795; trans. by William Cobbett from *Précis du droit des gens moderne de l'Europe,* Göttingen, 1788), for helpful documentation and references to earlier equilibrist works; and Heinrich von Ompteda, *Literatur des gesammten, sowohl natürlichen als positiven Völkerrechts* (ed. by Carl Albert von Kamptz, Berlin, 1817), for a small, but useful, bibliography. Quincy Wright, *A Study of War* (2 v., Chicago, 1942), has good bibliographical references in the sections dealing with the balance of power; see especially II, 743–766.

B. *Theorists*

Among the writers on the balance of power, chiefly in the period from 1700 to 1815, there is much material, which is by no means exhaustively treated in Chapters I–III of this study. These have attempted a synthesis of only the more important works, with occasional reference to some of the less important. For the most part the theoretical discussions of balance of power are rather short, and there seem to have been many more written in French than in any other language. Among the most notable are a group of articles by Henry, Lord Brougham and Vaux, to be found in his *Works* (11 v., London and Glasgow, 1855–57), VIII (1857): "Balance of Power," Jan., 1803, pp. 1–50; "Historical View of the Doctrines of Foreign Policy," Jan., 1843, 51–67; "General Principles of Foreign Policy," 1843, 69–102; and "War Measures as Connected with the Balance of Power" in three parts: I, Jan., 1807, II, Oct., 1808, and III, July, 1809, pp. 161–205. These essays place Brougham among the most intelligent, persuasive, and rewarding authors on the subject. Siour Favier, *Politique de tous les cabinets de l'Europe* (3d ed., ed. by M. Ségur, 3 v., Paris, 1802), offers one of the most important collections of material on the balance of power. Also among the important authors and works are Fénelon, François de Salignac de la Mothe-, "Supplément" to the "Examen de conscience sur les devoirs de la royauté," *Oeuvres de Fénelon* (3 v., Paris, 1835), III, 360–363; and Friedrich von Gentz, *Fragments on the Balance of Power* (London, 1806; trans. from *Fragmente aus der neuesten Geschichte des politischen Gleichgewichts in Europa,* Leipzig, 1806), a very impressive reassertion of the principles of the balance of power. These works of Fénelon and Gentz are justly renowned among the writings on the subject. Both are most interesting, and both have been used heavily in this study. David Hume, "Of the Balance of Power," *Essays: Moral, Political, and Literary* (2 v., London, 1875), I, 348–356, is an oft-cited, clear, and undistinguished essay by the outstanding Scottish philosopher; it is primarily concerned with the question of balance of power policies in the ancient world. Dominique de Fourt de Pradt, *La Prusse et sa neutralité* (London, 1800), has a lot of material on the balance; and Gaspard de Réal de Curban, *La science du gouvernement* (6 v., Paris, 1765), VI: *Contenant le traité politique par rapport au dehors et au dedans de l'état, et aux moyens de concilier les intérêts respectifs des puissances qui partagent la domination de l'Europe,* contains rather good material on balancing policies. Emmerich de Vattel, *The Law of Nations* (3 v., Washington, 1916; trans. by C. G. Fenwick from 1758 ed. of *Le droit des gens* . . .), esp. III, *passim,* gives the thinking of a great partisan on the balance of power. Not many of his pages deal with the subject, but those that do make his work an important one in this area. A contrasting point of view may be found in Johann Heinrich von Justi, *Die Chimäre des Gleichgewichts von Europa* (Altona, 1758), a denunciation of equilibrist policy. For perceptive material on and by Edmund Burke, one should consult his *Thoughts on French Affairs, Remarks on the Policy of the Allies with respect to France,* and *Letters on a Regicide Peace,* large excerpts from which may be conveniently found in Ross J. S. Hoffman and Paul Levack, *Burke's Politics, Selected Writings and Speeches of Edmund Burke on Reform, Revolution, and War* (New York, 1949), 402 ff. One of the few long eighteenth-century treatises on the balance of power is Franz Josias von Hendrich, *Historischer Versuch über das Gleichgewicht der Macht bei den alten und neuen Staaten* (Leipzig, 1796), where the author deals intelligently but not thoroughly with both ancient and modern materials and generally finds the balancing system desirable.

Short works by Rousseau and Kant are both of unusual interest and importance. Rousseau rewrote a work by an earlier writer and published it in 1761 as "Extrait du projet de paix perpetuelle de M. l'Abbé de Saint-Pierre"; it may be found in the first volume of C. E. Vaughan, *The Political Writings of Jean Jacques Rousseau* (2 v., Cambridge, 1915). Rousseau was struck by the raw competition within the state system and by the virtually automatic checks and balances. For further comment see above, pp. 84–85. Immanuel Kant was similarly impressed by the raw competitive struggle and its automatic checks but felt that it bred an inevitable evolutionary development toward stability. His argument is found in *Zum ewigen Frieden* in *Sämmtliche Werke* (ed. by G. Hartenstein, 8 v., Leipzig, 1867–69), VI (1868), 405 ff. For a convenient English translation, consult M. Campbell Smith, *Perpetual Peace: A Philosophical Essay* (London, 1903). Further comment on Kant's unique work may be found above, pp. 20–22. For one of the more valuable eighteenth-century treatments of the balance of power, see Abbé de Mably, *Collection complète des oeuvres . . .* (15 v., Paris, 1794–95), V: *Contenant les principes des negociations—pour servir d'introduction au droit public de l'Europe fondé sur les traités.* Johann Jacob Schmauss, *Einleitung zu der Staats-Wissenschaft und Erleuterung des von ihm herausgegebenen Corpus juris gentium academici . . .*

(2 v., Leipzig, 1741–47), I, is a self-styled history of the balance of power. It deals quite inadequately with the European state system from that standpoint up to 1740, with no special treatment of the theory of balance.

Many other works have been investigated. *An Appendix to the Memoirs of the Duke de Ripperda* (London, 1740) contains a useful little essay; and *Europe's Catechism* (London, 1741) is an amusing and revealing series of questions and answers on the balance of power. Moderately useful are René Louis de Voyer de Palmy, Marquis d'Argenson, *Considerations sur le gouvernement ancien et présent de la France* (Amsterdam, 1765); Comte d'Hauterive, *De l'état de la France à la fin de l'an VIII* (Paris, 1800); A. H. L. Heeren, *History of the Political System of Europe and Its Colonies* (2 v., Northampton, Mass., 1829; trans. from *Handbuch der Geschichte des europäischen Staatensystem und seiner Colonien,* Göttingen, 1811); Ewald Friedrich, Graf von Hertzberg, *Ueber den wahren Reichtum der Staaten, das Gleichgewicht des Handels und der Macht . . .* (Berlin [?], 1786 [?]); Charles Davenant, *Essays upon the Balance of Power . . .* (London, 1701); and J. Mallet du Pan, *Du péril de la balance politique de l'Europe* (London, 1789).

No attempt is made to incorporate in this work the sixteenth- and seventeenth-century works which touch on the balance of power. They form another area for investigation.

C. *General Works*

The best general work on the balance of power is Leonce Donnadieu, *Essai sur la théorie de l'équilibre* (Paris, 1900), which contains a good essay on the history of the European balance from its origins up to 1900, with a brief, but relatively good, section on the Congress of Vienna and a stimulating criticism of the balance of power. The author saw the concert as an inevitable development of, and improvement upon, the earlier balancing system, although he did not work out the details of that development. The fact that this book remained an essay and never grew into a detailed history of the balance of power will remain a disappointment to the student of the subject. Charles Dupuis, *Le principe d'équilibre et le concert européen* (Paris, 1909), argues that the eighteenth-century equilibrium failed, as indicated by Napoleon's conquests; that the balancing principle needed to be re-enforced by some improvement; that the concert served as this necessary, new device; and that the concert was derived from the equilibrist tradition. Thus Dupuis seems to have taken over Donnadieu's thesis, and indeed appears to owe much to Donnadieu's historical survey and his brief treatment of the Congress of Vienna, although Dupuis makes scant acknowledgment of this debt. The chapter by Dupuis on the Congress of Vienna comprises eighteen pages, most of which are given over to a few quotations which had previously been unearthed by Donnadieu.

Alexandre de Stieglitz, *De l'équilibre politique, du légitimisme et du principe des nationalités* (3 v., Paris, 1893–97), has a good section (I, 113–231) which deals with balance-of-power theorists and contains many fine quotations, especially from the writers on international law. See also Olof Hoijer, *La théorie de l'équilibre et le droit des gens* (Paris, 1917), for a reasonably good discussion of theory. Quincy Wright, *A Study of War,* has some stimulating essays on balance of power; and one of the supporting manuscripts in the preparation of Professor Wright's study is available for examination —A. F. Kovacs, "The Development of the Principle of the Balance of Power from the Treaty of Westphalia to the Congress of Vienna" (unpubl. MS, University of Chicago library). This manuscript, if put into shape for publication, could be a very handy introductory essay on the balance of power. It describes the evolution of a multiple balance in the eighteenth century out of the earlier Hapsburg-Bourbon dualism; it generally follows Rousseau's analysis of the balancing process, and treats the partitions of Poland as a natural and desirable outcome of that process. It contains also a helpful and interesting selection of excerpts from writers on the subject. Another intelligent, general examination of the balance of power, which has been consulted through the courtesy of its author, is Theodore H. Von Laue, "History of Balance of Power, 1494–1914" (unpubl. MS).

D. *Special Works and Articles*

There have been many articles on the balance of power, most of them utterly undistinguished and of slight relevance here. The following represent the best: Lothar Bucher, "Uber politische Kunstausdrücke, II. Politisches Gleichgewicht," *Deutsche Revue,* XII

(Sept., 1887), 333–340, not an especially good article, but useful for quotations from sixteenth- and seventeenth-century authors; Richard Cobden, "The Balance of Power," chap. iii of the pamphlet *Russia* (1836), reprinted in *Political Writings* (2 v., London, 1867), I, is probably the most powerful denunciation of the balance of power, stimulating and forceful; Sidney B. Fay, "Balance of Power," *Encycl. of Soc. Sciences,* moderately good, but limited and disappointing, when one considers that it came from one of America's most distinguished diplomatic historians. A. von Kirchenheim, "Politisches Gleichgewicht," *Deutsche Revue,* XL (Dec., 1915), 308–313, offers an intelligent, short commentary. H. O. Meisner, "Vom europäischen Gleichgewicht," *Preussische Jahrbücher,* 176 (May, 1919), 222–245, is a rather good article with a helpful discussion of the history of the balance of power. A. F. Pollard, "The Balance of Power," *Journal of the British Institute of International Affairs,* II (March, 1923), 51–64, is useful, careful, and stimulating—the wittiest of the articles on this subject. Adolf Rein has written one of the best of all articles in the field, "Über die Bedeutung der überseeischen Ausdehnung für das europäische Staaten-system," *Historische Zeitschrift,* c. 131, pt. I (1927), 28–90. This is a skilled article with stimulating interpretation and excellent documentation; it introduces new bibliographical material and contains material on the "framework" and on the relation of sea power to the balance of Europe. Alfred Stern, "Das politische Gleichgewicht," *Archiv für Politik und Geschichte,* IV (Jan., 1925), 29–37, is undistinguished but has moderately helpful documentation. Alfred Vagts, "Gleichgewicht und/oder Völkerbund," *Europäische Gespräche,* IV (Oct., 1926), 520–537, is helpful in clarifying the uses and misuses of the term "balance of power."

II. *Application of the Balance of Power, 1812–1815*
    A. *Bibliographies*
    Since there is no special bibliography on the balance of power for the 1812–1815 period, chief reliance has been placed on the standard bibliographies, which are familiar and demand little comment. The following have been helpful: W. H. Allison, S. B. Fay, A. H. Shearer, H. R. Shipman, and G. M. Dutcher (eds.), *A Guide to Historical Literature* (New York, 1937); F. C. Dahlmann and G. Waitz, *Quellenkunde der deutschen Geschichte* (9th ed., Leipzig,

1932); F. M. Kircheisen, *Bibliographie du temps de Napoléon comprenant l'histoire des États-Unis* (2 v., Paris, 1902–12); G. Parisset, *Le consulat et l'empire* (Paris, 1921); George Vernadsky, *Political and Diplomatic History of Russia* (Boston, 1936); Louis Villat, *La révolution et l'empire, 1789–1815* (2 v., Paris, 1936); K. Waliszewski, *La Russie il y a cent ans: Le règne d'Alexandre Ier* (3 v., Paris, 1923–25); and A. W. Ward, G. W. Prothero, and Stanley Leathes (eds.), *Cambridge Modern History* (14 v., Cambridge, Eng., and New York, 1902–12), IX (1906): *Napoleon.*

B. *Sources*

For treaty texts, the following have been of great help: Georg F. von Martens, *Recueil des principaux traités d'alliance, de paix, de trêve, de neutralité, . . . conclus par les puissances de l'Europe . . . depuis 1761 jusqu'à present* (2d enl. ed., by K. von Martens, 8 v., Göttingen, 1817–35), VIII (1835): 1803–1808; Georg F. von Martens, *Nouveau recueil de traités d'alliance, de paix, de trêve, de neutralité, . . . depuis 1808 jusqu'à présent* (16 v., Göttingen, 1817–42), I (1817): 1808–1814, II (1818): 1814–1815; M. de Clercq, *Recueil des traités de la France* (2 v., Paris, 1864); Feodor F. Martens, *Recueil des traités et conventions conclus par la Russie avec les puissances étrangères* (15 v., St. Petersburg, 1874–1909), an excellent collection with scholarly connective text between the document; and Great Britain, Foreign Office, *British and Foreign State Papers* (London, 1832–), I–III (London, 1838–41), covering the 1812–1815 period and containing correspondence as well as official papers. For special material on the boundary problems and changes of 1814–1815, I have relied on Edward Hertslet, *A Map of Europe by Treaty . . . since the General Peace of 1814* (4 v., London, 1875–91).

There are in addition several useful miscellaneous collections of documents: Comte d'Angeberg (Jakob Leonhard Boreyko Chodzko), *Le congrès de Vienne et les traités de 1815* (2 v., Paris, 1864), indispensable; J. L. Klüber, *Akten des Wiener Kongresses in den Jahren 1814–15* (9 v., Erlangen, 1815–35), similar to d'Angeberg but not as helpful; H. T. Colenbrander, *Gedenkstukken der algemeene Geschiedenis van Nederland van 1759 tot 1840* (22 v., 's Gravenhage, 1905–22), VII, containing useful British documents for the 1815 period; F. von Demelitsch, *Actenstücke zur Geschichte der Koalition 1814* (Vienna, 1899); and J. Holland Rose, *Select Despatches . . .*

relating to the Third Coalition against France, 1804–05 (London, 1904).

The period is generously supplied with important memoirs and collections of correspondence. The most useful of these have been: *Memoirs of Prince Metternich, 1773–1815* (ed. by Prince Richard Metternich, 2 v., New York, 1880; trans. by A. Napier from *Mémoires, documents, et écrits divers*, 8 v., Paris, 1880–84); *Mémoires du prince de Talleyrand, publiés par le duc de Broglie* (5 v., Paris, 1891–92)—in some cases use has been made of the translation by Raphaël Ledos de Beaufort: *Memoirs of the Prince de Talleyrand* (5 v., New York and London, 1891–92); K. A. von Hardenberg, *Denkwürdigkeiten* (ed. by Leopold von Ranke, 5 v., Leipzig, 1877); Harold Temperley and L. M. Penson, *Foundations of British Foreign Policy from Pitt (1792) to Salisbury (1902); or Documents Old and New* (Cambridge, 1938), for Pitt's "draft to Vorontsov"; C. K. Webster, *British Diplomacy, 1813–15* (London, 1921), an excellent selection of the most important British diplomatic correspondence in the period; Arthur Wellesley, Duke of Wellington, *Supplementary Despatches* (15 v., London, 1858–72), XI, especially helpful for the diplomacy of the summer of 1815; Charles W. Stewart, Third Marquis of Londonderry (ed.), *Memoirs and Correspondence of Viscount Castlereagh* (12 v., London, 1848–53).

In piecing out the picture of Russian policy, the following works were of assistance: E. Botzenhart (ed.), *Freiherr vom Stein: Briefwechsel, Denkschriften und Aufzeichnungen* (7 v., Berlin, 1931–37), which contains a rather generous sprinkling of documents relating to the balance of power; *Arkhiv Kniazia Vorontsova* ("Archives of Prince Vorontsov," 40 v., Moscow, 1870–95), volumes 8, 17, 18, 23, 29, 30, 35, 37, 38 containing moderately helpful correspondence in French for 1812–1815; A. Gielgud (ed.), *Memoirs of Prince Adam Czartoryski* (2 v., London, 1888), especially useful for Russian policy toward Poland, the mission of Novossiltsov in 1804–1805, and the equilibrist outlook of the author; and Karl Robert, Graf von Nesselrode, *Lettres et papiers, 1760–1856* (11 v., Paris, 1904–12), moderately useful.

C. *General Works*

In the reconstruction of the diplomatic history of the period and in the working out of the details of the practice of the balance of power, there have been a number of very useful works. Volume IX, *Napoleon,* of the *Cambridge Modern History* has been useful as well as the following: A. W. Ward and G. P. Gooch, *The Cambridge History of British Foreign Policy, 1783–1919* (3 v., Cambridge, 1922–23), I; A. Sorel, *L'Europe et la révolution française* (8 v., Paris, 1895–1904), VIII, the most helpful, single volume of the 1812–1814 period, attentive to the balance of power, and a splendid production of Europe's most brilliant diplomatic historian; Adalbert Wahl, *Geschichte des europäischen Staatensystems im Zeitalter der französischen Revolution und der Freiheitskriege, 1789–1815* (Munich and Berlin, 1912), containing basic information on the formation of the last coalition and helpful bibliography; Wilhelm Oncken, *Das Zeitalter der Revolution, des Kaiserreiches und der Befreiungskriege* (2 v., Berlin, 1884–86), II, excellent on the role of Prussia and Austria during the formation of the last coalition; Wilhelm Oncken, *Oesterreich und Preussen im Befreiungskriege* (2 v., Berlin, 1876–79), extremely useful for Austrian and Prussian policy and very helpful on Metternich; Heinrich G. von Treitschke, *History of Germany in the Nineteenth Century* (6 v., New York, 1915–19; trans. by E. and P. Cedar from *Deutsche Geschichte im neunzehnten Jahrhundert,* 5 v., Leipzig, 1890–96), I and II, the first volume being interesting for a very prejudiced and exciting statement of Prussian policy at the Congress of Vienna, and the second dealing at some length with the diplomacy of the Second Peace of Paris.

For Russian history, in addition to Vernadsky and F. Martens, parts of the following have been consulted: K. Stählin, *Geschichte Russlands* (4 v., Stuttgart, 1923–39), III; Theodor Schiemann, *Geschichte Russlands unter Kaiser Nikolaus I* (4 v., Berlin, 1904–19), I, on Alexander I; K. Waliszewski, *op. cit.,* II, scholarly and most helpful.

For a wider general perspective, one does well to examine Ranke's illuminating interpretive essay, "Die Grossen Mächte," on the history and role of balance-of-power shifts and practices from 1648 to the age of Napoleon; a translation may conveniently be found in Theodore H. Von Laue, *Leopold Ranke, the Formative Years* (Princeton, 1950), 181 ff.

D. *Special Works: (1) Biographies*

In addition to the works cited above, which contain a great deal of material on the individual statesmen, there are many useful biographies, most of which have occasional pages on the balance of power, in addition to careful information on the diplomacy of the statesmen in question. For Metternich the following have been helpful: C. S. B. Buckland, *Metternich and the British Government from 1809 to 1813* (London, 1932), a competent and very detailed study; H. Ritter von Srbik, *Metternich: Der Staatsmann und der Mensch* (2 v., Munich, 1925), I, very good for Metternich's equilibrist thought and action; E. L. Woodward, *Three Studies in European Conservatism* (London, 1929), pretty much a restatement of Srbik's thesis, with attention to the balance of power; and Helene Du Coudray, *Metternich* (New Haven, 1936), clear and intelligent, with a useful summary of Metternich's complicated diplomacy in 1813, as he detached Austria from Napoleon.

For Gentz and his relation to the balance of power, there are the following: Golo Mann, *Secretary of Europe: The Life of Friedrich Gentz, Enemy of Napoleon* (New Haven and London, 1946; trans. by W. H. Woglom) and Paul R. Sweet, *Friedrich von Gentz, Defender of the Old Order* (Madison, Wis., 1941), scholarly, readable, and critical, with considerable attention to the balance of power.

Talleyrand's commitment to the balance of power is briefly treated in Crane Brinton, *The Lives of Talleyrand* (New York, 1936), Georges Lacour-Gayet, *Talleyrand, 1754–1838* (4 v., Paris, 1928–34), and Guglielmo Ferrero, *The Reconstruction of Europe: Talleyrand and the Congress of Vienna, 1814–15* (New York, 1941; trans. by T. R. Jaeckel).

For Castlereagh, see Charles Kingsley Webster, *The Foreign Policy of Castlereagh, 1812–15* (London, 1931). Prof. Webster (now Sir Charles) has here produced one of the masterpieces of historical literature on European diplomacy. Together with its companion volume, which covers the period from 1815 to 1822, this work presents the findings of a careful re-examination of Castlereagh's decade of policy making in foreign affairs. The author establishes Castlereagh securely among England's great foreign ministers and brings out clearly Castlereagh's equilibrist approach to international relations.

For Hardenberg there is no adequate biography. Oncken, *op. cit.*, and Treitschke, *op. cit.*, are both helpful for the period of the War of Liberation, Treitschke being also helpful for the 1814–1815 period. The best collection of material on Hardenberg is, of course, his *Denkwürdigkeiten,* edited by von Ranke.

On Tsar Alexander, in addition to the works cited above, the following are helpful, although not sufficiently explicit on his relation to the balance of power: Pierre Rain, *Un tsar ideologue: Alexandre Ier, 1777–1825* (Paris, 1913); Grand Duke Nicholas Mikhailovitch, *Le tsar Alexandre Ier* (trans. by N. Wrangel, Paris, 1931); and A. Vandal, *Napoléon et Alexandre Ier: L'alliance russe sous le premier empire* (3 v., Paris, 1891–96), good on the pre-1813 period. Hannah A. Strauss, *The Attitude of the Congress of Vienna toward Nationalism in Germany, Italy, and Poland* (New York, 1949), has material on Alexander's relation to the principle of nationality in this period.

(2) *Diplomacy*

For the details of the diplomacy of the 1812–1814 period, chief reliance has been placed on the treaties of Martens, *op. cit.,* and the special works, already cited, of Oncken, Sorel, and Webster. In addition to these works, some specialized studies have been helpful: Max Lehmann, *Freiherr vom Stein* (3 v., Leipzig, 1905), for details concerning the Russian decision to follow Napoleon into Germany; Eli Heckscher, *Continental System: An Economic Interpretation* (Oxford, 1922), helpful on the Napoleonic overbalance, the position of Sweden, and the deterioration of Franco-Russian relations in 1810–1812; August Fournier, *Der Congress von Châtillon, 1814* (Vienna and Prague, 1900), an extremely fine study of the diplomatic complications of early 1814; F. D. Scott, *Bernadotte and the Fall of Napoleon* (Cambridge, Mass., 1935) and F. D. Scott, "Bernadotte and the Throne of France, 1814," *Journal of Modern History,* V (1933), 465–478, both of them excellent on the candidacy of Bernadotte in 1813–1814 and both illustrative of the high unconcern of Bernadotte for the balance of power. On the period leading up to the first Bourbon Restoration, E. J. Knapton, "Some Aspects of the Bourbon Restoration of 1814," *Journal of Modern History,* VI (1934), 405–424, is very helpful indeed.

The most useful of the standard accounts of the Restoration were: Pierre Rain, *L'Europe et la restauration des Bourbons, 1814–18* (Paris, 1908), and Charles Dupuis, *Le ministère de Talleyrand en*

1814 (2 v., Paris, 1919–20), an excellent monograph by a student of the balance of power. Dupuis does not link the Restoration to the balance. Among the other historians of the Restoration, the following were consulted: H. Houssaye, *1814* (41st ed., Paris, 1903); Marie, Marquis de Roux, *La restauration* (Paris, 1930); and Eduard Driault, *Napoléon et l'empire: La chute de l'empire* (Paris, 1927). Driault, among these, is very attentive to the balance of power but does not link it with the Restoration. For the diplomacy of the summer of 1814, the best account is in Webster, *The Foreign Policy of Castlereagh, 1812–15*, 288–323; see also the fine work of G. J. Renier, *Great Britain and the Establishment of the Kingdom of the Netherlands, 1813–15* (London, 1930).

Recent decades have witnessed a considerable increase in the attention of scholars to the Congress of Vienna, although there is not yet a comprehensive history of the congress which might be described as definitive. The documents, although incomplete, are in d'Angeberg and Klüber. The best short account of the congress itself is C. K. Webster, *The Congress of Vienna, 1814–15* (Peace Handbooks, London, 1919), skillful, informative, but necessarily brief. It was written as a background study on peacemaking for the British experts and delegates to the peace conference in 1919. It is not a thorough study and of course does not pretend to be. There are rather good accounts in the *Cambridge History of British Foreign Policy*, I, and the *Cambridge Modern History*, IX. Harold Nicolson, *The Congress of Vienna, 1812–22* (New York, 1946), does not satisfy the requirements of a comprehensive history, although it offers a most attractive account of the work of the congress statesmen by one of England's most intelligent and readable writers on diplomatic history. It has many small mistakes, but these by no means nullify the usefulness of the work.

Among the older, continental historians Treitschke, *op. cit.*, has an interesting but highly prejudiced account. The most thorough recent treatment of the general diplomacy of the congress may be found in Karl Griewank, *Der Wiener Kongress und die Europäische Restauration 1814–15* (rev. ed., Leipzig, 1954), a book which is not yet well known in this country and which came to hand too late to be of much use in the preparation of the present manuscript.

Attention has been given to the social side of the congress by Freiherr von Bourgoing, *Vom Wiener Kongress* (Munich and Vienna, 1943).

To supplement these works, see Bruno Gebhardt, *Wilhelm von Humboldt als Staatsmann* (2 v., Stuttgart, 1896–99), II, good on Humboldt and his conception of the "strong center" of Europe; G. Pallain (ed.), *Correspondance inédite du prince de Talleyrand et du roi Louis XVIII pendant le Congrès de Vienne* (Paris, 1881); August Fournier, *Die Geheimpolizei auf dem Wiener Kongress* (Vienna, 1913); and M. H. Weil, *Les dessous du Congrès de Vienne* (2 v., Paris, 1917), the last two very interesting, containing much of the atmosphere of the congress, the rumors, the night life, the entertainments, and occasionally more important tips.

For the summer and fall of 1815, there is a relative scarcity of good work. The best books are as follows: Webster, *The Foreign Policy of Castlereagh, 1812–15*, containing the best summary; Gebhardt, *op. cit.*, II, good on the narrative of events and the German aims; W. Alison Phillips, *The Confederation of Europe* (2d ed., New York, 1920), an unusual and excellent monograph on the early years of the concert of Europe, with useful material on the balance of power.

In addition to the work of Webster, the following are useful for the idea of guarantees: Sir E. Satow, *"Pacta sunt servanda* or International Guarantee," *Cambridge Historical Journal,* I, no. 3 (1925), 295–318, useful, but not as critical as Sir J. W. Headlam-Morley, "Treaties of Guarantee," *ibid.,* II, no. 2 (1927), 151–170, scholarly and clear. For the Holy Alliance, see William P. Cresson, *The Holy Alliance* (New York, 1922); Hildegard Schaeder, *Die dritte Koalition und die Heilige Allianz* (Königsberg and Berlin, 1934); E. J. Knapton, "An Unpublished Letter of Mme. de Krudener," *Journal of Modern History,* IX (1937), 483–492, for a fine bibliographical comment; and E. J. Knapton, *The Lady of the Holy Alliance* (New York, 1939), an excellent biographical study of a very interesting person and a careful re-examination of the origins of the Holy Alliance.

The books in this bibliographical comment on the 1812–1815 period have been chiefly useful for the diplomatic narrative and only secondarily useful for what they contain on the balance of power. On the whole, they contain surprisingly little on the latter, although what they do contain is often very helpful. When all the odds and ends are synthesized, they make an intelligible whole and do much to illuminate the theory and practice of the balance of power in that period.

Index

Aberdeen, Lord, 135-136, 137, 138, 146
Absolutism, 68, 69, 298
Acte additionnel, 267
Aix-la-Chapelle, Congress of, 285, 293-294
Alberg, Duc d', 186, 187
Alexander I of Russia, 105, 134, 137, 189, 201, 276, 286, 289; and Napoleon's Russian campaign, 99-103; European policy of, 103, 104n, 108-109n, "Tilsit" policy of, 104; sends Novossiltsov to London, 105-106, 281; and Napoleon, 106, 169, 190n, 191; and Pitt, 106, 143; and Prussia, 107, 108, 109, 110; and Metternich, 115, 117, 118, 120, 146, 149, 191, 197, 223; and Polish question, 122, 190-192, 195, 200, 211-212, 215, 216-217, 232, 237; and consolidating alliance, 135; and Castlereagh, 145, 182n, 197, 211-212, 216-218; and Congress of Châtillon, 146, 147; and balance of power, 156, 170-171; and march on Paris, 162; and moderation toward France, 163, 275, 277, 279; and advocacy of Bernadotte, 166, 167, 170, 190; and Bourbon Restoration, 166-168; in London, 180-181; at Congress of Vienna, 186-261 *passim;* policy at Congress of Vienna, 189, 193, 197; idealism of, 197-198; and Saxon question, 197, 245; and Francis I of Austria, 223; and Talleyrand, 227n; and general guarantee of peace, 281, 282, 286; and renewal of Treaty of Chaumont, 283, 285, 288-289; and Ottoman Empire, 284; and Triple Alliance, 289; and Congress of Aix-la-Chapelle, 293, 294; favors intervention, 294; disappearance of, 295-296; and nationalism, 303
Alliance: as balance-of-power device, 58-62, 77, 297; distinguished from coalition, 78, 80, 88, 306
Alliance balance, 82, 83n, 84, 85, 86,